CHINESE HUMAN SMUGGLING ORGANIZATIONS

SHELDON X. ZHANG

Chinese Human Smuggling Organizations

Families, Social Networks, and Cultural Imperatives

STANFORD UNIVERSITY PRESS

STANFORD, CALIFORNIA

Stanford University Press
Stanford, California

© 2008 by the Board of Trustees of the Leland Stanford Junior University.
All rights reserved.

Printed in the United States of America on acid-free, archival-quality paper

Library of Congress Cataloging-in-Publication Data

Zhang, Sheldon.
 Chinese human smuggling organizations : families, social networks, and cultural imperatives / Sheldon X. Zhang.
  p. cm.
 Includes bibliographical references and index.
 ISBN 978-0-8047-5741-6 (cloth : alk. paper)
 1. Illegal aliens—United States. 2. Human smuggling—United States. 3. Human smuggling—China. 4. United States—Emigration and immigration. 5. China—Emigration and immigration. I. Title.

E184.C5Z429 2008
364.1'3—dc22
2007029374

Typeset at Stanford University Press in 10/14 Janson

For my parents

Contents

Tables, Figures, and Maps

MAPS

Preface

Illegal entry into the United States by Chinese nationals is not new; organized Chinese human smuggling activities, however, began to emerge only two decades ago. This phenomenon did not receive much public attention until in November 1993 the *Golden Venture*, a Honduras-registered freighter with 286 illegal Chinese immigrants on board, ran aground on New York's Long Island (Fritsch 1993). Ten immigrants drowned while trying to swim ashore. Although this was the most publicized story about undocumented migration from China in the 1990s, it represents only one incident in a much larger context of clandestine smuggling of Chinese nationals to the United States (Liang and Ye 2001, 187). Nonetheless, the *Golden Venture* incident was a watershed event in transnational human smuggling for several reasons. First, it signified the beginning of a tidal wave of illegal Chinese immigrants to the United States after China and the United States resumed their diplomatic relationship. Second, it brought to the front page the potential threat to U.S. national security and the U.S. immigration system of an influx of illegal immigrants from a country bustling with one-fifth the world's population. Third, it compelled U.S. law enforcement and social service agencies to acknowledge the problem of illegal Chinese immigrants as real and serious, and to mobilize resources that were previously directed mostly at curbing illegal migration from Latin America. Fourth, it showcased the tenacity and capability of the smugglers and their transnational networks in moving human cargoes around the world.

Transnational migration has become a global phenomenon that affects practically every nation. Growing international commerce, greater integration of world economy, and advances in communication technology and mass transportation have not only expanded global exchanges of goods and services, but also spurred the movement of laborers seeking employment opportunities. About 175 million people currently live outside their native countries (roughly 3 percent of world's population), and almost 10 percent of the population in developed nations is made up of foreign-born migrants (United Nations 2002, 2). Currently legal and illegal migrants account for 15 percent of the population in some fifty countries; and the trend of population movement is expected to continue well into the future (National Intelligence Council 2000, 23). The globalization of the marketplace and the integration of manufacturing and distribution processes worldwide can only encourage the movement of laborers, and in turn propel the undercurrent of illegal migration. The pressure for outward migration has already created a booming economy, with brokers and facilitators taking advantage of legal loopholes, forging identity documents, and exploiting loosely guarded borders to assist fee-paying migrants to reach their destination countries.

Human smuggling is a multi-billion dollar business. Unlike their counterparts from Mexico, who generally pay a few hundred to a few thousand dollars to enter the United States illegally (Cornelius 2000), illegal Chinese immigrants must pay tens of thousands of dollars to human smugglers for the journey (Chin 1999). People involved in the smuggling business have demonstrated surprising resiliency in developing new transportation strategies that allow them to stay one step ahead of law enforcement agencies. After the events of September 11, 2001, many suspected that illegal immigration would be significantly curtailed as governments at all levels shored up security measures. The newly established U.S. Department of Homeland Security quickly evolved into a mega-organization, taking on a wide range of functions previously performed by different federal agencies including border security, customs inspection, transportation safety, and emergency response. Inspections at all ports of entry have intensified. Billions of dollars have been spent, but the impact of the nation's security measures on illegal immigration and concomitant human smuggling activities remains in doubt. Recent news reports suggest that illegal entry by foreign nationals, either individually or in an organized manner, has remained largely unabated. Most notably, a *Time* magazine investigation alleged that the 9/11 events had failed to bring about effective measures to tighten the nation's borders and that the situation of illegal immigration had actually become worse (Barlett and Steele 2004). The report estimated that in excess of three million illegal immigrants entered the United States in 2004, "enough to fill 22,000 Boeing 737-700 airliners, or 60 flights every day for a year" (Barlett and Steele 2004, 51).

Although Mexican nationals continue to make up the majority of the illegal immigrant population, U.S. Border Patrol agents are encountering a growing number of nationals from other countries or other than Mexicans (OTMs, in Border Patrol parlance) entering from Mexico. They reportedly come from Brazil, Guatemala, China, India, Pakistan, Afghanistan, Bulgaria, Russia, Egypt, Iran, and Iraq. The Border Patrol's records indicate a rapid increase in the apprehension of OTMs, from less than 2 percent of all arrests in 1996 to more than 13 percent a decade later in 2005. Law enforcement agencies increasingly worry that the illegal channels developed by human smugglers will also be used by terrorist organizations to deploy their members.

My fieldwork in China and the United States also suggests that human smugglers continue to find ways to transport their clients and settle them in the rapidly expanding Chinese communities across the country. A drive through towns, large and small, can provide a glimpse of the growing demand for cheap laborers to work in the kitchens of the many successful Chinese buffets. Only a handful of scholars have taken an interest in illegal migration from China, and scholarly literature related to human smuggling is just emerging (Liang and Ye 2001), partly because human smuggling is not a traditional racket of choice for criminal organizations. More important, for many years illegal Chinese immigrants have remained largely "invisible" because of linguistic differences and cultural barriers posed by ethnic enclaves in the United States. As long as these communities' problems do not spill into the mainstream society, few outsiders have reason to pry into these ethnic enclaves.

Much of our knowledge about human smuggling and illegal Chinese immigration is based on information provided by the immigrants themselves, rather than by smugglers. Willard Myers (1994; 1996), an immigration lawyer who worked with many undocumented immigrants, claimed that a global network of Taiwanese criminals controlled much of the human smuggling trade; he warned about the threat of this influx of illegal Chinese nationals to U.S. national security. Peter Kwong (1997) wrote a book, based on personal interviews in New York City and a trip to China, about the illegal work force in the underground economy and argued that the increase of Chinese illegal immigration was tied to unfair American labor practices. A few other researchers have also produced scholarly work on Chinese human smuggling (Bolz 1995; Wang 1996). Still, empirical studies on human smuggling and illegal immigration by Chinese nationals remain rare in the United States. Thus far, only two studies have gathered systematic empirical data on a large scale to explore the causes and processes of Chinese human smuggling activities to the United States. One of these studies was funded by the National Science Foundation (NSF) and conducted by Ko-lin Chin and Robert Kelly (1997), who interviewed three hundred smuggled Chinese immigrants in New York in 1993. Among their major findings are:

- Almost 90 percent of the subjects were from the three townships of Changle, Tingjiang, and Mawei. Most were young, married men with little formal education and few professional skills.

- The majority of the subjects admitted that they came to make money, not because they were politically persecuted in China.

- Almost half (48 percent) of the respondents flew into the United States. Another 40 percent crossed the U.S.-Mexican or U.S.-Canadian border overland. Only 12 percent arrived by boat.

- Chinese human smuggling activities were not dominated by traditional crime syndicates, such as China-based secret societies, Hong Kong-based triads, Taiwan-based organized gangs, or even U.S.-based tongs and street gangs.

- Of the 143 respondents who arrived by plane, only seven flew directly from China to the United States. Most had to travel through multiple transit points in other countries; it took on average 106 days for the 143 by-air respondents to complete their travel.

- Most of the respondents who arrived by boat endured horrendous suffering during their voyage. Women were often raped and men beaten by the enforcers on the boats. More than ninety human cargo ships left China between 1989 and 1993. Few were ever detected or intercepted.

- Those who crossed into the United States on land also faced a variety of risks and hardships. The majority first traveled to Mexico or Guatemala by boat. They suffered not only during the voyage but also while crossing the border.

- Although 37 percent of the study subjects were detected and detained by U.S. authorities at point of entry, only 11 percent of the border-crossing immigrants were caught. Those who traveled by air had a much higher rate of apprehension, at 64 percent. However, all those who were detained at points of entry were immediately released after they filed for political asylum.

- Upon arrival, respondents were kept in safe houses by debt collectors until they paid the entire smuggling fee. Many of those who failed to deliver the payment promptly were tortured by their captors. The average smuggling fee for the whole sample was $27,700.

- Most of the respondents worked in restaurants, garment factories, or construction firms, where they made about $1,400 a month. On average they paid off their smuggling debts in less than three years.

The 1993 survey in New York City conducted by Chin and Kelly (1997) was significant in many aspects. It was the first large-scale empirical effort to gather information on the characteristics of the tidal wave of illegal Chinese immigrants, which started in the mid-1980s and accelerated after the crackdown on the democracy movement in Tiananmen Square in 1989. Chin's study and subsequent book (1999) provided critical firsthand information on the nature and extent of Chinese human smuggling.

The other study, which Ko-lin Chin and I worked on with researchers in the city of Fuzhou, was underwritten by the National Institute of Justice (NIJ), the research arm of the U.S. Department of Justice (Zhang and Chin 2002a). Fuzhou and its adjacent counties have long been considered the capital of Chinese human smuggling activities. The vast majority of illegal Chinese immigrants who arrived in America in the 1980s and 1990s came from this region. Data collection activities for the NIJ study, which the current book project is based on, were carried out between 1999 and 2001. Unlike most other studies, which gathered data from illegal immigrants about the smuggling process, our research team interviewed smugglers in New York, Los Angeles, and the Fuzhou area. Multiple strategies were employed in the data collection, including face-to-face interviewing, field observation, and researching government documents and press reports.

The objective of this book is to uncover the inner workings of Chinese human smuggling organizations and the patterns of their operations, and to provide a conceptual explanation of how these individuals, who come from a wide range of backgrounds, were able to engage in group-oriented transactions and to deliver their services with surprisingly high levels of success and efficiency. There are two major components to this book. The first is to shed light on the elusive players behind this illicit enterprise by means of a descriptive narrative about who these smugglers were, where they came from, how they perceived themselves, and how they conducted their smuggling business. The second is to give a conceptual analysis of how and why these otherwise ordinary individuals were able to turn human smuggling into a global business. I construct a theoretical paradigm to attempt to provide a better understanding of small group transactions and the smugglers' remarkable ability to thrive in a hostile and uncertain market environment.

In Chapter 1 I present a historical overview of illegal entry by Chinese nationals to the United States as well as discussing recent trends in the operation of illegal smuggling enterprises. I also provide a synopsis of some of the most prominent explanations of the causes of international migration, and offer my own understanding of the unique characteristics associated with illegal Chinese migration from Fujian Province to the United States.

Chapter 2 provides a descriptive analysis of the human smugglers interviewed in this study. I have also added to this description other smugglers whom I encountered over the years before and since the NIJ study. In this chapter, I present their basic demographic characteristics, describe their varied pathways into the business, and discuss their perceptions of the roles they played in the smuggling process.

In Chapter 3, I present the various strategies and methods used by smugglers to recruit and prepare their clients for the journey to America. The emphasis of the chapter is on smuggling activities inside China.

Chapter 4 discusses the funneling effect of successive outward migrations by Chinese nationals, which has spread across the globe. I describe the methods employed by human smugglers to move their clients slowly and methodically along the many way stations to their eventual destinations. Many illegal immigrants were stuck in transit countries, often for years. The emphasis is on smuggling activities in transit countries.

In Chapter 5, I describe the U.S.-based smugglers and highlight the differences between them and their counterparts in mainland China. The emphasis is on the arrival and payment collection processes of the smuggling activities.

In Chapter 6, I present the scant information we gathered from this study on profits of the business, the cost of doing business, and how partners shared the smuggling fees.

Chapter 7 analyzes the organizational and operational patterns of these human smugglers. In this chapter, I also describe how human smugglers looked for market opportunities and formed alliances with others to pool resources to carry out specific smuggling tasks. I also describe the specific roles involved in smuggling operations and their corresponding structural arrangements.

Chapter 8 presents a conceptual framework, the *dyadic cartwheel network*, to explain how structural patterns emerged from these human smuggling organizations and how these unique structures provided efficient ways for smugglers to protect themselves and to maximize potential profits. I place my theoretical discussion within a comparative context of two major theoretical approaches in organized crime literature—the corporate model and the enterprise model.

Chapter 9 offers a brief review of traditional Chinese criminal organizations—Hong Kong triads, Taiwan criminal organizations, U.S. tongs and Chinatown gangs—and provides an analysis of the connection (or lack thereof) between human smugglers and traditional Chinese crime groups. In this chapter, I describe the structural and organizational differences between these two criminal entities, and examine the market conditions and organizational factors that may explain the absence of any large-scale involvement by traditional Chinese criminal organizations in transnational human smuggling activities. I argue that traditional criminal organizations are ill equipped structurally to deal with the uncertainties and challenges common in an enterprise-oriented market environment.

Chapter 10 presents a group of female subjects in this study who were active participants in human smuggling, and analyzes the important role that gender may play in this illicit business. I put forth the argument that it was no accident that a sizable group of women, some of them with worldwide notoriety in both law enforcement and immigrant communities, became involved and even successful in this business, a departure from traditional racketeering activities.

Finally, Chapter 11 presents my thoughts on the future of illegal Chinese immigration to the United States and what the authorities in China and in this country can do to best manage, if not necessarily eliminate, the flow of illegal immigrants, which has been the main lifeline for maintaining a vibrant underground economy in the United States. I also include smugglers' own assessments of the future of their business, and discuss the challenges confronting policy makers and law enforcement agencies in both China and the United States. I also highlight areas of interest for future research on transnational Chinese human smuggling.

Acknowledgments

I am grateful to many individuals who have contributed to the data collection for this study and to the production of this manuscript. First of all, I want to thank Ko-lin Chin of Rutgers University, a personal friend and the co-principal investigator in the project that laid the foundation of this manuscript. Ko-lin played an instrumental role in the design, planning, and implementation of this study. Our collaboration has led to several conference papers and journal articles. It was only after he became overwhelmed by his many other research and writing obligations that he asked me to assume the sole authorship. Still, I consider this book a product of our joint effort, although I take full responsibility for the views presented herein, as well as any errors and omissions that I may have overlooked.

Therese Baker-Degler, my mentor for many years, encouraged me from the beginning to consider producing a book manuscript from this multi-year project and sending it to Stanford University Press as a possible outlet. She edited and polished several earlier papers based on this study, and reminded me to steer away from academic jargon and parlance unique to the human smuggling trade so that this book could reach a larger audience.

I want to thank Feng Chen and Baihua Chen in Los Angeles for their connections in the immigrant community, which helped me get in touch with many prospective subjects. I appreciate their stories about human smuggling activities, both in China and in the United States, which illuminated the inner workings of this business.

Special thanks go to Darwin Tchan, Jorge Guzman, Scott Morris, Jim Hays, Roger Thompson, and Jeannette Chu of the former U.S. Immigration and Naturalization Service (INS) for their assistance in this study and for sharing their insight into and knowledge of federal anti-smuggling efforts. Their sustained support and interest in my project over the years have provided much-needed encouragement.

I want to thank the subjects, in particular, for entrusting me and the members of my team with the most sensitive information about their involvement in this illicit business. I also want to thank my fellow researchers in China, whose familiarity with local cultural nuances greatly enhanced my understanding of the social context of the smuggling business. Without these individuals, whose identities I am not at liberty to disclose, this study would not have been possible.

Muriel Bell, my editor at Stanford University Press, nurtured this book project from the beginning. I greatly appreciate her measured advice and editorial suggestions. I want to thank Kirsten Oster for keeping the project on track and for chasing reviewers for their feedback. Carlo Morselli at University of Montreal and Chu Yiu Kong of Hong Kong University helped sharpen the analysis and argument in several parts of this manuscript. Their enthusiastic endorsement and support of this project are much appreciated. I also want to thank the anonymous reviewers of this manuscript for their helpful comments.

Special thanks go to Jennifer Bursik, who cheerfully agreed to review and polish this manuscript on short notice. Her words of encouragement over the years on my other works are greatly appreciated.

Many other people helped in the production of this manuscript. Donna-Marie and Jack Cruickshank, Philip Gay, and Robert Winslow have read, edited, and improved drafts of this manuscript. I very much appreciate their comments, their suggestions, and most important of all, their friendship. Although their suggestions have been valuable and are incorporated into the final text, I may have inadvertently overlooked some. Again, I am solely responsible for any errors and omissions in this final product.

Finally, and most important, I thank my wife, Susan, for her unwavering support and understanding during this protracted intrusion, and for pulling double duty in taking care of our young children while I was away doing fieldwork. I am also grateful to my in-laws, Ken and Iva, for providing much-needed childcare on numerous occasions.

Major financial support for this study was provided by a grant (1999-IJ-CX-0028) from the National Institute of Justice (NIJ), Office of Justice

Programs of the U.S. Department of Justice. Lois Mock, my grant manager at NIJ, provided administrative oversight for this study. The opinions expressed in this book are solely mine and do not necessarily represent the views or policies of the U.S. government. Parts of this study have previously been presented at conferences and published in journals.

PART ONE

Snakeheads and Human Smuggling Operations

CHAPTER I

Coming to America

Illegal Chinese Migration to the United States

Introduction

When the Chinese communists took control of mainland China in 1949, the emigration of Chinese nationals to the outside world all but ceased. The country was practically closed off. For most Chinese, the idea of going to the United States, let alone going through illegal channels, was as unthinkable and as remote as going to the moon. Going abroad (or *chuguo*) was something that high-ranking officials in Beijing could do and that the ordinary citizens could read about in the newspaper.

After the United States resumed diplomatic relations with mainland China in 1978, Chinese nationals resumed legal immigration to America (Zhou 1992). Many wanted to come, but few had a legitimate opportunity to do so, because of limited immigration quotas. The lure of higher U.S. living standards, combined with restrictive U.S. immigration policies, quickly built up a demand for alternative venues. A lucrative enterprise began to emerge in the late 1980s, initially in southern China, in which brokers or facilitators helped fee-paying customers leave China and move overseas. These entrepreneurs are collectively called "snakeheads" both in China and in Chinese communities overseas.[1] Today the business of human smuggling has gone global, and the list of destination countries has stretched beyond the handful of countries to which Chinese historically migrated.

Law enforcement agencies and policy makers view human smuggling as a criminal activity replete with human rights violations and grave political and social implications. However, those who engage in the business of transporting people across borders and those who are smuggled generally do not share the same view. Human smuggling carries little social stigma in either the sending communities in China or the receiving communities elsewhere. Most view it simply as a business involving willing participants—those who have the connections and resources to get people to where they want to be, and those who desire such services and are willing to pay for them. At most, human smuggling is viewed as a *mala prohibita* crime, made so solely by government regulations.

This book is based primarily on a three-year study (Zhang and Chin 2002a). Unlike studies that gathered data from illegal immigrants about the smuggling process, this project relied on interviews with smugglers in New York, Los Angeles, and Fuzhou in southern China (see map, Appendix A). This study employed several strategies in its data collection, including face-to-face interviews, field observations, and collection of government documents and press reports. Researchers involved in this study interviewed a total of 129 individuals (or snakeheads) in the United States and China who were directly involved in recruiting, organizing, and transporting Chinese nationals illegally into the United States. Also interviewed were a number of key informants in the communities who either were familiar with human smuggling activities or had friends or relatives in this business, as well as many law enforcement officials in both countries. To date, this remains the only study to systematically gather firsthand data from individuals directly involved in organizing and transporting Chinese nationals from mainland China to the United States. A detailed description of the research methodology is provided in Appendix B.

Illegal Chinese Immigration: A Historical Overview

The first sizable Chinese group to enter the United States arrived more than 150 years ago. By most historical accounts, the Chinese were probably the first Asian immigrants to come to the Pacific coast of the United States. Stories about the early settlement of Chinese nationals in the United States and the explanations of their arrival tend to vary somewhat depending on the historical accounts and the authors' interpretations. There were two recurrent themes: railroad construction and the California Gold Rush.

Political turmoil and economic troubles that brought famine and devastation to millions are cited as a major push for farmers in Southern China to seek employment overseas (Jones 1992). In addition, news of high wages and the need for laborers for the westward expansion of the railroad have been cited as a major pull factor. Many early Chinese immigrants came as "coolies" to work on railroad construction (Jones 1992). Other historians have cited the lure of the Gold Rush, coupled with the efforts of trans-Pacific steamship companies to drum up business among Chinese by hyping the prospects of instant wealth (Lee 1960; Tsai 1983).

The demand for cheap labor, in California and other western states, in other sectors of the fledging economy were additional pull factors for early Chinese immigrants, who were hired for cooking, laundering, farming, fruit growing, tideland draining, mining, and other labor-intensive activities in the frontier communities (Tsai 1983, 13). Although the majority of early Chinese settlers lived close to urban areas and formed their own enclaves, some reportedly braved warring Indians and ventured as far as the Idaho Basin in search of gold (Zhu 1997).

While cheap labor was in short supply and job opportunities in service occupations abundant, the employment of Chinese coolies laying the railroad tracks and toiling in mines and agricultural fields went largely unnoticed. Laborers from southern China (mostly Guangdong Province) continued to arrive on the West Coast in large numbers (Jones 1992). After the completion of the transcontinental railroad in 1869, Chinese who had been employed in the West moved en masse to the East Coast in search of jobs. White society began to take notice (Rhoads 2002). With their conspicuous linguistic, cultural, and physical features, they soon drew attention from other immigrants, who were largely European, and were blamed for a host of social problems, from decreased wages to unemployment. The hostility took on an immediate racial tone, as the Chinese laborers were viewed as incapable of assimilation into mainstream society and its customs (Jones 1992, 213). Union members, many of whom were themselves recent European immigrants, staged protests and acts of mob violence against the Chinese. The political activism of white immigrants quickly won widespread support, leading to a series of discriminatory court decisions and ultimately the passage of the Chinese Exclusion Act in 1882 by the Congress. This was the first American immigration legislation to bar a particular group of people based on their race (Rhoads 2002). This law signaled a formal shift in U.S. immigration policy away from allowing free and unhindered movement of immigrants to imposing limitations on the number as well as the racial characteristics of those it chose to admit.

Except for a few exempt classes (merchants, students, diplomats, travelers, or children of U.S. citizens), legal immigration from China practically came to a halt during the exclusion era (1882–1943) (Wong 2000; Chin and Chin 2000). Open hostility and discrimination against Chinese immigrants who were already in the United States forced many to return to their home country (Jones 1992). However, America remained a strong magnet for many other Chinese seeking to improve their lot. Entry into the country through illegal channels thus emerged as a response to the exclusion laws. Although Chinese already living in the United States made legal and political attempts to repeal the exclusion laws, most of these efforts were ineffective. The majority of the working-class Chinese expended their energy on devising strategies to circumvent the laws (Lee 2003, 189).[2]

Because of immigrants' perseverance and the corruptibility of immigration officials, illegal migration became a booming business. By exploiting legal loopholes and gaps in government enforcement practices, Chinese nationals were able to devise strategies to circumvent the exclusion laws, and effectively became the first entrepreneurs to start the business of transnational human smuggling.

Smugglers employed a number of schemes to smuggle immigrants into the United States. The most well-known was probably the "slot racket" or "paper son" scheme (Lee 1960). Under this method, those entering the country either posed as the sons of U.S. citizens by native birth or assumed the identities of others. In an era of no photo identification or fingerprint cards, assuming someone else's identity was easy. All the applicant had to do was to memorize the information on the purchased papers and pass an interrogation at the port of entry. It is not clear when the scheme was first started. Some have speculated it was probably when the American-born children of early railroad workers returned to China to get married and have children in their home villages (Chin and Chin 2000). Official documents designated these children as sons or daughters of Chinese Americans, or "derivative citizens." These documents soon became a hot commodity to be sold and resold to those who wanted to come to America.

The paper son scheme hit an all-time high in 1906, when the earthquake and ensuing fire in San Francisco destroyed many government buildings and incinerated most birth and citizenship documents. The loss of official records gave thousands the opportunity to launch successful claims to citizenship or declare they had sons or wives in China eligible to immigrate. Because the government was unable to contradict their claims, thousands were granted citizenship (Ngai 1998). Thousands more led so-called "paper lives," constructing and reconstructing their personal histories according to the paper trail that allowed them to enter the country in the first place (Wong 2000, xi). It is estimated that by 1950, at least 25 percent of the Chinese American population were illegal (Ngai 1998). The use of fraudulent documents became so prevalent that U.S. immigration officials launched a so-called Chinese Confession campaign, offering legal status to anyone who would come clean by exposing the paper trails that perpetuated the paper son scheme. This simply created more paper families, however, as illegal Chinese immigrants stepped forward to confess and thus became legalized and eligible to petition for the immigration of other family members. These newly legalized families were now armed with authentic immigration documents, which provided additional opportunities for the paper son scheme.

Another method employed to circumvent interrogations and other restrictions at the port of entry involved making illegal border crossings from neighboring countries (Zhu 1997, 189). There are many vivid accounts of how Chinese immigrants turned crossing the border from Canada and Mexico into a booming business during the exclusion era. Aided by Canadian, Mexican, and American smugglers, some 17 thousand Chinese immigrants crossed into the United States from Canada and Mexico from 1882 to 1920 (Lee 2003, 151).

Because of lax immigration control, both countries became attractive way stations for Chinese immigrants. Taking advantage of trafficking routes already established for alcohol, opium, and other contraband along the Canadian border, smugglers used boats and railcars to transport Chinese immigrants for a fee (Lee 2003, 157). Along the largely unguarded Mexican border in the south, organized and experienced Mexican smugglers procured fraudulent documents, provided transportation and safe houses, and even provided illegal Chinese immigrants with native clothing so they could pass as Mexicans (Lee 2003, 160-161).

Although few historians have discussed these early-day illegal immigration activities as organized crime, the extent and scope of the paper son racket, the systematic manner in which immigration papers were bought and sold, and the elaborate arrangement of border crossings exhibited clear patterns of highly organized activities. These illicit activities were carried out mostly by groups of individuals—often blood relatives or people from the same village—or entrepreneurs. The illegitimacy of the paper son scheme brought forth blackmailers, extortionists, and informers who sought to take advantage of those involved in the illegal immigration business (Lee 1960). Tongs and clans became involved in providing protection services and settling disputes to ensure that knowledge of the racket did not spill outside the Chinese communities (Lee 1960, 303). From the extensive involvement of members of a particular community and their sophisticated arrangement of coordinated activities, McIllwain (1997; 2003) argues that the business of immigrant smuggling during this period was indeed an organized enterprise.

The Chinese Exclusion Act of 1882 probably bears the chief responsibility for bringing about the enterprise of transnational human smuggling. However, even before the exclusion era, human smuggling had already been practiced, for a different reason. Because the vast majority of early Chinese immigrants were male, women being generally barred from independent entry, females were recruited to come to the United States as prostitutes (Stevens 2002; Tsai 1983). Women were often brought over as "wives" of merchants, or "daughters" of U.S. citizens—one of the few legal venues for women to immigrate to the United States (Stevens 2002). In one historical account, more than half of the Chinese women in Boise, Idaho, in 1880 (although their numbers were small in reference to their male counterparts) were prostitutes (Zhu 1997, 188). In 1875, the prostitute traffic between Hong Kong and San Francisco was so heavy that the U.S. Congress passed the Page Law, barring women of "disreputable character" from entry (Tsai 1983, 19).

These early Chinese settlers came to the United States searching for better economic opportunities, a motive not much different from that of present-day illegal immigrants. The restrictions imposed by the government were merely obstacles to overcome, the same way that they were required to endure long voyages over the vast ocean, and then venture into a world that was not only alien but also hostile. In their culture, labor and hardship were an expected price to pay for a better life.

Illegal Chinese Immigration: The Contemporary Situation

Like those who came before them more than a century ago, illegal Chinese immigrants today must overcome many obstacles in search of a better life. Beginning in the early 1980s, ordinary mainland Chinese were once again allowed to leave the country. Once the door was open, the Chinese soon discovered that legitimate venues to move abroad were too few and restrictive. Consequently, illegal channels were developed to meet the demand (Chin 1999).

The rapid growth in global commerce has brought about greater exchanges of not only goods but also people from different countries. As Passas (2000) and Williams (1994) point out, increased transnational commerce works not only to weaken social controls, but also to enhance cross-border criminal activities. No one knows when the modern day human smuggling from China to the United States began, although one human smuggler in New York City claimed that he and some of his friends were smuggled into the country in 1985 by paying off the captain of a freighter. According to this source, quite a few people came to the United States as stowaways in the early and mid-1980s. Soon, idle fishing trawlers in Taiwan were recruited to transport illegal immigrants over the open seas with hundreds crammed beneath the decks. Criminal organizations and individual entrepreneurs from Taiwan have been implicated in most of these maritime smuggling operations (Hood 1994). Stories began to appear in newspapers in the early 1990s about suspicious boats unloading people on the shores along the Pacific coast (Brazil et al. 1993). The *Golden Venture* incident in 1993 shocked the nation with photos and televised images of people wrapped in blankets walking in long lines under the watchful eye of U.S. law enforcement officers on New York's Long Island.[3] The nation was besieged by fears of massive waves of illegal immigrants from the world's most populous nation.

No one knows the true extent of illegal Chinese immigration to the United States. In widely cited testimony before the U.S. Senate, Willard Myers, an immigration lawyer who worked with many illegal Chinese immigrants, estimated that around 100,000 illegal Chinese immigrants may be smuggled into the United States each year (Myers 1994). Other sources, including those in the U.S. intelligence community, put the estimate at around 30,000 a year. One researcher in China has provided a more accurate estimate by conducting a survey in the greater Fuzhou area (including the adjacent counties). Based on the completed questionnaires, the total number of people who were smuggled into the United States in the ten-year period between 1991 and 2000 numbered around 300,000; this is close to the annual figure provided by U.S. intelligence.[4] The survey also reported that about half of those who went to the United States in the 1990s were smuggled during one three-year period (1991, 1992, and 1993). Since then, the figures have steadily declined, probably due to increased crackdowns by the Chinese government and frequent interceptions on the seas by U.S. law enforcement officials. Aside from this survey, which focuses on Fujian only, no other studies have provided a systematic estimates of the number of Chinese nationals being smuggled into the United States.

An analysis of 150,655 undocumented immigrants apprehended at the nation's borders found only 182 who were from mainland China, or 1.2 per thousand.[5] Based on this figure, the figures for illegal Chinese immigration seem insignificant compared to the number of illegal immigrants from Mexico. In a report on irregular Chinese migrants in 2000 for the International Organization for Migration, Ronald Skeldon (2000) points out that, despite their small number, illegal Chinese immigrants are the source of great anxiety in Western countries, for several reasons. First, Chinese human smuggling has been orchestrated by highly organized groups of individuals capable of transporting people over vast distances. Second, because Chinese immigrants are willing to pay high prices, the tremendous profitability of this business only serves to reinforce smuggling activities. Third,

Western law enforcement agencies have long had difficulties in infiltrating and combating Chinese smuggling networks. Finally, because China is the world's most populous nation, there is an underlying fear of the prospect of uncontrolled migration.

In the years since the *Golden Venture* incident, the U.S. government has significantly stepped up its border control and mobilized resources, from high-tech underwater listening devices to overseas diplomatic posts, in an attempt to curb the influx of illegal Chinese immigrants (Gross 1996; Marquis and Garvin 1999; Offley and Connelly 1999). The Congress has also passed laws to increase penalties for criminals caught smuggling illegal immigrants, and has expanded the authority of law enforcement agencies to combat human smuggling (Chin 1999, 151). Federal authorities have successfully prosecuted several human smuggling groups as racketeering enterprises (Gold 1995). But the wave of Chinese nationals arriving illegally does not appear to be receding. Instead, a complex web of international smuggling networks appears to have formed. Human smugglers of different nationalities operate around the world, facilitating and organizing the movement of illegal Chinese migrants to the West. The discovery of the bodies of fifty-eight Chinese migrants inside an air-tight refrigerator truck in Dover, England, in June 2000 is a case in point (McAllister 2000). These illegal immigrants originated from Fujian and traveled through many European countries with the help of Dutch and Turkish smugglers before they boarded the ill-fated truck.[6]

Three main strategies have commonly been employed by smugglers to bring Chinese nationals into the United States. The first is to travel to Mexico or Canada "by some means" and then illegally cross the borders into the United States (Asimov and Burdman 1993). The second involves flying into the United States either directly or via several transit points outside China. These by-air illegal immigrants usually have fraudulent documents to allow them to board the plane and enter the country (Lorch 1992). The third strategy is to transport Chinese nationals in fishing trawlers or freighters and dock at a U.S. port (Zhang and Gaylord 1996; Chin 1999). Human smugglers often employ a combination of these methods. Some transportation strategies appear to be more popular than others at certain times. Since the *Golden Venture* incident, significant changes have taken place in the smuggling business, and new trends have emerged in several directions. The following examples reflect some of the trends in recent years.

CHANGES IN SMUGGLING METHODS AND ROUTES

Illegal Chinese immigrants are increasingly being transported into the United States through means other than fishing trawlers heading directly to the mainland. The sea route is still used, but increasingly smugglers are going to peripheral locations to unload their human cargo, among them the U.S. Virgin Islands, Guam, Ensenada (Mexico), and British Columbia (Canada). Within the first four months of 1999, five ships were intercepted off the waters of Guam and a total of 625 Chinese nationals were detained (Wang 1999). In the first five months of 1999, more than a hundred illegal Chinese nationals were detained in the U.S. Virgin Islands (Associated Press 1999). In August of 1999, about 130 illegal Chinese immigrants landed at the southern tip of Queen Charlotte, an isolated island off Canada's Pacific coast (Reuters 1999). In June and August of the same year, Mexican authorities detained more than two hundred Chinese nationals in Ensenada, in Baja California, after suspicious neighbors tipped off officials to the location of their safe house (Lau and Dibble 1999). These stories represent only a few failed cases that caught the attention of the authorities.

Chinese human smugglers have developed other methods to infiltrate the defense lines erected by the Coast Guard. They now use cargo containers to transport illegal immigrants directly to U.S. ports (Jablon 1999; Zahniser 2004). In January 2000, three Chinese migrants were found dead inside a container on a freighter that arrived in Seattle from Hong Kong (Hervocek 2000). In another incident, twenty-one illegal Chinese were detained at the port of Long Beach after arriving on Christmas Day on board a Danish freighter, and nine others were caught at neighboring Los Angeles Harbor after arriving on Christmas Eve on board MS *Sine Maersk* (Jablon 1999). The two groups traveled in soft-top containers (i.e., canvas-covered) that were equipped with food, water, battery-powered lights, portable potties, cell phones, and ladders for climbing out. In January 2005, three weeks before the Chinese New Year, thirty-two illegal immigrants were found in two containers aboard a ship arriving from Hong Kong at the port of Los Angeles; the authorities did not believe the crew knew about the stowaways (Associated Press 2005). Despite increased inspections in recent years at all U.S. ports, containers are still a frequent choice of transportation by smugglers. Few fishing trawlers are used for human smuggling purposes these days.[7]

INCREASED DEMAND FOR THE AIR ROUTE

Although far more expensive than using fishing trawlers, smuggling operations via the air route have significantly increased in recent years. In fact, the air route has become the preferred transportation choice for those with sufficient connections and financial resources.

Since the *Golden Venture* incident, there have been many stories of fishing trawlers or freighters being intercepted off of U.S. waters, landing hundreds of illegal Chinese immigrants in jails in countries such as Mexico and Canada. Since 9/11, U.S. customs agents have also expanded their shipyard cargo inspections, further restricting smugglers' maritime activities. In response, smugglers have developed way stations and transit points in many countries to move immigrants through various "legitimate" channels. Most often, smugglers arrange "business" delegations to visit either the United States or other transit countries. Fraudulent marriages with U.S. citizens are often promoted and sought after by prospective smugglers and clients respectively. Although some smuggling operations by air do land in the United States directly, many more fly to Canada, Mexico, South Korea, or Japan, or simply enter by way of international transfers at a U.S. airport, where upon arrival the Chinese passenger would seek political asylum. Such incidents have become commonplace in many U.S. ports of entry. The sea route, reserved mostly for villagers from small towns, is usually considered unacceptable to urban dwellers and better-educated clients.

GROWING SMUGGLING COMMUNITIES IN CHINA

The presence of Chinese migrants overseas (both in North America and Europe) seems to be trending in two directions (Pieke et al. 2004, 200). First, because of the cumulative nature of transnational migration, the immigrant-sending area in China has grown from a few counties in Fujian Province to include many other parts of China. For years the vast majority of illegal Chinese immigrants to the United States had come from Fujian Province, located in southeast China directly across the strait from Taiwan.

In recent years, the Wenzhou area in Zhejiang, the province that borders Fujian to the north, has supplied a rapidly rising number of immigrants. For years Wenzhounese had been known to migrate to European countries, but now they are also heading to the United States in large numbers. Illegal immigration from other parts of China, including Beijing, Shanghai, Tianjing, Shenyang, Dalian, and such interior regions as Hubei Province, has also increased. With China's estimated surplus labor force of more than 100 million people (Goldstone 1997), clandestine migration may, as Massey (1999, xiii) has suggested, "produce a flow of immigrants dwarfing that now observed from Mexico."

A second trend in human smuggling activities has been an expansion of the territory in which smugglers are operating within the United States. Smugglers no longer restrict settlement of illegal immigrants only to major metropolitan areas with large ethnic communities where Chinese historically resided. These immigrants have become more mobile inside the country, following better-paying jobs or setting up their own take-out restaurants—and this activity in turn encourages further smuggling activity.

CHANGES IN THE SOCIOECONOMIC BACKGROUND
OF ILLEGAL CHINESE IMMIGRANTS

In the past, most illegal immigrants were young males from farming villages, for whom life in China offered poor prospects (Zhang 1997; Hood 1994). In recent years, because of massive layoffs resulting from China's economic reforms, a growing number of illegal immigrants are former employees of government agencies or state-owned businesses. They tend to be well-connected and oftentimes are able to obtain "authentic" documents through "proper" channels. Not much is known about how this trend has affected smuggling activities or how the settlement process for these more educated and skilled workers may differ from that of earlier arrivals.

RISING SMUGGLING FEES

Fees charged for the illegal journey to the United States have been increasing significantly. The 1993 survey in New York City found an average of $27,745 per client, with a range of from $9,000 to $35,000 (Chin 1999). The average in 1988 was $22,956, and it has increased steadily ever since by about $2,000 a year, shooting up rapidly in the early 1990s. In 1992, the average fee was $29,688. In 1993, it surpassed $30,000. In July 1999, a few would-be migrants who were waiting to take off in Fuzhou reported that their fee was about $52,000. In January 2000, a snakehead waiting for his connecting flight at the Taipei Airport claimed that his smuggling price was $60,000. News reports have confirmed the steady increase in smuggling fees. For instance, Lau and Dibble (1999) reported a smuggling fee of $51,000, and Jablon (1999) reported a smuggling price of $50,000. In late 1998, when a major smuggling ring across the Canadian-U.S. border through a Mohawk Indian reservation was broken up, the smuggling fee was reported to be $47,000 per person (*San Diego Union Tribune* 1998). Figures obtained in this study, since the summer of 2000, have ranged between $55,000 and $60,000. In 2006, we were unable to find a price of less than $60,000.

These trends indicate significant changes in the pattern of illegal migration in response to changes in market and socio-legal conditions in recent years, possibly affecting immigrants' settlement patterns, lifestyle, employment, health, and access to social services. The steady increase in smuggling fees seems to reflect extreme imbalances between the availability of capable smugglers and increases in the number of those who desire their services. Changes can also be attributed to the effect of other market constraints such as law enforcement activity and the increased demand for transportation methods safer than the once-popular, but accident-prone, maritime method.

The Causes of Transnational Migration

The factors that initiate and sustain transnational migration are manifold and have shifted over time (Massey et al. 1993, 1998). Population migration has become a global phenomenon in the past century. In the past, it was mainly Europeans who left their home countries in search of a better life overseas. Now migration mostly originates from developing nations in Africa, Asia, and Latin America to industrialized countries in North America and Europe (Massey 1999). In the latter half of the twentieth century growing international commerce disrupted the livelihood of many in traditional economies and accelerated their movement in search of better economic opportunities.

In *neoclassical economic theory*, differences in wages between sending and receiving countries are seen as the most important factor motivating people to migrate (Harris and Todaro 1970; Mahler 1995). Laborers migrate from lower-wage countries to higher-wage countries. International population migration thus becomes an equalizing mechanism to balance the distribution of economic resources across countries (Massey et al. 2002, 9). Sharp discrepancies in the supply of labor between countries have long served as a magnet to draw people from developing countries to developed countries. In China, in much the same way, farmers from the interior have migrated to coastal regions, where a red-hot economy employs a migrant population in excess of 150 million (Bian 2002). Employment opportunities and higher wages, along with a breakdown of the state welfare system and limits in the amount of farmland, have become the primary driving force behind China's domestic population migration. Because there are few restrictions on domestic travel, such a massive population movement inside China is considered not only legal but vital to sustain the economic growth in coastal provinces.

In contrast, the *micro-economic theory* views migration as a collective act to increase a family's income and minimize risks against a variety of financial uncertainties and market failures (Stark and Bloom 1985). Migrants decide to leave their home countries based mainly on a favorable cost-benefit calculation. However, wage differences are not the only motivation. The decision to migrate also involves larger units of inter-related people such as families or households and sometimes an entire community (Stark 1991). By sending family members abroad to work, households diversify their sources of income and gain protection against the risk of unemployment, crop failure, or price inflation (Massey 1999).

The money sent home from overseas allows households to make major purchases, such as building houses. In China, in an era of diminishing state-guaranteed welfare benefits, going abroad for many serves as a safety net against natural disasters, crop failures, and unemployment. Having a family member, preferably a son, in the United States is akin to creating a financial shelter or a private pension system that minimizes the risk of poverty in old age. Higher wages and greater opportunities abroad have thus been the core explanation for transnational Chinese migration. The prospect of accumulating more wealth than one can ever dream of making in China impels individuals to emigrate.

Other theories look at the influence of the interdependency and integration of a global economic system. For instance, the *world systems theory* proposes that immigration is a result of the expansion of capitalism from its core in Western Europe, North America, Oceania, and Japan to other peripheral countries. Incorporation into the world market economy disrupts traditional economic activities and causes population dislocation in these peripheral regions (Morawska 1990). Massey (1988) argues that international migration is not caused by a lack of economic development but by development itself, because historically it has not been the poorest countries that have dominated international migration, but countries that have experienced economic development.

The *dual market theory* of international migration, in turn, emphasizes the pull factors in receiving countries, where there is a chronic need for cheap foreign workers due to structural and demographic changes (Piore 1979). Labor markets in post-industrial nations have become bifurcated, with high pay and steady jobs on one end, low pay and unstable jobs on the other. In cities such as Los Angeles and New York, a concentration of managerial, administrative, and technical jobs produces a steady demand in the service industry, and provides a structural incentive and market for low-wage foreign workers (Massey 1999). In agreement with this perspective, Skeldon (2000) cites two factors that contribute to the unidirectional movement of population from poor countries to the developed world. The first is the low fertility rate in much of the developed world, which means fresh laborers must be imported to sustain economic growth and contribute to the existing system of welfare and other social benefits. The second factor is rising levels of education among the populace in the West, which diminish the pool of native workers willing to accept low-paid, low-skill, and insecure jobs. Although most western countries have found ways to import both skilled and unskilled workers, there appear to be many unmet needs that draw large numbers of irregular or illegal migrants. More significantly, although regular and planned migration seems to follow the expansion or contraction of the host economy, irregular and illegal migration appears to be independent of the demand for labor and economic growth in those desirable destination countries (Skeldon 2000).

Studies of the causes of international migration have traditionally focused on such economic or market factors as cost-benefit calculations, employment opportunities, and the rearrangement of capital and human resources. This dominant perspective was revised by Massey et al. (1993) with the so-called "new economics of migration." However, theories with an emphasis on economic factors cannot adequately explain why illegal (or irregular) migration has remained largely unchanged, irrespective of the economic conditions or labor market changes of the host countries; nor can it explain adequately the specific direction and timing of migratory flows (Pieke 1999). For instance, illegal Chinese immigrants in the United States came largely from one geographical region, the greater Fuzhou area in China's Fujian Province for many years. In Europe, its many large and well-established Chinese communities drew their members primarily from the Wenzhou and Qingtian regions of southeastern Zhejiang Province. Economic explanations cannot explain why people from these townships and villages decided to migrate en masse, but not those in neighboring villages in similar or worse economic condition.

Economic factors may provide the original impetus for people to leave their home countries in search of a better life abroad, but to explain large-scale and sustained transnational migration, non-economic factors must be considered. Some researchers suggest that the spread of migrant networks and the development of ethnic communities overseas (or infrastructure) make additional movement more likely; this process is known as cumulative causation (Taylor 1992; Massey et al. 2002). In this context, human smugglers are merely brokers and facilitators who provide the logistics necessary to sustain the movement of migrants. The fundamental cause, though, lies in the expansion of a global economy and commercial exchanges within a formally bordered world.

The picture of transnational migration is a complex one. Although most migrants would cite economic reasons as the main motive for leaving their countries, the actual configuration of how and why migration occurs goes beyond merely changing residences for the sake of a better life. Kinship and community ties, legal barriers and human smugglers, airlines, railways, and shipping companies, and even law firms, human rights groups, and anti-immigration activists are all part of this complex picture. Each group plays a role that directly or indirectly affects the flow and direction of legal as well as illegal migration. Pieke (1999, 9) proposes that emphasis be placed on the role of family members, kin, and fellow villagers as key factors in explaining migration flows, choice of settlement, and overseas community building. In other words, economic factors alone are insufficient to explain the patterns of international migration.

International migration is typically started by a few pioneers, who land in a foreign country either fortuitously or deliberately in search of better economic opportunities. Once these pioneers have established a stronghold, they make contact with their home community to recruit labor and business partners. As newcomers arrive, they tend to work for these early settlers. Soon an internally stratified community grows up around these pioneers in the adopted country (Thuno 1999). One's family and kinship network plays a vital role in deciding who should embark on the far journey and when, as few Chinese will travel the long distance and endure the hardship just for their own sake. A collective and family-based decision can impel an individual to make the long and arduous journey to a foreign country (Hood 1997, 82).

FACTORS UNIQUE TO ILLEGAL MIGRATION BY FUJIANESE

Aside from the social and economic aspects discussed above, there are other factors unique to the Chinese context. Although the number of illegal immigrants from other parts of China appears to be rising, one fact remains largely unchanged: the majority of illegal Chinese immigrants in the United States are Fujianese (Zhang 1997). Such a large number from such a geographically concentrated area is rare in U.S. immigration history. Several factors account for it.

First, after two decades of reforms starting in the 1980s, China went from a command-driven economy to one that relies on market adjustments. This economic transformation has greatly improved the efficiency and productivity of its economic system, but also resulted in serious disruptions to traditional livelihoods. Millions left their hometowns and migrated to urban, and particularly coastal, regions in search of jobs. The gradual abolition of the *hukou* (residential registration) system has further spurred the movement of migrant laborers. They now number approximately 150 million, and are free to change residences without having to obtain permission from the authorities (Mackenzie 2002; O'Neill 2002). The *hukou*, which bound Chinese people to their places of birth for guaranteed provision of various socio-economic benefits (e.g., employment, schooling, food rations, and distribution of farm land), has been described as the broadest experiment in population control in human history (O'Neill 2002). Rural dwellers can now move to cities and compete with urban residents for all social and welfare benefits. The massive numbers of rural laborers, willing to work for lower wages and in poor conditions, rapidly displaced native workers in coastal regions like Fujian. Many Fujianese in turn searched for better economic opportunities elsewhere, namely abroad. Raising a sum of tens of thousands of dollars for the journey to the United States is not something that impoverished peasants from the interior of China can accomplish. In fact, most illegal immigrants are not destitute by any Chinese standard.

Second, Fujian has a long history of sea-based smuggling, secret societies, and outward migration (Liang and Ye 2001). These traditions date back to the seventeenth century, when the Fujianese rebelled against the domination of the Manchurians from the north, who had overthrown the Ming rulers in 1644 and formed the Qing dynasty. Following its conquest of China, for several decades the Qing government banned people from leaving the country, through various edicts threatening death by beheading, in order to place a firm control over the remnant supporters of the Ming Dynasty. The ban was in large part enacted to stem migration to Taiwan, which before 1683 was under the control of the Ming general Zheng Chenggong and his family (Tsai 1983).

Even after the Qing government conquered Taiwan and ordered all Ming citizens to return to the mainland, the anti-migration edicts remained in effect, and people from Guangdong and Fujian provinces who wished to go abroad were required to apply for permits under strict conditions (Tsai 1983). Still, because of political oppression, population pressure, and scant farmland, natives of Guangdong and Fujian risked the high seas and harsh governmental punishment to migrate to Taiwan and Southeast Asia in search of a better life (Hood 1994). These migrants often used bribery and other unlawful practices to escape mainland China (Tsai 1983). Today the majority of Taiwanese natives and of the overseas Chinese communities in Indonesia, the Philippines, and Malaysia can trace their ancestral roots back to Fujian and Guangdong.

Third, because of its long history of outward migration, Fujian has a "culture of migration" in which sending communities are often dependent, economically and psychologically, on their brethren overseas. For centuries, the migration of one or more family members (typically married men) has set in motion the outward movement of the kinship or clan. These men settle in a foreign land, accumulate wealth for the family, and then explore opportunities and prepare for the eventual migration of the whole family. As more members of the kinship network join the pioneers, the economic base of the family expands and provides an infrastructure enabling others to migrate. At the center of this culture, what remains are kinship and family groups, circles of mutual obligations that sustain both legal and illegal international migration. Remittances and return trips home (especially around major Chinese holidays) serve to reinforce migrants' continued membership of these groups (*guxiang*).

Macro and cultural factors have combined to push Chinese to make the illegal passage to the United States. Cultural-specific factors take the form of motive and family pressure; macro-structural factors include both push factors (adverse socioeconomic and political conditions) and pull factors (greater opportunities abroad). Though structural factors help explain the prevalence of illegal migration, cultural factors determine who will actually participate and when.

Human Smuggling and Human Trafficking

Before we discuss the activities and organization of Chinese human smugglers more fully, I need to differentiate two terms that are often used in discussions of this subject—*human smuggling* and *human trafficking*. Journalists and even law enforcement representatives often use the two terms interchangeably to describe any organized illegal transportation of human beings from one country to another. To the general public, these two terms are often indistinguishable from one another. However, the United Nations and many governments including the United States have established a clear distinction between human smuggling and human trafficking. The former involves the willing participation of an illegal immigrant, whereas the latter involves involuntary participation, and is considered a violation of human rights. The U.S. government, recognizing the threat to national security, has formed an agency comprising members from the departments of State, Homeland Security, and Justice to crack down on human smuggling, terrorist travel, and trafficking in persons (Human Smuggling and Trafficking Center 2005).

According to U.N. protocol, *human smuggling* refers to "the procurement, in order to obtain, directly or indirectly, a financial or other material benefit, of the illegal entry of a person into a State Party of which the person is not a national or permanent resident" (United Nations 2000a). The U.N. declaration is intended to address the burgeoning global business of illegal immigration facilitated by either enterprising agents or organized criminal groups who provide services for a fee to move customers across borders. The key factor is the voluntary relationship between the two players, whereby a potential migrant contracts with a smuggler to be moved to a country through illegal means (Shelley 2005). It is possible the migrant may experience worse conditions during transportation than he or she was promised earlier, be charged extra fees, or be given a more stringent payment schedule than the original agreement. News and government reports have documented many abuses of illegal immigrants at the hands of their smugglers, but the business arrangement remains a consensual one.

Human trafficking also involves the transportation of illegal immigrants across borders, but the term applies specifically to the recruitment, purchase, and transferring of persons (mostly women and children) for the purpose of prostitution, brokered marriages, forced labor, or other slavery-like practices and entails the use of real or threatened force, abduction, fraud, deception or coercion, or debt bondage (United Nations 2000b). Trafficking victims most often are young women who are coerced into the sex trade or duped into believing they are going to work in well-paying jobs overseas. Victims are often lured by fraudulent job recruiters with phony contacts and transported to foreign countries where they are sold to brothels or held under bondage to work off significant debts (Shelley 2005).

In practice it is often difficult to tell where smuggling ends and trafficking begins, some researchers have found, as few victims are abducted outright by force from their villages (Arnold and Bertone 2002). However, most agree that when force, fraud, and coercion are used to force migrants into any type of bondage or indentured labor, the nature of the business is changed. In this book, the term human smuggling is used consistently, to distinguish it from human trafficking and to indicate that the smuggling activities examined here involve only willing participants.

CHAPTER 2

Becoming a Snakehead

Snakeheads have remained the most elusive group in the Chinese human smuggling chain. Little research has been conducted on the composition and precise operations of this group, for obvious reasons. For many years, U.S. law enforcement agencies have assumed two things about snakeheads: that they are connected with traditional organized crime groups (such as gangs, tongs, and triads) in Chinese communities, and that they have elaborate international networks. Much of our current knowledge about these smugglers has been based on interviews with illegal immigrants, who, in most cases, know little about how their smugglers operated and how smuggling transactions are made between and among various collaborators.

A few studies have attempted to describe Chinese human smugglers, most notably *Smuggled Chinese*, by Ko-lin Chin. Based on a New York survey in 1993, Chin (1999, 29–32) found that illegal immigrants often group the smugglers into two categories: "big snakeheads" and "little snakeheads."

Big snakeheads are the investors, planners, and supervisors involved in smuggling operations. Typically they are overseas Chinese, who are seldom known to the people being smuggled. They are often perceived as capable businesspeople with power, wealth, formidable reputations, and connections in the community. Their place of origin is usually the areas adjacent to Fuzhou, the capital of Fujian Province, in southern China, and they have settled in the United States, Hong Kong, or Thailand. Taiwanese from Taiwan, Brazil, Panama, and Bolivia are also alleged to be major organizers in human smuggling.

Little snakeheads, for their part, are mostly local residents rather than overseas Chinese, and they serve mainly as middlemen and recruiters. They usually live in or around the sending communities in China, and their main responsibility is recruiting clients, making referrals, and collecting down payments. Little snakeheads are usually the relatives or good friends of big snakeheads. If little snakeheads are unable to recruit clients themselves, they turn to members of their extended families and friends to act as members of what can be called the "second tier" of little snakeheads. This is especially true in the case of maritime smuggling operations, in which they must gather hundreds of clients in a short period of time to fill a boat. Often, former clients who have made the journey successfully to America are asked by their snakeheads to recruit from among their friends and relatives in China.

The word *snakehead* can be applied to anyone who brokers services and facilitates getting people to foreign countries through irregular channels. This may include a long list of social contacts, business associates, friends of friends, and even acquaintances who may not even know they are aiding illegal migration. Sometimes these people provide assistance for a fee; other times, they simply consider it a favor. A narrower use of the term refers only to those who knowingly provide smuggling services for a fee to assist someone to emigrate. In practice, the concept of a snakehead can be a slippery one. One snakehead in this study described how he came to define those involved in the smuggling trade:

> It's not easy to define a "snakehead." There are many government officials who work with snakeheads. Many snakeheads were themselves smuggled abroad before, like a friend of mine who went to Japan as a "foreign student." He paid a snakehead a lot of money. When he got to Japan, he worked at a Chinese-run bakery. After he befriended his boss, he came back

to recruit people to go to Japan on student visas and send them to work in his boss's bakery. His goal was simply to earn back the money he had initially spent for his trip to Japan. I came to the U.S. through a fraudulent marriage arrangement. When my immigrant status is secure, I will do the same thing. I will get a divorce and go back to China to marry someone for a fee. I definitely want to have the opportunity to earn back the money I spent on getting here.

Among the subjects in this study, the distinction between big and little snakeheads appeared to be rather blurred. Snakeheads came from diverse backgrounds. Unlike their clients, smugglers interviewed in this study did not usually refer to one another as "big" or "little" snakeheads. However, some definitely appeared more successful than others, and were occasionally referred to as "big snakeheads" or "doing big businesses." By and large, it was difficult to discern the big players because of the secrecy surrounding most of their activities. Most subjects in this study were working with other snakeheads, who in turn worked for still other snakeheads. Sometimes, the distinction was purely made on appearance or one's self-promotion. Those who appeared to be well connected (that is, knowing a lot of people) and spending lavishly would be honored with the title of "big snakehead."

Snakehead Demographics

We interviewed a total of 129 individuals who claimed to have participated in the transportation of Chinese nationals into the U.S. As shown in Table 2.1, the majority of the subjects were male (82 percent), with a high school education or less (90 percent). They were generally in their thirties or forties (about 79 percent) and married (about 79 percent). The majority of the subjects (75 percent) described themselves as either unemployed or self-employed. Of those who said they were unemployed, most were actually self-employed, engaging in a wide variety of income-generating activities. They considered themselves unemployed only in the sense that they did not hold a salaried job, or because it was difficult for them to describe how they drew their main income. None of the subjects were by any means destitute.

Of the seventy subjects interviewed in the United States, forty-five (64 percent) entered the country in 1993, the year of the *Golden Venture*

Table 2.1. Demographics of snakehead subjects

	Frequency	Percent
Interview format		
Formal	111	86.0
Informal	18	14.0
Total	129	100.0
Gender		
Male	106	82.0
Female	23	18.0
Total	129	100.0
Education		
No formal education	5	4.2
Grade school	29	24.2
Junior high	31	25.8
High school	43	35.8
College	12	10.0
Total	120	100.0
Marital status		
Married	100	78.7
Single	21	16.5
Divorced/separated	6	4.7
Total	127	100.0
Age		
21–30	18	14.1
31–40	65	50.8
41–50	36	28.1
51 and older	9	7.0
Total	128	100.0
Employment		
Employed full time	28	21.7
Self-employed	57	44.2
Unemployed	40	31.0
Retired	4	3.1
Total	129	100.0
Citizenship/Immigration Status		
U.S. citizen	29	22.5
U.S. green card holder	24	18.6
U.S. legal non-immigrant	17	13.2
U.S. illegal immigrant	12	9.3
Chinese citizens only	47	36.4
Total	129	100.0

NOTE: Percentages are rounded.

incident, or before. The remaining twenty-five subjects (36 percent) came later. Of this group, forty-four (63 percent) entered the country through legal channels, and the rest were smuggled into the United States illegally. Surprisingly, the majority (73 percent) of these snakeheads claimed to have entered the United States directly from China. More than two-thirds of the U.S.-based snakeheads were either citizens or green card holders; at the time of the interviews only about 11 percent were illegal immigrants.

Smugglers and Their Backgrounds

People of diverse backgrounds were found in the smuggling business. The number of different jobs held by the subjects in this study was close to 70, including restaurant owners, waiters and waitresses, housewives, handymen, masons, taxi drivers, farm laborers, seafood retailers, garment factory workers, hair salon owners, and fruit stand owners. This assortment of jobs was collapsed into 14 categories and presented in Table 2.2.

With a few exceptions, the majority of the subjects did not hold salaried jobs in state-run entities or established corporations. Based on these self-reported occupations, the business of human smuggling did not seem to attract people who would prefer predictable and routine activities. Although a few subjects were employees of government agencies or educational institutions (e.g., middle school teachers), by far most of them were entrepreneurs of some sort, making a living in occupations (such as small retail stores, vending outlets, and other independent or commission-based businesses) in which uncertainties and risk-taking were the norm.

Table 2.2. Subjects' employment status

Job Category	Frequency	Percent
1. Owner of large business	1	.8
2. Education-related employee	3	2.3
3. Small Business employee	1	.8
4. Farmer	4	3.1
5. Full-time smuggler	8	6.2
6. Government employee	3	2.3
7. Housewife	5	3.9
8. Illicit business worker	2	1.6
9. Illicit business owner	4	3.1
10. Self-employed worker	8	6.2
11. Service-sector worker	16	12.4
12. Small business worker	1	.8
13. Small business owner	37	28.7
14. Unemployed worker	36	27.9
Total	129	100.0

NOTE: Percentages are rounded.

Through interviews and interactions with these individuals, I discovered that behind these snakeheads were still other people of diverse backgrounds. Subjects often mentioned names in reference to other circles of friends or acquaintances that they claimed to be working with. As one snakehead in Queens, New York, explained:

> Ah Chen (one of the subject's partners) is from Hong Kong, but he lives in Shenzhen. His parents and brother live in Hong Kong now. He knows many people who work in police agencies. We are friends. I have known him for many years. He has a high school education and was originally in some financial business in Shenzhen. My other partner in the U.S. also graduated from high school in Fuzhou. He knows many people in Fuzhou and owns a hair salon there. Because of our (smuggling) business and frequent travel back and forth, he has quit managing his hair salon and asked his cousin to take care of it.

Although some of these social networks consisted of Chinese immigrants commonly found in Chinese enclaves, others claimed to have partners of higher visibility. One subject in New York said:

> Among our partners, some hold crucial positions in the police divisions in charge of processing travel permits. Others are involved in government agencies in charge of tourism. I first got to know these people because I came in frequent contact with them in my business. Later we have become friends. But we are not relatives.

These human smugglers were different from one another in almost every aspect, but shared one common interest: making money. The business of transnational human smuggling required no special skills or training and was open to just about anyone with the right connections and enough courage. One of the subjects commented, "Wherever there are Chinese, there are snakeheads. Snakeheads are people who are willing to take risks (of being arrested) for money." Another subject in Brooklyn, New York described some of his smuggling partners:

> Our partners in China have only a grade school education. None have any social status worth mentioning. I can't tell you any details about the background of my partners in the U.S. Let me just say that they are all from Fuzhou and have made a lot of money. None have had much education. Some of them have families and others don't. Besides doing human smug-

gling activities, they all have other businesses, such as financial offices, restaurants, and nightclubs.

Among the study subjects, the youngest was twenty-four years old. Those under thirty made up only about 14 percent of the sample. They were mostly recruiters and musclemen (debt collectors), roles peripheral to and on both ends of a smuggling operation. The majority (close to 80 percent of the subjects) were married with families. Although there were no age limits for participating in human smuggling, this business appeared to be dominated by those who were considered "established" culturally (meaning married with families). One may ask why prospective immigrants and their families should care about the age or marital status of their smugglers. For one thing, the Chinese culture in general considers young and unmarried people to be inexperienced and unreliable and thus less trustworthy. Individuals with families and children are considered to be interconnected with the community and bound by their many social obligations, thus assuring prospective clients that their smugglers would not simply take the money and disappear.

Entry into the Smuggling Trade

For most subjects in this study, entry into the smuggling business was not deliberate. Instead, it was rather fortuitous, and the subject was often abetted by friends, relatives, or acquaintances who happened to know one or more snakeheads. A 36-year-old subject, who also owned a brick factory, described how he got involved in the human smuggling business:

> First of all, many of my relatives went to the U.S. with the help of snake-heads. They are doing very well there. Secondly, I know people who are in the human smuggling business. So I have become involved.

A summary of the experiences of how subjects in this study first became involved in human smuggling activities, appears to show two main routes: (1) the family/friend route, and (2) the snakehead route.

THE FRIEND AND FAMILY ROUTE

More often than not, those in a smuggling organization belonged to a family or a close social circle. As Table 2.3 shows, half of all the subjects became involved in the business through their relatives, friends, or business associates. Direct recruitment by snakeheads accounted for one-third of the subjects in this study. Interestingly enough, about the same portion of these subjects also claimed that their main source of clients was their friends and relatives.

Going through one's social network appears to be the most logical route to enter the trade, because human smuggling is essentially a business of social networking. Entry into the smuggling world is a two-way street: either a smuggling "wannabe" approaches his or her friends or relatives, expressing an interest in getting involved, or the person is approached by others because of his or her occupational connections or social position. A

Table 2.3. Involvement in smuggling activities

	Frequency	*Percent*
Introduced to smuggling business by		
Relatives and friends	55	50.0
Other snakeheads	38	34.5
Other	17	15.5
Total	110	100.0
Sources of clients		
Relatives and friends	54	49.1
Referrals from other clients	14	12.7
Referrals from specific regions	25	22.7
Recruiter network	17	15.5
Total	110	100.0
Motives in smuggling business		
Money	64	57.7
Money and to help friends	37	33.3
To help friends	8	7.2
To pay debt	2	1.8
Total	111	100.0
Quit previous job after involvement in smuggling business		
No	53	48.2
Yes	57	51.8
Total	110	100.0
Time commitment in smuggling Activities		
Full-time	39	36.4
Half-time or part-time	23	21.5
Sporadic	45	42.1
Total	107	100.0

NOTE: Percentages are rounded.

45-year-old subject in Flushing, New York, described how he entered into this business:

> I got into this business through friends. It was back in 1995, when I was working as a coordinator at a container shipyard. I was responsible for informing my (smuggling) partners about who were on duty at the yard and what uniforms they were wearing. I would then provide the clients with the uniforms of the day so they could blend in when they approached their designated containers.

Such an informal recruitment process seems to give just about anybody with the right connections or in the right social circles the opportunity to enter the business. Such was the story of a teacher in Changle County who became involved in the business because her husband was without a stable job at one point. Hearing that people could make a lot of money in the United States, she approached her aunt, who in turn put her in touch with a snakehead. Soon her neighbors found out about her organizing a smuggling trip and asked if they could tag along. In her words, "Without even knowing it, I became a snakehead overnight, and I didn't even get paid a penny by these people."

THE SNAKEHEAD ROUTE

A sizable number of the subjects in this study, about a third, reported that they became involved as a result of knowing people already in the smuggling business. They were different from those who came via the family route in that the snakeheads who introduced them to the smuggling business were neither relatives nor members of their social circles. One snakehead in New York's Chinatown, who was primarily responsible for receiving and delivering clients and collecting payments, described his entry into the smuggling trade like this:

> I was smuggled into the U.S. myself. I went through many countries before arriving in Canada. From there, I was loaded into a cargo truck and driven into the U.S. Since I became acquainted with the snakehead who smuggled me into this country, I asked to join his smuggling group. I used my personal stories to recruit other clients.

Complementary needs appear to be what brings otherwise unrelated individuals into a smuggling network. One subject in New York, who entered the

country through a marriage fraud, described how he got to know a snakehead and became involved in this business:

> It was back in 1997, when I was working as a barber in a hair salon in China-
> town. A customer of mine was a snakehead and asked me if I could help him
> collect payment from his clients. He said he would pay me 30 percent of
> the collected money. I agreed because I wanted to find something else to do
> on the side to earn more money. My motive was quite simple. I didn't make
> much money as a barber and needed another job. At first, the snakehead
> gave me two or three names and told me each of them needed to pay their
> smuggling fees in $1,200 installments. I usually phoned the clients in the
> evenings to inform them when and where to deliver their payments. A lot
> of times these clients claimed to have no money to pay me. I'd tell them, "If
> you don't pay, your family members back in China will be in trouble." That
> statement would usually cause them to worry and most would figure out a
> way to come up with the $1,200.

In a few other cases, recruiters themselves were prospective immigrants
who were either instructed by their smuggling handlers to bring in more
clients or voluntarily participated in the recruitment effort to reduce their
own costs or to save up for their eventual trip. As one subject in Changle
County said:

> I was a taxi driver and knew many people, so one day I asked a local snake-
> head if I could be smuggled to the U.S. He said yes. I told my family about
> my plan, and several of my relatives heard about it and wanted to join the
> trip. They told me that we could look after each other on the boat. So I
> asked the snakehead if these relatives of mine could also come along. He
> said yes and my costs would be lower.

In addition to these two common routes of entry, a few subjects claimed
that they ventured into the human smuggling business solely on their own
initiative and had no direct solicitation or assistance from any others whatsoever. One subject in Philadelphia, who immigrated to the United States
with his family in the 1970s through his U.S. citizen father, told about joining the smuggling business:

> It was back in 1986. I was losing money in my restaurant business. During
> this time, I spent a lot of time hanging out in Chinatown travel agencies just
> to kill time. It was in these places I heard a lot of stories about human smug-
> gling and paid attention to the conversations, and gradually figured out the

details of the process. Then I decided to try this business myself, and I used my brother-in-law as my guinea pig and helped him to apply and obtain a tourist visa to Thailand. I did his case through my various contacts in those travel agencies. Once I got started doing this business, I had no interest in any other type of work.

Motives for Participation in Smuggling

For a large majority of the snakeheads interviewed in this study, the primary motive for becoming involved in the human smuggling business was money. In fact, 92 percent of the respondents cited money as either the primary or one of the primary reasons for becoming involved in human smuggling. Many subjects considered human smuggling an easy way to make a living. One snakehead in New York City said:

> Before I got involved in this business, I was manning a mobile produce stand, selling fruit and vegetables. It was a hard life. You had to put up with all kinds of weather, rainy days, cold windy days, and hot summer days. In 1998, I was successful in helping some friends arrange business delegations to the U.S. Then I realized how easy it was to do this business. Since then, I stopped selling produce.

For newly arrived immigrants who can only work on menial, low-paying jobs in Chinese communities in the United States, human smuggling offers a way to make easy money and improve their living conditions. One subject in New York, who entered the country with a false visa on a Hong Kong passport in the 1970s, said he started smuggling immigrants in the 1980s, mostly by using photo-substituted passports, bringing clients into either Toronto, Canada, or the United States directly. He attested that the smuggling business was a quick way to make money:

> I had no other motives than making money. My wife was pregnant at the time and I knew we would need a lot of money. I just didn't make enough, about $30 a day, in a garment factory pressing clothes all day long. Once I started doing this business, I quit my garment factory job. There was no time for other jobs.

It was not uncommon to find desperate individuals who joined the smuggling business because there were no other viable options to make some quick money. Some snakeheads in this study claimed that they were in debt and needed to come up with some money fast. One 24-year-old debt collector in New York described how he joined a smuggling group to pay his own smuggling debt:

> I was smuggled into the U.S. on a boat and only had $20,000 to give to my snakehead. I owed another $30,000, plus $10,000 in interests. A total of $40,000 and I must pay back in four years. I had worked for two years for my smugglers as a debt collector and a guard at a safe house. I still have two more years to go before I finish paying the debt.

Still, a third of the subjects in this study made it clear that making money was not their only reason to get involved in this business. These smugglers claimed that helping friends and relatives was just as important. One subject, who owned a successful clothing business in China and specialized in bringing "business delegations" to the United States, explained how he got involved in the smuggling business:

> Because of my business, I would travel to the U.S. several times a year. Because it was easy for me to obtain U.S. visas, I began to bring a few clients with me. That was the beginning of my smuggling business. Although my primary reason was to make money, it was also a good thing to help out my friends and relatives who wanted to come to the U.S. I could kill two birds with one stone. Now, about every six months, I bring a group of clients with me to the U.S. I am still running my clothing company because I need the company to organize these business trips.

How Human Smugglers Perceive Themselves

As Chin (1999) found in his New York survey, smuggled Chinese nationals often consider snakeheads either philanthropists who want to help others or "ordinary business people" who merely want to make money. Data from this study suggest that most snakeheads do not think what they are doing is criminal and consider their smuggling activities legitimate ways of providing alternatives to those who would have few opportunities to advance in China. One snakehead reflected:

> Yes, my motive in this business is money, but I am also helping people to go to America and give them a chance to rise above poverty. They have no way to make money and even those with jobs only bring in a few hundred

Chinese yuan a month. But in America they can make $1,000 a month. Why not do them the favor? It is a good thing that I am helping my relatives and friends as well as others.

It was clear that most subjects expressed some apprehension about their involvement in this business and, because of widely publicized crackdowns by the authorities, were fully aware of its illicit nature. However, they simply could not see how their participation in this business would qualify them as criminals. In most cases, the subjects seemed to be more concerned about the headaches and money issues of the business, and even about their responsibility to their clients, than about the morality of their entrepreneurial ventures. A subject in New York City who owned a hair salon made it clear that his legitimate business was only his "open identity" and he could make far more money from smuggling immigrants:

> I personally bring clients into the U.S. from China through Thailand. I also take care of many things in smuggling operations, such as obtaining legal status, acquiring ID cards, registering with local authorities. This is a risky business, and any mistakes can land me in jail. I could lose a lot of my years and even my life if caught. But the money is good in this risky business. So I think it is worth it. I deserve to be rich.

In general, snakeheads tend to have positive opinions about themselves. They see themselves as upstanding businesspeople or even "do-gooders" who help their friends and neighbors to get a better life. Some even claim

Table 2.4. Views on involvement in smuggling activities

	Frequency	*Percent*
Mutual benefit	7	.2
Reputation as a businessman	4	4.1
A lot of responsibility	20	20.6
Try to do my best	11	11.3
Hard work and lots of fun	3	3.1
Necessary work	8	8.2
Only do proper/legal things	4	4.1
Work for good pay	19	19.6
Safety and profit	10	10.3
Forced to do smuggling	3	3.1
Not easy—lots of headaches	8	8.2
Total	97	100.0

NOTE: Percentages are rounded.

that their involvement in human smuggling ventures helps solve some of China's pressing social problems, such as overpopulation and unemployment. One snakehead in Fuzhou proudly proclaimed:

> I have nothing to feel bad about being a snakehead. I don't lie to my clients, nor do I ask for additional payments after they arrive in America, nor do I physically abuse anyone. In fact, I feel like I am doing something positive for China. There are so many unemployed people here, and we have a huge population. We not only help China to solve these problems but also increase the amount of foreign currency being sent back from overseas.

The large number of Fujianese living abroad does appear to have both raised standards of living for those left behind and reduced rates of unemployment or underemployment, as large remittances are sent home each year, to the delight of local Chinese government officials (Pieke et al. 2004, 26). Although helping the government solve pressing social problems seems to be a cover for their true intention, snakeheads nonetheless are quite firm in their belief that they are making an honest living. One subject in Fuzhou emphatically said:

> My family is proud of what I am doing. You need to have a good reputation in this business. Most snakeheads are overseas Chinese who come back to Fuzhou to do this business. Like Sister Ping, her clients are extremely comfortable having their money in her hands because she has such an impeccable reputation.[1] People know that she will never take the money and run. Many people envy us, and their eyes turn red whenever they see us making so much money. I don't steal nor rob people. Nor do I lie to my clients. I have no uneasy feelings about what I am doing.

The fact that neither illegal migrants nor snakeheads consider human smuggling a crime, and that many view it as a good thing instead, might help explain why so many otherwise law-abiding people, including reputed business owners and community leaders, have been found in the smuggling trade. Another important reason is, of course, the seduction of the tremendous profits one may make from an "occupation" that many of the subjects in this study consider a godsend because it requires neither fixed working hours nor special skills.

Leaving the Smuggling Business

Venturing into the human smuggling trade was fortuitous for most of the subjects in this study, but when they left the business they followed predictable paths. About half (52) of the 111 subjects with valid responses had already quit the smuggling business at the time of their interviews. Of the remaining 59 active snakeheads, 46 (about 77 percent) had been involved in the business for less than three years. In fact, about one-third (19) of these snakeheads were in the business for about one year or less at the time of their interviews. There were, however, a few exceptions. One subject claimed to have remained active in the business for twenty-two years. On the one hand, the wide variation of years in business could partially be an artifact of the study's design, which sought to include in the study as wide a variety of snakeheads as possible. On the other hand, the variation may well reflect the business's fundamental lack of stability. The majority of the snakeheads who quit the business did so after about six years. This finding suggests that human smuggling is not a long-term career for very many. Furthermore, although most snakeheads entered the business through close friends, the three most common reasons for leaving the business were a growing concern for personal safety, an inability to maintain reliable smuggling networks, and bad luck.

GROWING CONCERN FOR PERSONAL SAFETY

First, some smugglers were no longer willing to continue being involved in this risky enterprise because of a growing concern over threats to their personal safety. These threats stemmed from mounting pressure from law enforcement authorities. Some witnessed the arrest of their relatives and became scared. One subject, who was running a fast food restaurant in Washington, D.C., said that she quit her smuggling activities because she was increasingly nervous about the crackdowns and tired of dealing with corrupt officials in China:

> I started doing the smuggling business in 1996. I had many contacts in
> China of various backgrounds. All of them were well connected socially. In
> the first half of 1999, I quit because too many people were doing this business. There were also many crackdowns by authorities in China and the
> U.S. I was also tired of having to travel so much. My contacts in China and

other transit countries were all very corrupt. It was exceedingly difficult for me to continue. It was also a lot of responsibility. There were so many contingencies and unpredictable events along the way; and there was always the possibility of being caught. Both my clients and I could lose a lot of money, and a failed operation would cause lots of headaches to me and my clients.

Other snakeheads who had quit the smuggling business said they became increasingly preoccupied with other successful enterprises. One snakehead in Fuzhou said:

> I was mostly recruiting and screening clients. I relied on friends and neighbors to find would-be clients who were financially well-off and referred them to the snakehead, who was a good friend of mine. I also served as a financial guarantor. Once the clients arrived in the U.S., I helped collect the payments in China. I was doing the smuggling business on the side, mainly to help my friends. Now I am too busy with my own business to do the smuggling thing.

INABILITY TO MAINTAIN RELIABLE SMUGGLING NETWORKS

Second, in contrast to those who *chose* to leave the business, some of the subjects were forced out for reasons beyond their control. They did so mostly because they were unable to maintain their networks or retain the connections crucial for the continuation of their smuggling activities. One snakehead in New York's Chinatown, who specialized in acquiring passports with temporary green card stamps for photo substitutions, explained why he quit the business:

> I did this business for seven full years and quit in December 1999. Towards the end, it became very difficult because we were unable to bribe the border security officials who manned the checkpoints in China. They were afraid of taking bribes from us because the Chinese government was cracking down hard. Also, new immigrants now must have a separate green card in addition to their Chinese passport, making the process more complicated.

Other subjects had to quit when they lost a crucial member in their smuggling network. Unable to replace the severed link, the group's remaining members inevitably fell apart and went their own way. Such was the story of a snakehead in Brooklyn, New York, who claimed to have made $420,000 in the three years he was in the business. His smuggling scheme involved purchasing Dominican Republic passports to bring illegal immigrants from mainland China into Hong Kong, then loading them onto U.S.-bound cargo ships:

> I used to work in the export business in Hong Kong, selling quartz watches to Mexico. I did not stop my export business because I only did smuggling part time. I was responsible for bringing clients from China into Hong Kong and delivering them to my partner. He worked with a captain and made arrangements to get them onto the freight boat. I was in the smuggling business for three years. Unfortunately my partner died of cancer in 1998. He did not introduce me to this captain, so I could not continue the business. I was too honest and did not go behind my partner's back to acquaint myself with the captain. Otherwise, I could have continued on my own.

The loss of a crucial network member was a common reason for the breakdown of many smuggling organizations. A subject in Bronx, New York, described how his job as a customs inspector in China made him a critical partner in a smuggling organization; in one year he earned profits worth twenty times the annual income of a regular government employee. However, after his scheme was discovered and he was placed under internal investigation, with an arrest warrant pending, he had to smuggle himself out of China and came to the United States:

> It was between 1995 and 1996. I was making a decent living, but wanted more money. A snakehead friend agreed to give me $10,000 a person in exchange for my assistance to escort his clients onto an outbound freighter. My primary responsibility was to "inspect" the boat, and certify it as "safe" to leave China. Every two to three months, he would have a group of eight to ten clients going through my jurisdiction, and I would file a fraudulent inspection report to clear the boat for departure. In 1996, I was informed of an investigation into my inspection work and realized I had been followed. Fortunately I escaped in time. Otherwise I could lose my life. I heard that an inspector from the same port district was implicated and sentenced to death. Now I am a cook in a restaurant and can never go back to China. My only hope now is to make money to send back home to raise my son. I shouldn't have taken the money from this snakehead. I only have my own greed to blame.

BAD LUCK

Third, there were the unfortunate snakeheads who, in spite of their best efforts to conceal their activities, were caught and thrown in jail. Not only did their smuggling careers come to an abrupt end, but many also lost a fortune in the end. One subject, a transit escort residing in Queens, New York, described how he quit the business:

> I got involved in this business in 1994. Prior to that, I was working in a clothing factory in New York's Chinatown. My main motive was to make money. I got to know a snakehead who asked me to accompany his clients to exit China and enter the U.S. For each client I accompanied, I would receive $3,000. One day in December 1998, while passing through an airport in France, my client was stopped by French immigration officials because his fraudulent visa was detected. That client confessed to French authorities that I was his escort. I was arrested and jailed in France for four months. It was a terrible experience. After I returned to the U.S., I quit the business.

For the purposes of this study, research contacts in China were able to interview a few incarcerated snakeheads. One of these imprisoned subjects, a specialist in arranging tours to countries such as Vietnam and Laos for transit purposes, described how he was arrested:

> I was caught when I was escorting six clients onto a bus to cross into a border town in Yunnan Province. I was so close to finishing the job because we had already acquired the border-crossing passes. These six clients were each fined 3,000 Chinese yuan (about $370). My partner from Laos and I were fined 30,000 yuan each (about $3,700) because we were the snakeheads.

In sum, human smuggling is a business that requires neither fixed hours nor special skills, and anyone with the right connections and enough "guts" can develop a profitable niche in the business. Individuals become involved in this business mostly through their fortuitous social connections. Money is the most important motive for the vast majority of snakeheads, although many think they are also doing a good deed by helping their friends and relatives. Regardless of their motives, snakeheads in general consider it an easy way to make money. Although subjects in this study were not randomly selected and are therefore not necessarily representative of any snakehead population, many snakeheads had several attributes in common; they were

- Male
- Marginally educated (usually with less than a high school education)
- Married

- In their thirties or forties
- Self-employed
- Engaged in the trade on a part-time basis or sporadically
- A member of a tight social network
- Dealing with smuggling partners individually, on a one-on-one basis
- Making money for their specific services, with little or no control over how other members of the operation went about their tasks.

None of the subjects in this study considered themselves criminals. On the contrary, many considered themselves do-gooders. This positive self-image may help explain why many otherwise law-abiding people, including reputable businesspeople and community leaders, have become affiliated with the human smuggling trade. However, despite their positive self-perceptions, many snakeheads did not remain in the business for long and were aware of the illicit and temporary nature of their involvement.

CHAPTER 3

Recruitment, Preparation, and Departure

The business of human smuggling is as varied in its arrangements and operations as the backgrounds of the individuals participating in the trade are diverse. For each general pattern I present below, there are exceptions. For instance, smuggling operations usually follow time-consuming processes that involve smugglers working in concert with other smugglers to get documents ready and trips planned. In a few cases, the planning and execution of the operation were so efficient and secretive that the would-be immigrants were working on their regular jobs one day, disappeared the next day, and two days later their relatives showed up at their workplace to gather their personal items and announce their safe arrival in America to stunned office mates.

Most smuggling operations are carried out in three basic stages: (1) recruitment and preparation, (2) the journey, and (3) the arrival. All three stages, although interconnected and dependent on each other, involve specific activities aimed at attaining different objectives. Because snakeheads employ different modes of transportation with different levels of complexity, what I discuss in the following sections represents broad characterizations of the major phases; additional steps may be involved in an actual operation.

Recruitment

The process begins when prospective clients and their smuggling handlers meet. Unlike traditional racketeering activities (e.g., prostitution, loan shark-ing, or fencing stolen goods), which often take place in locations known to their prospective customers, human smugglers have no established venues or neighborhoods to conduct transactions with prospective clients, although there have been some exceptions to this general pattern. For instance, for a few years in the late 1980s and early 1990s, many so-called "going abroad consultation" agencies openly advertised their services in assisting people to move abroad. These businesses quickly drew the attention of law en-forcement agencies. Because they lacked continued personal or familial connections within the smuggling communities, they found it hard to re-cruit would-be immigrants. As a result, these agencies were either closed or mutated into something else. One subject in Fuzhou related:

> My husband was doing this "going abroad consultation" business, and I started out by helping him respond to inquiries and prepare agreements. Most of those who came to our store were merely checking us out to see if we could actually help them go to other countries. Later my husband set up an organization for cultural activities in another city and used the outfit to send delegations abroad for "cultural exchanges."

By and large, most snakeheads and their prospective clients find one an-other through their mutual social circles. More specifically, the majority of prospective clients know only the recruiters, and few know all the snake-heads in a smuggling organization. Depending on their personality and role in the smuggling operations, some snakeheads seem eager to interact with their clients, while others never reveal their identities. One snakehead in Fuzhou explained her reasoning:

> I don't deal with my clients directly. In this business, we are all one-on-one. You recruit clients for me and I turn to my next partner. To protect myself, I never let my clients know who I am, because if any of these clients ever are arrested and sent home, I can get into big trouble. I hold my recruiters responsible for dealing with my clients.

The recruitment process can evolve in many ways. In some cases, prospective clients are approached by relatives or friends who happen to know people in the smuggling business and want to make money by making referrals. In other cases, eager clients look for contacts who can include them in a smuggling trip. Such was the case with a middle school teacher in Minghou, a county to the west of Fuzhou, whose friends wanted to go to the United States:

> I was talking to a colleague of mine one day and she told me her friends wanted to go to the U.S. She asked if I had any contacts in this business who could help. I had many friends in Changle County, and the smuggling business was widely known there. So I told her I would help. I made a few phone calls to my friends and got her in touch with a snakehead.

A mason in Mawei, a township in the suburbs of Fuzhou, said that he was approached by recruiters already working in the smuggling business:

> I was playing cards one day, and a neighbor of mine came looking for me and asked if I could find anyone interested in going to the U.S. by boat for $36,000 a person. If the trip was successful I would earn commissions. Since this was the first time, I had no idea how much I would be paid for a referral. But I knew someone who wanted to go to the U.S., so I gave this neighbor of mine the contact number. Later this client actually made it to the U.S. The second time I was approached by this snakehead, I asked first how much he was going to pay me before I made any referrals. I agreed to help him when he told me he was willing to pay me $1,000 per client.

Without formal channels for advertisement or regular meeting places, snakeheads typically must rely on a good reputation spread by word of mouth. Prospective clients all have their own ways to evaluate their smuggling handlers. Some do it on the basis of social standing in the community or the worth of the legitimate enterprises in which the snakehead is involved. Success in one area often serves as a measure of one's capability as a snakehead. One recruiter in Changle, who at the time of the interview was trying to smuggle himself into the United States, described what he knew about his snakehead:

> This guy used to operate a karaoke bar and made a lot of money in the town. He has been smuggling for quite some time. Many people said he was quite successful and his clients almost always reached the U.S.

The most effective way for a snakehead to convince prospective clients of one's capability, however, is through testimonials from relatives of successful clients, or by having them check out a former client's family in the village whose son made it into the United States safely because of him. It appears that a reputation can advance rapidly, after just one or two successful operations, as the mason in Fuzhou related as he continued his story:

> The first group of clients that I was involved with went to the U.S. by boat. The second group got there by plane with all legitimate travel documents. Because these two groups all arrived in the U.S. safely, many people came looking for me. This last time, for instance, I was prepared to refer only one person; but several of his relatives and friends showed up at the meeting place, expecting me to introduce them to my (snakehead) partner.

Low-level snakeheads (i.e., recruiters), although eager to make easy money from referrals, are also concerned about the credibility of the snakeheads they work for; because their clients are mostly friends and relatives, they scrutinize them carefully. Word of mouth and personal referrals again are crucial in establishing a snakehead's credibility and verifying his or her competence. The occasional scam makes such careful screening at both ends of the business necessary. Unscrupulous individuals posing as credible snakeheads from time to time round up unsuspecting clients, only to turn them in to the police for a cash reward. For many years, law enforcement agencies in Fujian have offered financial rewards to people who tip them off about human smuggling operations. One of the subjects in this study was the victim of such a scam:

> I was in the wholesale business, selling watermelon seeds, and met someone at a business contact's home who claimed to have been a snakehead for more than ten years and very successful. He asked if I could introduce him to some clients and he would pay me 3,000 yuan for each client. My business was slow at the time, so I agreed to help him. I knew little about this person and his background. He contacted me only through his cell phone to give me instructions. He told me that our clients would depart from Quanzhou (a coastal city about 100 miles south of Fuzhou) by boat and go directly to the U.S. I spent two weeks recruiting seven people. When we arrived at the bus station and boarded the bus for the port of Quanzhou, this guy asked to borrow my cell phone to call his boss. Within five minutes the police arrived. Only then did it dawn on me that this whole thing was a setup.

Many of the subjects in this study reported having either directly encountered or heard of such scams. However, their stories about smuggling scams were often presented in the context of their efforts to present themselves as straightforward and truthful in their business conduct. As I discussed in Chapter 2, snakeheads generally think of themselves as honest business people providing needed services to those who can pay. A good reputation is a vital asset that snakeheads are most eager to acquire and maintain. One restaurant owner in Philadelphia, who quit his eatery business to become a full-time smuggler, explained:

> In this business, your clients rely on you to get them to their destination and you get to make money from it. If I can't get them there, I should return all their deposits. My clients are all referred to me by my friends. When they succeed in arriving in the U.S., their families will refer more relatives or friends to me. Reputation is very important in this business.

With China's large surplus population and the eagerness of its young to seek opportunities abroad, one might think that there would never be a shortage of prospective clients in China, and that the demand for smuggling services would be endless. In reality, only a relatively few Chinese have the financial wherewithal to pay to be smuggled into a foreign country. Most can only dream of such a journey. But having enough money does not guarantee that a snakehead will come forward to offer his or her services. Snakeheads screen their clients for a variety of reasons. As one snakehead in Fuzhou who specialized in arranging "business delegations" to the United States said:

> I have to screen my clients, not always by myself, though. There are two types of clients I don't want—those who are *tuqi* (behaving like country bumpkins) and those who are very good-looking. Both types attract attention from border checkpoint inspectors. I like clients who are as plain looking as possible, so they do not attract any attention. I want the border checkpoint inspector to ask as few questions as possible. I usually ask my clients to come to Fuzhou and my recruiter will come with them and tell them his boss (me) would like to talk to them. I will then talk to them and ask them questions. I don't want anyone who can't answer questions quickly or respond to my inquiries with proper answers. The slow ones will be rejected. There have been few rejections because my recruiter screens clients first and he knows what kind of clients I want.

Because of the obvious illegality of the smuggling business, snakeheads and their prospective clients are keenly aware of potential payment issues when none of the agreements are legally enforceable. Accordingly, recruitment involves a two-pronged screening process in which both the prospective client and the snakehead assess each other. The client must be certain that the snakehead can be trusted; the snakehead must be certain the client can pay the smuggling fees. One snakehead in Fuzhou, who owned an aquaculture business and also did construction work, explained the screening process:

> There are two basic rules in this game. Clients must have money or no smugglers will take them. Then the smuggler must have a success record or he will never get any clients. In most cases, all parties know each other through friends and relatives, making it easy to build a mutual trust.

Because there are always more prospective clients than snakeheads, smugglers in general are more careful screeners of prospective clients than prospective clients are of snakeheads. More than anything else, in the initial interactions with prospective clients, snakeheads (often through their recruiters) must come to a decision regarding the financial capability of their clients. No snakeheads want to take on clients on a promise that once in America they will work off the debt in installments over many years. Again, as with differences in snakeheads and differences in mode of transportation, the scrutiny of clients' financial abilities varies widely.

Snakeheads can obtain assurance of payment in several ways. In many cases, relatives already in the United States will vouch for the smuggling fees. Because referrals often take place within a small social circle, it is fairly easy to find out whether a prospective client indeed has relatives overseas, particularly in America. Oftentimes a snakehead's own social network extends to the Chinese communities in the United States, where he can easily verify the existence of these relatives. Snakeheads will either receive phone calls from or make phone calls to the United States for verification purposes. In other cases, clients use bank accounts to verify their savings and their ability to come up with sufficient funds to pay the fees. A third way is to find a guarantor in China, usually someone inside the prospective client's close social or familial circle, who promises to pay the expense once the journey is completed. These guarantors are not only well off financially, but widely respected in the community, and most of them have relatives in America themselves.

As a last resort, families of would-be immigrants may, either single-handedly or collectively, take high-interest loans from people in their village. Surprisingly, few lenders seem to mind the illegal nature of this practice and the possibility that the borrowers might default on payment. People in the sending communities were actually found to be quite willing to lend money to would-be immigrants. The interest rate for these loans can run up to 24 percent annually. One government official in a village in Lianjiang County, where most, if not all, families had relatives in the United States, explained that:

> If you want to open a business, say, in buying and selling fresh fruits in China and want to raise some seed money, nobody will give you a penny because they don't know whether you will make it or not. Such lending will never happen because people have no faith in these kinds of ventures in China. But if you tell them you want to go to the U.S. and want to borrow money to pay for the trip, most are willing to lend you the money because everyone who gets to the U.S. will find a job and work hard to send money home.

Maritime smugglers appear to place less stringent financial requirements on prospective clients than do snakeheads using other modes of transportation, however, because of the large number of people required to fill the cargo space for each trip. Many recruiters reported that multiple clients (mostly relatives) would be gathered at the port of departure and sent off to catch the boat. Still, such gatherings of would-be immigrants for maritime operations are not random and casual but restricted to small social circles. As one recruiter explained, "I rely on people whom I know very well to refer clients to me. These clients are usually neighbors of one another or from the same village."

Because maritime smugglers try to maximize their profits by filling the boat to its capacity, it is likely that some immigrants without adequate financial means will manage to get on board. In addition, maritime snakeheads do not always have the time to carefully screen their clients before letting them get on the boat. Stories of torture and beatings, as reported in the news media and detailed in Chin's 1993 survey in New York (Chin 1999), illustrate what can happen when illegal immigrants cannot make payment upon arrival. For this reason, the majority of the subjects in this study claimed to spend much time scrutinizing their clients' ability to pay. As one snakehead in Fuzhou explained:

> I ask my recruiter to do a lot of investigation in the village to find out if the client has the ability to pay the fees. A friend of mine once smuggled a client, a single child of an older couple who, it later turned out, couldn't pay. What can you do about him? This client told my friend that he had relatives in the U.S., and he was the only child, so his family was able to save a lot of money. But once he got there, none of his relatives were willing to lend him the money. His parents were in their seventies. No one in the village was willing to lend them the money because who knew if the older couple could live long enough to pay off the debt? This client told my friend that he was willing to work in a restaurant of his choice and would not draw any wages until the debt was paid. Who in their right mind would want such an arrangement? Getting paid in small installments over years? What about all the costs my friend had to pay to others who were part of the deal? So my friend lost a lot of money on this case. I make sure that my recruiter has a clear understanding on this issue. I always warn him if there is any problem with payment, I will hold him responsible. There are several ways to check a person's ability to pay, such as a house, some type of business, or close relatives in U.S. (like brothers). I also must find out if this family has a good reputation or is in good standing in the community. These things are very important. My recruiter knows that I will hold him responsible for the payment issue, so he is careful in selecting and referring clients to me.

Such careful screening of clients was a common practice among the subjects in this study, particularly among those whose smuggling business involved complex arrangements using legal and illegal routes and assorted types of documents. One snakehead in New York's Chinatown, who specialized in acquiring Indonesian passports in Jakarta, said that during the years he was active in the business (between 1996 and 2000) he had to spend a lot of time in Fuzhou screening his clients and contacting them to make sure they actually had the money. To most snakeheads in this study, a prospective client's ability to pay was the first and most important concern.

Preparation

Preparations for the journey usually commence shortly after the screening is completed and an agreement is reached between the snakehead and the client. However, the actual smuggling process does not begin until the down payment is made. As a general rule, recruiters do not get paid until their clients reach America. The down payment serves two main purposes: (1) to secure the prospective client's commitment to working with the same snakehead, and (2) to cover basic costs such as securing travel documents. Depending on the smuggling method, the preparation phase may be as simple as following instructions to congregate in a coastal village to wait for small boats to ferry them out to sea, where they will meet with the transoceanic ship. A complex preparation, such as assuming the identity on a photo-substituted passport, may involve language training, memorizing biographical information on the passport, and mock interviewing to prepare for possible inquiries at the port of entry.

Maritime operations appear to involve the least amount of client preparation. When clients decide to work with a particular snakehead, they wait to be notified of the location and time to meet. These operations often involve illegal landing of passengers in Canada, Mexico, South American countries, or peripheral U.S. territories where no legal documents are needed. Even less preparation is necessary if members of a smuggling group also own and operate the transoceanic fishing trawler. Most maritime smugglers must work with willing captains, who, in turn, hire a crew for the journey. Leasing a boat and preparing for the transoceanic trip often take months. A snakehead from Fuqing (south of Fuzhou), who also ran a leather products business, claimed that once he had enough clients, it usually took his group another two to three months to lease a boat and stock the necessary supplies.

Snakeheads who specialize in arranging "business delegations" often make elaborate preparations and establish training procedures to ensure that their clients can respond to questions by immigration officials, both in China and in the United States. Snakeheads who exploit fraudulent travel documents all conduct some type of training to prepare their clients before departure. Clients in "business delegations" must either assume someone else's identity or travel with an altered passport. Training sessions can be as elaborate and complicated as learning about a company (for which the delegation is formed) or as simple as memorizing the basic biographical information printed on the passport. In many cases, clients must also learn a few English words to appear educated. These days English language schools have sprung up in the townships of many sending communities in Fujian Province. Advertising flyers, often in the form of hand-written notes, offering intensive English language training can be found pasted on brick walls in many places. One female snakehead in Fuzhou reported usually sending her clients to Chengdu, the capital of Sichuan Province, where they would be included in legitimate business delegations. Pre-departure training was mandatory, she explained:

> Before departure, all my clients must go to Sichuan to receive training. They must learn about the companies that organize the delegations and their "official" positions. For instance, one client was assigned an accountant position in a delegation. He had to learn about the company's profit and loss situation, staff structure, and payroll. All my clients must also learn provincial vital statistics such as names of the leaders of the province, the population, major geographical locations, and agricultural products. There is a lot to learn. That is why I screen my clients carefully and make sure they can learn these things and be able to respond to questions at the airport.

Departure

The method of transportation determines the departure process. There are probably as many detailed departure arrangements as there are snakeheads, as each smuggling organization develops its own unique procedures and makes its own transportation decisions. The methods for exiting China are essentially the same as the methods for entering the United States: by sea, land, or air. Most snakeheads employ a combination of these methods.

DEPARTURE BY AIR

Departure by air is by far the most risky method in terms of being detected and detained, because of the tight security at international airports. At the same time, it is also the most sought-after route of departure because of its convenience and relative safety. Because Fuzhou has only limited international flights, such as those to Hong Kong, snakeheads often launch transit operations. Many of the subjects of the study claimed to have sent their clients to other cities in China for their initial international flights. By and large, these departure cities are in the coastal provinces and have many international flight connections. One snakehead in Lianjiang County described the transit used by his group:

> I know my snakehead boss is a U.S. citizen. He brings his clients to Shenyang (a city in Liaoning Province in northeast China) and from there they fly to South Korea, sometimes to Japan, and then to Los Angeles.

A former snakehead whose two sons were both in the United States and whose main business was importing and exporting fresh fruit described how his photo-substituted clients left China:

> I mainly worked with little snakeheads (recruiters) and directed them to bring their clients from around Fuzhou to Guangzhou by train. My boss in Guangzhou would take over and bring the clients through Hong Kong to Canada. I know these clients would be transferred to the U.S. I know the big snakehead was in the U.S. The one I was working with was a business-man in Beijing.

Direct flights to America by far are the clients' most preferred method of travel. However, because of immigration officials' and airlines' tight passport control, illegal migrants must often hold genuine documents of their own or assume the identity of someone else having genuine travel documents. Although they are still available, fraudulent documents are becoming more difficult to produce as more countries employ state-of-the art counterfeit technology. As one snakehead in Fuzhou who was active in acquiring and altering foreign passports described:

> I have done a lot of things in this business. At one time I specialized in acquiring and altering passports. We call it *huantianshu* (changing the heavenly book—or altering a passport). At the beginning I was doing it with a friend. He bought the original equipment and chemicals from overseas. You have to be very careful when peeling off the lamination. The temperature has to be right. I ruined a couple of passports in the beginning. Later I became very good at it. I mostly changed Chinese passports. Foreign passports were not easy to change and had to be sent out to Guangdong Province to get the job done. I think the passports were actually altered in Macao. But I was not privy to those details. Passports are more difficult to alter these days and I don't do them anymore. I simply buy them from people who come back from the U.S., Taiwan, Japan, or Korea. These days instead of *shatou* (lopping off one's head, or replacing the passport photo), we simply

do a *diaobao* job (switching the bags, or assuming someone else's identity). *Diaobao* is much easier.

Resourceful snakeheads can acquire genuine travel documents and U.S. visas, thus improving their clients' chances of successful departure and arrival. These snakeheads usually use their extensive networks and contacts to get their clients placed into companies or agencies that have legitimate business in the United States. In one such story, a twelve-year-old Chinese girl who was supposedly participating in a space camp in Alabama disappeared soon after arrival at the San Francisco International Airport and later showed up at her relatives' residence on the East Coast (Gaudette 2002). As a precaution against possible defection, the girl had signed an affidavit proclaiming that she had no relatives in the United States. Local law enforcement agencies launched a massive search for two days and an Amber Alert was issued by the California Highway Patrol, notifying all motorists on California freeways of a possible kidnapping. It was clear that her snakehead had been able to work through the organizing agency in Beijing to get the girl included in the group while planning and coordinating transfer details with her relatives in the United States.

Another way that genuine travel documents are used to leave China is via the fraudulent marriage. Although this is a time-consuming process, fraudulent marriage offers probably the most advantages in terms of ensuring one's entry and legal status in the United States. Because spouses of U.S. citizens are given special treatment and put on a fast track to enter the country with full immigrant benefits to work and travel, many people find ways, often through smuggling groups, to enter into fraudulent marriages. The underground economy of marriage fraud has thrived for many years, catering to those who temporarily trade in their bachelorhood for tens of thousands of dollars and to those who are willing to pay tens of thousands more for a guaranteed entry and legal status in America. Service providers (including government clerks, recruiters, matchmakers, and immigration lawyers in China and the United States) are more than happy to provide the necessary paperwork for a fee.

Surprisingly, fraudulent marriages frequently involve people already married and often with children in China. In this scheme, married couples in China file for divorce and thus become eligible to remarry. An eligible unmarried person is recruited in the United States and sent to China to "acquaint and engage" with the prospective bride or groom. After registering with the local government, the "couple" then hold a wedding ceremony to formalize the union. All proceedings are photographed and videotaped for legal evidence. The client, together with any underage children, then becomes eligible for immigration to join his/her U.S.-citizen spouse. Because of his/her marriage to a U.S. citizen, the client obtains a temporary (or conditional) green card valid for two years. Although these reconstituted families almost never live together, they keep joint bank accounts, addresses, utility bills, and even albums of "family pictures." In time, immigration lawyers will be hired to prepare all the necessary paperwork for adjustment from temporary immigrant status to a permanent green card, and eventually to U.S. citizenship. Clients are carefully coached before their mandatory face-to-face interviews with U.S. immigration officials.

After three years of a marriage to a U.S. citizen, an immigrant is eligible to become a U.S. citizen, but the actual length of time varies depending on the backlog of applications in a particular state. Once citizenship is finalized, the immigrant can divorce again and become eligible to remarry the ex-spouse. Although seemingly foolproof, this process often takes years to complete and comes with a high price. At the time of this study, the price for a fraudulent marriage in the Fuzhou area was $70,000 for an individual and more than $100,000 if underage children were involved. To many, the prospect of providing one's spouse and children a guaranteed ticket to America is well worth the cost and sacrifice. Ironically, fraudulent marriages are mostly considered perfectly "legal" in many sending communities around Fuzhou. One rather respectable figure in a township in Lianjiang County, whose wife and two children went to New York through a fraudulent marriage, was quite open about how he viewed the scheme:

> Fraudulent marriages are considered acceptable and legal in this region.
> People are open about their desire to leave the country via these "legal
> means." Let me tell you a true story. A man in his fifties from the U.S., who
> had previously married three times and been dumped three times by his
> young brides, recently came back to look for yet another young bride. This is
> an extreme case. He is not doing it for the money, so he said. He just likes to
> marry a young woman. You know what, all the eligible women in this town
> ship are lining up for an interview with him. Even the female clerk process
> ing his paperwork at the local Public Security office wants to marry him.

It is almost impossible to stop smuggling schemes such as fraudulent marriages and business delegations at the port of exit or entry, because the traveler holds genuine documents and the only thing illegal is his/her intention. Less resourceful snakeheads often use fraudulent travel documents to leave China, which increases the likelihood of being detained at security checkpoints. The scheme of *maiguan* (buying the checkpoint, or bribing the checkpoint security personnel) is often used to ensure clients a safe exit. This is a common practice in the human smuggling business because, except for a few boat-based operations, all illegal migrants must pass through some checkpoints, either over land or at an airport. One snakehead in Fuzhou who arranged for photo-substituted clients to go through airport checkpoints told her story:

> *Maiguan* is very expensive. There are only a few places along the coast you can bribe the security personnel. Fuzhou is not on the list. Beijing, Shanghai, Guangzhou are the three big ones. Each deal costs about 60 to 80 thousand yuan (about $7,300 to $9,700). The price can only go up. These contacts are really hard to develop and they make the easiest money. Airports with direct flights to the U.S. are the most expensive to bribe and also the most risky, because every person caught and sent back by the U.S. authorities can be traced to the specific checkpoint where the document was inspected. When the risk of detection is the highest, corrupt border control officials also charge the most. *Maiguan* can also be accomplished at land border checkpoints. These border crossings are relatively cheap because many people pass through each day and the risk of being caught is low. It usually costs 10 to 30 thousand yuan in these places.

All parties involved in *maiguan* procedures know very well that these illegal migrants may be caught as soon as they land in the United States or some other country. As a result, a practice called *taitou* (lifting one's head, or as soon as the airplane takes off) has emerged as a way to protect both the corrupt security personnel and the snakehead. In this case, the snakehead makes it clear to the client that as soon as the airplane leaves the ground, all payment must be made. The checkpoint security personnel involved must also be paid immediately. One snakehead in Fuzhou explained how *taitou* works:

> I know who is on duty today and at which inspection booth. I will stand in the back while watching my clients lining up. The officer in the inspection booth sometimes knows the names of the clients, while at other times he

will see me standing in the distance. All parties in this scheme know what to do and no instructions are needed. The inspector will examine the travel document and let my client pass. As soon as the airplane takes off, I will pay out the *maiguan* money. The entire smuggling fee will also be settled immediately. In this scheme, both the smuggler and the clients are fully aware that they are holding fake or altered passports that will likely be detected at the U.S. immigration control. They often tear up their travel documents and flush them down the toilet, and surrender to U.S. officials as soon as they touch down and apply for political asylum. Some clients try their luck with a falsified passport to pass the U.S. immigration inspection (or *chongguan*). While their applications for political asylum are pending, these clients are bailed out by our contacts for about $5,000 each.

Depending on how convincing their stories are, the majority of illegal Chinese migrants detained at the U.S. port of entry are afforded an opportunity to appear in front of a federal judge, at which time they often become eligible to be bailed out. Unfortunately not all *taitou* clients are so lucky. Some are repatriated immediately on a return flight on the same airline. When immediate repatriation occurs, there will be trouble for all involved in the smuggling operation. The female snakehead in Fuzhou described the possible aftermath of her clients being caught and returned to China:

> Chinese authorities will track down those who were on duty on that day when these clients passed through. The inspectors on duty must explain to their supervisors what had happened, although they always claim innocence by saying they did examine the documents but were probably not paying enough attention to the details. Because the border security force (or *bianjian*) is a part of the Armed Police (or *Wujing*), which is considered part of the military system, these border inspectors are soldiers. The worst thing that can happen to a soldier is to be discharged (or *fuyuan*). That's why these corrupt officers must charge as much as they can, sometimes up to 100,000 to 120,000 yuan (about $12,000 to $15,000) per person, thinking that this may be a one-time and career-ending deal. Keep in mind that the money is not paid to one inspector. We must bribe up to seven people in the unit, from the inspector in the booth to the supervisors and even plain-clothes officers roaming the international terminals at these airports. They work in packs. You can't just bribe one person. It won't work. Furthermore, because of frequent rotations, these soldiers usually leave in a few months. So they are also in a hurry to make as much money as they can while in power.

Using the *taitou* method to leave China has one major drawback: clients must often spend months in immigration detention, waiting for their cases to be heard in a federal court and bail to be set before they can disappear into the underground economy.[1] These clients enter the country knowing that they will be detained. Many stay in detention facilities for a year or even longer, remaining idle when they could have been making money in a restaurant or garment factory. Although the drawbacks are infamous, human smugglers have also improved the *taitou* strategy over the years, as the same Fuzhou snakehead explained:

> I am sending my *taitou* cases through Canada now. Canadian authorities don't lock up illegal immigrants for long, probably one month at most. If they can't find evidence to prove that you intentionally entered the country illegally, they will give you refugee status, which allows you to work. Once you are released, there will be people waiting outside the jail to pick you up and arrange for your transfer to the U.S. The main difference here is the length of incarceration. Many of my clients now want to go to Canada for transit purposes.

The term *maiguan* has long been a widely understood concept inside the Chinese smuggling community. Smugglers and would-be clients know immediately that the term implies bribery of officials at border checkpoints. Over the years, *maiguan* has evolved into complex and sometimes even double-blind procedures for protection purposes. One snakehead in Fuzhou explained how a recent *maiguan* operation worked:

> Contact A knows Officer B, who works at an airport checkpoint. Smuggler C knows Contact A. C will pay A to make arrangements at the airport, who finds out when and where Officer B will be on duty. Contact A then notifies Officer B to go easy with people going through his inspection booth on certain days or even for certain flights. Contact A then notifies Smuggler C to instruct his clients to line up in a specific lane for inspection. Neither Contact A nor Officer B knows who the clients are. Smuggler C does not know who Officer B is. The clients know neither Officer B nor Contact A.

Such a scheme can provide a good alibi in the event these clients are caught and repatriated, because the inspection officer was going easy on everyone during the shift. The officer will have no knowledge of or prior connection with any of the illegal migrants. In recent years, however, the

Chinese government has instituted mandatory and frequent rotations of border inspectors to combat official corruption. Some subjects in this study reported that they quit the smuggling business because of the loss of such crucial contacts. As a backup strategy, some smugglers these days are more interested in cultivating relationships with supervisory officers at airports rather than inspectors. The above snakehead explained the shift in networking emphasis:

> All secondary inspections or interrogations are conducted by supervisors, who make decisions either to clear or detain suspicious travelers. For instance, an inspector refers a suspicious guy to his supervisor, who will conduct interrogations and double-check the travel documents. The supervisor then clears the passenger for departure. If the inspector refers several suspicious passengers to this supervisor only to have them released, he will know something fishy is going on. In most cases, the inspector will not report this matter to a higher level of command because there is usually no evidence and there are no witnesses to substantiate such speculations. He may make it known to the supervisor that he is aware of what is going on. In most cases, the supervisor knows well enough to ask the intermediate or the snakehead to invite the inspector to dinner and to *baiping* (even things out by paying the bribes to all parties). The supervisor often will not be present when such transactions take place. This way, the less each party knows about what the other party has received the better, because if both the inspector and his supervisor collaborate knowingly, when one goes down in a corruption investigation, the other probably will also be implicated.

DEPARTURE BY LAND

Leaving China by land usually requires that snakeheads bring their clients to border regions and get them out making many crossings into neighboring countries along the long borders in the north with Russia and Korea, or to the south with Hong Kong, Vietnam, Laos, and Burma. Because of the bustling commercial activities in border regions, human smugglers often exploit border crossings, particularly in Yunnan and Guangxi provinces in the southwestern corner of China. Travel documents are still required for border crossings, although the inspection is not as strict as at an international airport. Because the Fujianese are notorious for illegal emigration, passports and other identification documents issued in Fujian Province usually invite greater scrutiny than those from other parts of China. Many would-be migrants will therefore arrange to transplant themselves to other provinces in order to acquire non-Fujianese identification cards and passports. One snakehead in Fuzhou complained that to improve her chance of success she had to move all her clients to other provinces:

> I have to move my clients to another province to place them in business delegations. You can't do it in Fujian anymore. No one wants to see a Fujian passport. It costs at least 20,000 yuan to move a person to Dalian (a city in northeast China) to obtain the necessary official paperwork. You need to create his entire history with the company from job classification to payroll. You must also bribe the municipal officials in charge of reviewing and approving foreign travel. You see, these government officials have to interview members of official business delegations. If you don't have connections with these officials, and they ask to interview your clients, you will be caught immediately, because your clients can never master the local accents. So you have to have connections to get foreign affairs officials to waive the interviews.

Those who use a land route to send their clients abroad are limited in their smuggling capabilities, because transporting migrants from Fujian Province to any of the border areas in China is cumbersome and arduous. Since few snakeheads share their trade secrets or contacts with each other, they find it hard to improve their smuggling skills and specialties or become more efficient over time. A smuggling network, once formed, will probably stay the same until it ceases to function. Evolution or expansion rarely occurs within an existing smuggling unit.

One subject in Mawei, who was smuggled to Canada many years previously and became familiar with different transportation methods and routes, reported that his smuggling group would fly clients from Fuzhou to Kunming (the capital of Yunnan Province) first; there these clients would obtain local border region tourist documents and travel overland, then cross into Laos. Once inside Laos, his Laotian snakehead would transport the clients to Vietnam, where they would be flown to Singapore, then to Indonesia, and finally to Canada. His partners in America would transport the clients from Canada into the United States. Sometimes his clients would cross into Vietnam from Guangxi Province. On one occasion, he and his Laotian partners, together with their six clients, were detained by border police in Mengla, a border town close to Laos. After paying their fines, he still managed to take his clients through another border town into Vietnam.

Despite the difficulties, snakeheads still use land routes. For many years, they used cities bordering on Laos, Burma, and Vietnam to circumvent the need for exit permits, an emigration control mechanism. In order to thwart these activities, the Chinese government required all new passports be stapled with the exit permit from the specific country to which the passport holder originally applied to travel. This was to prevent a passport holder from going to any country that he was not authorized to travel to. The measure failed to work, however, because once a passport holder completed the initial trip, the exit permit was often removed, so the passport could then be used to travel to any country. Human smugglers quickly figured out that by sending clients to these neighboring countries their passports could be transformed into a more flexible travel document. Thus exit permitting was futile in curtailing illegal emigration; it was later abandoned by the Chinese government.

DEPARTURE BY SEA

Maritime smuggling activities, prominent in the late 1980s and early 1990s, have lost much of their draw in recent years. Increased surveillance and interceptions on the open seas appear to have significantly reduced the success rate of these sea-based operations. The hardship on board the smuggling ship and the perils of the rough seas have dashed any remaining enthusiasm among prospective clients. Even in villages where throngs of individuals eagerly await a chance to leave, few locals desire to be stuck beneath a boat's deck for weeks. Veterans of this practice in America often tell of their bitter experiences and attempt to discourage their relatives and friends from following in their footsteps. One recruiter in Changle County related one horror story he had heard:

> A friend of mine told me that his son was totally deceived by a snakehead. Before the trip, the snakehead told him that there would only be a dozen or so clients on the boat and that the boat was well-equipped and stocked with lots of supplies. In reality, more than a hundred people were crammed into the boat, and they had little to eat or drink. The crewmen were physically abusive to the clients at will.

Maritime smuggling operations proceed in several stages. First, the recruiters need to gather prospective clients through their friends and relatives; meanwhile, other organizers work to secure small boats for ferrying clients to the mother ship for crossing the Pacific. Then the mother ship, oftentimes a fishing trawler or a freighter, must be leased and stocked with supplies. Still other snakeheads work to coordinate overland transportation to get clients to the loading point on the coast. In most cases, maritime smugglers pick up multiple groups of clients at several locations along the coast. A recruiter working in one location typically knows little about who else is contributing to the boatload. He only knows that the clients are heading for the United States and that he is responsible for bringing them to the rendezvous point. One recruiter in Fuzhou said:

> I told my clients when and where to meet. They usually took the bus to Fuzhou and I met them at the bus station and introduced them to my partner. Then my part of the deal was completed.

A snakehead in Los Angeles claimed that he and his partners had worked out a better way to ship clients by boat:

> You don't need a visa to go to America. I have many friends who arrived on container ships. No, they did not hide in any containers. They passed as crews. They usually came in groups of five or ten. When night fell, these clients would congregate at a meeting place and get transported by small boats to a dock alongside the container ship. After their secret signals matched, the container ship would lower its bridge and the clients just walked up onto the deck. Then the crew would tell them which rooms they were assigned to.

Not all boats depart from the coastlines of Fujian. Illegal immigrants also depart from neighboring provinces such as Zhejiang or Guangdong. One snakehead in Fuzhou, who came to the United States in 1988 by going through Cambodia and then returned to China in 1992 to join the human smuggling business, said there were many things to consider when transporting clients on boats. He claimed to have undertaken a variety of tasks in a maritime operation, leasing boats, hiring the crew, and stocking supplies:

> When negotiating the lease on a boat I have to spend 100 percent of my effort to prepare for the trip, including how much space there is, the fuel capacity, and where to find the captain experienced enough to navigate to

the U.S. I have to find engineers and other experienced and responsible staff. Even the musclemen on board must be able to control the crowd and prevent riots from breaking out. There are many headaches during a trip such as mechanical problems or shortages of water or food on board. I can get supplies from other countries or get a different boat. The biggest worry happens when the ship loses communication with people on the mainland.

One subject in New York described how he acted as an escort for illegal immigrants brought in on smuggling ships. The 40-year-old father of one daughter said that after he came to the United States through a marriage fraud, he could not find a decent job. With neither formal education nor job skills, he eventually got involved in a gambling business with a few friends from Fuzhou. He claimed to have participated in maritime smuggling activities more than ten times:

> My boss at the gambling den liked me and asked if I could help him escort his clients on a boat to the U.S. In return, he was willing to give me 20 percent of the gambling business's income. I would fly back to Fujian twice a year on average, usually in December and February. The snakeheads there would tell me where to board the boat. There were usually two to three local escorts also. So we would round up the clients and move them to the bottom of the boat. We usually spent about a month at sea, and as soon as the boat reached the U.S. I would leave the clients to our local partners. I was only doing this part time and to keep my share of the gambling business.

For years, snakeheads and illegal immigrants have reported a steady decline in maritime smuggling operations. More and more snakeheads are sending their clients by air or over land to transit countries such as Thailand or Korea. Some subjects in this study claimed that it only took a few media reports of maritime smuggling accidents or a few horror stories circulated in the village to scare away prospective clients. These snakeheads recalled the early years of maritime smuggling, when clients had to pay a down payment before they could board the ship. Now, to attract clients, maritime snakeheads usually promise to pay fines and repatriation expenses if the operation fails.

Cargo containers outfitted by snakeheads to transport illegal migrants have also attracted wide attention in recent years. With the ports so porous along the U.S. west coast, where millions of containers arrive each year, snakeheads and other organized criminals alike have discovered that ports are a convenient channel for the transport of contraband. Even after 9/11, after which port security in the United States supposedly improved, the vast majority of commercial containers entering the country still receive little or no inspection. One subject in this study, formerly a customs inspector in China, explained how he helped illegal immigrants through commercial seaports:

> In the beginning, I was approached by a snakehead who promised to pay me $1,000 a client. This was a lot of money at the time when I was making practically nothing as a customs inspector. So I agreed to collaborate with him. The snakehead would travel from the U.S. to China and make his arrangements in Fujian. Each operation consisted of eight to twelve clients. After the snakehead told me the number of people involved and the time they would want to leave, I would make sure to "inspect" their boat, certify the paperwork, and file the proper documents. The snakehead always paid me right before the boat left the port. In one year, I made off with more than $30,000. But much of the money was confiscated after my scheme was discovered, and I only took a small amount with me when I left China.

These methods of client recruitment and departure strategies represent only a few of the many means whereby people are smuggled out of China. Snakeheads have devised and exploited many other schemes, but those detailed above nevertheless reflect the ingenuity of their collective entrepreneurial efforts in safeguarding business transactions as well as preventing unnecessary exposure to law enforcement agencies. Leaving China is only the beginning, however. A myriad of challenges await snakeheads and clients before they reach their final destination. The road to the United States can be easy and safe or arduous and perilous, depending on the resourcefulness of the smugglers.

CHAPTER 4

Smuggling Activities in Transit

Participation in a business delegation, marriage to a U.S. citizen, or conceal-
ment aboard ship, either in a cargo container or as a member of the ship's
crew—these are the only ways to get to the United States without passing
through transit countries. Only a few snakeheads command the resources
to forward their clients through direct routes on a consistent basis. By far,
most Chinese emigrants must go through other countries, often via a combination of overland, maritime, and air routes. A few illegal immigrants are
able to make it to the United States without undue delay. The rest, relying
on complicated smuggling routes and transportation strategies, must exert
great effort, endure horrendous hardships, and even undergo physical abuse
to reach their destination.

Global Network and International Collaboration

Chinese human smugglers have been able to evade most law enforcement efforts through their extensive global networks, and can move Chinese nation-

als successively through various parts of the world, with the United States as the most sought-after destination (Zhang and Gaylord 1996; Zhang 1997). International cooperation in human smuggling has reached an unprecedented level, with overseas Chinese and their collaborators in foreign countries working hand in hand to move illegal migrants to their destinations.

The collaborators involved in moving Chinese nationals across borders into various transit or destination nations come from a long list of countries, including Thailand, Japan, Australia, Hungary, Italy, the Netherlands, Mexico, Panama, and Canada. Authorities in these countries have long noticed the presence of large numbers of undocumented Chinese now residing in these countries (Boyd and Barnes 1992; Dubro 1992; Eager 1992; Lee 1992; Tam 1992; Gross 1996; Marquis and Garvin 1999). Even countries where, historically, few Chinese have resided are implicated. For instance, Czech citizens have been accused of using the country's "green border" to smuggle Chinese nationals into Germany (Ceska Tiskova Kancelar 2004).

More than a decade ago, U.S. officials claimed that Chinese smuggling rings had connections in fifty-one countries that were involved either as part of the transportation web, or as manufacturers of fraudulent travel documents, or both (Freedman 1991; Mydans 1992). According to an official U.S. source, "at any given time, thirty thousand Chinese are stashed away in safe houses around the world, waiting for entry" (Kinkead 1992, 160). This global network of human smuggling activities has only grown in size in recent years. Around the globe, many countries serve as intermediate stops for smugglers and their clients on their way to the United States or western European countries. In Southeast Asia, countries such as Thailand and the Philippines are well-known staging areas, as are Cambodia and Vietnam.

For U.S.-bound smuggling operations, Canada and Mexico are the most popular staging areas, because of their geographical proximity to the United States. Other countries far from North America have also become an integral part of global smuggling networks, as snakeheads and their foreign collaborators are constantly exploring new routes and transportation strategies. For example, members of the U.S. intelligence community cite numerous accounts of a high volume of Chinese smuggling operations being staged from Russia. Figures as high as "hundreds of thousands" have been reported (Thompson 2000). Chinese smuggling organizations have been able to tap into the global population migration movement, developing transportation routes through countries large and small. Even remote and obscure countries are being exploited. For instance, Surinam, a small country in South America, has become a major way station for Chinese human smugglers. The Surinamese government reportedly issues tens of thousands of "work visas" to Chinese nationals each year, far in excess of the number of jobs actually available. When questioned by U.S. officials regarding this practice, Surinam authorities reportedly responded that it wasn't their problem, because the Chinese nationals didn't stay in Surinam (Thompson 2000). High-ranking government officials in Panama, including President Ernesto Perez Balladares, have also been accused of selling thousands of tourist visas to Chinese human smugglers so that their clients can make their way to Mexico and slip across the U.S. border (Marquis and Garvin 1999).

From time to time, the news media report apprehensions of illegal Chinese immigrants in far-flung corners of the world. Most of the time, such interceptions simply go unnoticed. The following are a few examples of places where Chinese human smuggling operations have been staged:

- In August 2000, law enforcement agencies in South Africa intercepted 232 illegal immigrants in Johannesburg. Subsequent investigations found that forty-eight of them were Chinese nationals heading for the United States (Thompson 2000).

- The Belgian Federal Police reported that a Chinese-run company in the Congo used Hong Kong, Switzerland, and Belgium as transit points to move migrants towards the United States and Canada (Interpol 2003). Chinese nationals holding Japanese look-alike passports were arrested in Brussels in 2003, reportedly after staying in Abidjan in the Ivory Coast for several weeks and arriving in Belgium via Liberia.[1]

- Finnish authorities reported that Helsinki's Vantaa Airport was frequently used as a transit point for Chinese illegal migrants. They would often travel in small groups of two to six persons. They would hide their original passports and be equipped with several flight tickets, each of which they used for only a part of the trip (Interpol 2003).[2]

- Zurich in Switzerland is another transit point frequently used by Chinese smugglers to transport clients to the United States and Canada (Interpol 2003). A popular route is Hong Kong via Kuala Lumpur to the Zurich airport and then to Miami. Large numbers of illegal Chinese immigrants have also arrived at the Zurich airport from Douala, Cameroon, holding forged passports or visas, which can be purchased for $800 to $1,200.[3]

Transnational human smuggling on such a large global scale, with routes stretching to all corners of the world, would be impossible without the overt or tacit assistance of corrupt foreign government officials and businesses. Media outlets and law enforcement agencies have long reported collaborations between Chinese human smugglers and natives in transit countries. Forming business relationships with foreign nationals to carry out illicit activities is nothing new. It can be traced back to the Exclusion Era, between 1882 and 1943, when Canadians and Mexicans along their respective borders charged hefty fees to help Chinese smugglers ferry or guide illegal immigrants into the United States (Lee 2003). This same international trade has continued today with a new generation of entrepreneurs. In 1998, after an eighteen-month investigation of a tip by the Royal Canadian Mounted Police, law enforcement agencies from both the United States and Canada (including federal, local, and tribal agencies) broke up a large smuggling operation in the Buffalo, New York, area along the U.S.-Canadian border. The smugglers took advantage of the sparsely policed Native American tribal territories to move illegal Chinese immigrants from Canada into the United States. The collaborators included Canadian and U.S. nationals including Mohawk and Navajo Indians. Subsequent arrests were made in Philadelphia, New York City, and upstate New York (*San Diego Union Tribune* 1998).

In a more recent case, forty-two current and former Mexican government officials (many of them immigration enforcement agents) from at least one-third of Mexico's thirty-one states were arrested on charges of aiding and collaborating with human smugglers to smuggle Cubans, Uruguayans, Brazilians, Asians, and Central Americans into the United States (Castillo 2004). These officials allegedly provided smugglers with information about police raids, illegally freed captured migrants, and allowed passage of persons with falsified documents. Illegal immigrants were often brought into Mexico from the southern border (such as the states of Chiapas and Quintana Roo), kept in safe houses, and gradually transported to northern states bordering the United States (Castillo 2004).

Subjects interviewed in this study also reported extensive collaborations with foreign nationals in transit countries. One 50-year-old snakehead in Long Island, New York, who claimed to be the head of a smuggling organization, recalled the years he spent developing contacts with police and border control officials, first in his home county of Changle, then in Hong Kong and Thailand. He even claimed to have developed contacts inside the U.S. Consulate in Hong Kong who made it possible for him to obtain tourist visas for his clients. He started this smuggling business long before the United States or the Chinese government became aware that large numbers of Fujianese were being smuggled abroad. After a few years of successful operations, he invested his ill-gotten gains in legitimate businesses. He quit both smuggling and his other, legitimate ventures in 1993 because of a heart condition. When probed about how he developed and cultivated his smuggling methods, he said:

> We took advantage of the ignorance of the U.S. government. I believe it was only after 1993, the U.S. government realized that many Fujianese were entering the country and discovered many of the smuggling methods. In the early years, I sent my assistants back to China to work and interact with border patrol and customs officials. I also worked through a retired captain to develop contacts in Thailand's shipping business. This captain figured out ways to bribe Thai shipping companies and their captains to help move my clients. I still remember my first big operation of thirty clients in 1983. I recruited the captain of a Thai oil tanker and his crew. The oil tanker docked in a Chinese port, loaded these clients, and then headed for New York. Back then, I only charged $22,000 a person. It is a lot more expensive now. Sometimes I sent my clients to Thailand by boat. From there, my local contacts used fraudulent passports to fly them to the United States. Other times, I had clients sent to Germany by boat, and from there they would fly to the United States on fraudulent documents. In short, I had to vary my routes to avoid attention from the governments.

One common theme that emerged in this study is that collaborators in transit countries frequently provided travel documents that enabled illegal immigrants to continue their journey. A 52-year-old snakehead in New York's Chinatown, who was smuggled by boat to the United States in the late 1980s and later became a U.S. citizen after gaining political asylum, explained how his Indonesian contacts assisted him to get proper documents such as bank statements, passports, and visas:

> There was this group of people in Indonesia who helped me. I supplied them with the photos of my clients and their personal information. These

people would help me create identification documents and then Indonesian passports for my clients. They charged $10,000 for these documents per person. My clients would then leave China using these fraudulent documents and posing as overseas Chinese from Indonesia to enter Indonesia. My contacts would then acquire authentic verification statements from a bank, for $5,000 a person, attesting that my clients "owned" properties and had sizeable bank deposits in Indonesia. With the bank documents and passports, my clients would apply for tourist visas to the United States. It was not 100 percent guaranteed. For every ten people, seven would obtain visas through this method.

The importance of collaborators in transit countries—particularly with their contribution to and provision of basic logistic support—is hard to overstate. In many of these countries, local citizens provide transportation (such as cargo trucks or passenger cars), food, and shelter—even guide service, selecting appropriate locations to cross borders. Motivated by money and bound by nothing more than the shared goal of delivering the "cargo" and getting paid, people of different nationalities, cultures, and religions have teamed up to transport not just Chinese but migrants of other nations to wherever they desire. In a 2004 conference at the Interpol Headquarters in Lyons, France, representatives from countries such as Slovenia, Serbia, Montenegro, and the Czech Republic, where there were no historical settlements of ethnic Chinese, reported rapid increases of Chinese nationals entering and leaving these regions, often with the help of local guides and drivers.[4] For example, in December 2003, thirty-four Chinese citizens, allegedly visiting Croatia as tourists, failed to show up at the airport when they were scheduled to return. Eight members of this group were later arrested in Slovenia (Bozic 2004). Slovenian citizens and organized crime groups allegedly provided accommodations for these illegal migrants in flats in the area of Ljubljana, and arranged for drivers and guides to help them cross into neighboring countries.

THE FUNNEL EFFECT

Many migrants do eventually reach their destinations, but many more have been stranded in transit countries for months or even years. According to one report, some illegal immigrants thought they were on their way to their destination countries but found themselves stuck in countries such as Indonesia and wound up working in local Chinese-owned businesses (Agence France-Presse 2004). Illegal migrants who leave China intending to reach either the United States or another western country but encounter insurmountable obstacles must therefore seek shelter in transit countries. Subjects in this study told many stories of unsuccessful smuggling operations in which clients had been stranded in one location after another and of other clients who had been gone for years and whose families still had not heard from them. One snakehead in Fuzhou's Mawei district who was running a retail propane store shared this story:

> I heard that a teenager from my hometown was supposed to fly to the U.S. But he was stuck in Thailand and was forced by his snakehead to call home to tell his parents that he had arrived in the U.S. so that the smuggling fee would be paid. The parents heard the child crying on the phone and demanded the snakehead to provide a U.S. phone number so they could call back to verify. They called the number only to find out their son was not there.

Migrants stranded in a transit country face two choices: either return to China to face possible fines and jail time, or settle in this less desirable place and make a living there on their own. Their unsuccessful journeys have had a self-reinforcing effect: as tens of thousands leave China each year en route to developed countries around the world, the exodus fuels the growth of overseas Chinese settlements along their migration routes. These settlements in turn provide an excellent cover and infrastructure and act as a way station for future smuggling operations. The U.S. intelligence community has long known that the existence of these overseas Chinese communities provide an opportunity for "pay as you go" schemes, allowing migrating Chinese nationals to work off part of their smuggling fees at each stage of the trip (Thompson 2000). These pay-as-you-go journeys can take several months or several years to complete. The staging locations, mostly within ethnic Chinese enclaves, become smuggling "bazaars" where illegal immigrants and snakeheads alike barter with one another to develop and cultivate viable transportation routes and business opportunities for each other. So far, no research has been done on this pay-as-you-go scheme. It is just one of the many methods of payment in the human smuggling business.

A snakehead in Los Angeles said that for many years he specialized in moving people through transit countries, mostly through Europe. He came to the United States a few years ago and lived in Louisiana for some time before relocating to the Los Angeles area. At the time of the interview, he was looking for a restaurant to buy. He described some of his favorite transit points:

> The best transit country now is Korea. But if you want to go to Europe, the easiest way to go is through Russia. Other easy transit countries include the Czech Republic, Belgium, and Hungary. Many people want to go to Germany and England, because there is more money to be made. In London, a good salary would be 1,300 pounds a month. Still, most people want to come to the United States because it is where the most money can be made.

According to this subject, many illegal Chinese immigrants were stranded in transit countries because their snakeheads ran out of contacts and strategies to move them forward. In many cases, clients were simply abandoned when the smuggling operation broke down. In these cases, the snakeheads simply disappeared. He added:

> I have several friends in Brazil who want to come to the United States. There are many people who are stuck in Brazil. There is little money to be made there. They only make about $150 a month. If I had reliable contacts in the United States, I could make a lot of money bringing these people in.

Unfortunately, this snakehead had tried for years to develop a reliable route to the United States but failed. He helped only one person to come to the United States in his entire smuggling career. He claimed that he had tried for a long time to cultivate a route to this country and at one time worked hard with a partner to develop a transportation scheme via Hong Kong, but said that his partner there, after taking more than 800,000 yuan (about $97,000) as a deposit, could never deliver and later simply disappeared. He offered his experience as a transit expert:

> This was really rare. Most of us (snakeheads) are really concerned about maintaining a good reputation, and we hardly ever defraud each other. I think this friend of mine in Hong Kong probably spent all the money trying to make it work. In the end he didn't have the money to repay me, so he simply disappeared. I was totally discouraged by the prospect of ever developing a reliable route to the U.S. I know there is much money to be made, and I have many clients. I just cannot build a reliable network. Europe is a lot easier. It is easy to get there. I have done it mostly through temporary labor export programs. There are many levels of government agencies

involved in arranging and organizing temporary labor exports for foreign countries. I can tell you all of them are involved in the smuggling business. We would apply for a number of permits and then use them again and again for multiple groups of people. The cost to go to Europe is 100,000 yuan, not much compared to what it costs to come to the U.S. This is all relative. The more money you can make in a country, the more expensive it will be to get you there. For places like Brazil, you probably can do it yourself.

TRANSIT OPERATIONS

What is least understood about the smuggling process is what happens when illegal immigrants are in the transit countries between China and their destination. Because in human smuggling most people are responsible only for their specific tasks, rarely does a snakehead know exactly what goes on at the next stage or with whom the next partner in line works. For instance, one snakehead in Fuqing claimed that his snakehead partners spent months preparing the boat while he and other recruiters were looking for and screening clients. The boat typically would land in Guam, where the clients would apply for political asylum and then wait to be bailed out or for their cases to be processed. In another case, the snakehead, who was a fisherman and responsible for recruiting and ferrying clients to the mother ship on the open seas, claimed that more than a hundred of his clients were sent to Argentina and Canada.

Surprisingly, when they were probed, many snakeheads in China or the United States claimed to know what was happening in transit to their clients. Upon close examination, it became clear that they were mostly using secondhand information from their collaborators to fill in the blanks. A snakehead in Fuzhou shared what he claimed to know about his partner and how the transit process worked:

> Once I was working with a snakehead who bought a Japanese passport from somewhere. In order to make use of this document, he asked me to recruit a client who could speak some Japanese but wanted to go to the U.S. Through some referrals, I found a client who once worked in Japan for six years and could speak the language. This client used this passport and flew out of the country from Shenyang (a city in northeastern China) to Korea and from there on to the U.S. I learned that his total smuggling fee was $50,000. I made $2,000 for this referral.

One businessman from Taiwan who was operating a shipping company told what he knew about transit operations:

> I was running a cruise boat company before I got involved in smuggling. Once I became active in this business I sold off most of my speedboat company's shares. In the smuggling business I was in charge of transporting clients, but only to Taiwan. I know my clients were all destined for the U.S. and other boats would get close to the U.S. waters and smaller speedboats would arrive to pick up the clients.

Nearly all the subjects in this study operated at the two ends of the smuggling process—the sending and receiving communities. Therefore, their knowledge of what went on in transit countries was mostly what they had heard from snakeheads at the next stage or from clients once they reached their eventual destinations. Stories of transit operations were also shared in the sending communities, because the majority of the subjects interviewed in China had never gone abroad. In some cases, subjects learned about transit activities from their failures. Such was the case of a snakehead in Fuzhou, who specialized in arranging business visas through transit countries. For years, she never had to bother with what went on in transit countries because few of her clients ever ran into problems. However, in 2000, two of her clients were detained in the Philippines. She recalled the troubles she had to go through to save her clients and herself:

> Two of my clients were arrested in the Philippines, together with my collaborator, a Taiwanese woman with U.S. citizenship. My clients left China with travel documents to go to Vietnam. Their first leg was to go to Hong Kong, supposedly for transfer. When they arrived in Hong Kong, they joined this 30-year-old Taiwanese woman and flew to the Philippines through the method of *duirentou* (matching two heads, or making passports with look-alike clients) with Taiwanese passports. When they arrived in Manila, an immigration inspector suspected the authenticity of the passports the two clients were holding and questioned them. The Taiwanese woman, already through the checkpoint, returned to assist these two clients by acting as their interpreter and trying to explain away their situations. All three were detained.
>
> The Taiwanese woman did not handle the situation wisely. She thought as a U.S. citizen she did not have to show much respect to the Filipinos. She insisted that she did not have to answer any questions posed by the inspector.

She claimed that she got to know these two passengers (my clients) during their trip to Manila and she was there only to help as an interpreter. Even during the detention, she felt that because she was a U.S. citizen, she would be released soon. Interestingly, at several points during their detention, several border control officials told her that she could pay $9,000 for each person to get them out of detention. She insisted she would not pay since she'd done nothing wrong. So these two clients of mine were locked up for three months there. During this time, I asked her repeatedly to just pay the fees to get them out before the Philippines authority contacted the Chinese authority. She refused to do so at first. Then she asked me to pay the fees. I refused because we had previously agreed that all expenses during transit were her responsibility. So we argued back and forth and did not reach an agreement. During this time, I made many phone calls to my two clients in the Philippines. There was this nice prison guard, whose ancestors came from the southern part of Fujian, who would allow my clients to answer my phone calls. You know how expensive these international calls were, and each call lasted a long time.

Eventually I had to pay an attorney over there to represent my clients. The Philippine authorities finally released the two to the Chinese authorities. My clients were flown back to Shanghai under the security of the airline. After they were returned to Fuzhou, they were again locked up, and were released after they paid the repatriation expenses and fines, about 19,000 yuan RMB each (about $2,300). I had to pay these expenses plus their detention costs. I gave the money to my recruiter, who in turn gave the money to the relatives of these two clients in the village. All together I lost more than 160,000 yuan (about $20,000) on these two people. I got very scared and stopped doing this business. Fortunately, these two clients did not reveal any of us. But I was really concerned about my safety. That's one main reason I don't live in Changle County anymore and don't deal with clients directly. The only person who can sell me out is my recruiter.

According to the few subjects in this study who were directly involved in transit operations, operations in these intermediate countries are not as simple as many snakeheads lead their prospective clients to believe. Although stories about transit operations are usually limited to a specific country or region and to one specific aspect of an operation, they nonetheless offer vivid glimpses of what may occur while migrants in transit are in these countries. A school teacher turned snakehead in Fuzhou, for example, told a story of how she once escorted a client from mainland China to Hong Kong for transit purposes and nearly got arrested. The following was her account of what happened at the Hong Kong airport:

In 1997, I was escorting a client to Hong Kong. This was a photo-substitution case (or *duirentou*). First, I acquired a passport from Sichuan Province with an authentic U.S. visa. Then I screened my clients and found one that looked somewhat like the picture on the passport. This client had genuine travel documents to go to Vietnam, which were easy to get. So I arranged for him to make the transfer in Hong Kong. There were few places in China with direct flights to Vietnam at that time. My client and I flew to Hong Kong from Fuzhou. During the flight, I gave him the passport and a ticket to the U.S. He gave me his own travel documents and his Fuzhou-to-Hong Kong roundtrip ticket. We were both waiting at the Hong Kong airport. We arranged our flight from Fuzhou to Hong Kong deliberately close in schedule to a flight from Chengdu (capital of Sichuan Province) to Hong Kong so there wouldn't be any suspicion. It was just my bad luck that day. Very few passengers checked in that day at Singapore Airlines in Hong Kong. I was waiting around and hoping that there would be a line in front of the check-in counter, and perhaps the airline clerk wouldn't have time to pay much attention to my client. But there was never a line. We waited and waited. I became nervous because there were plain clothes policemen roaming around the airport, and if you stayed in one place too long, you might be interrogated. Finally there were a few people forming a line at the Singapore Airlines counter. My client decided to try his luck. But by the time he stepped up to the counter, there was no one waiting behind him. Three airline staff members congregated at this one counter, probably out of sheer boredom, and they each took a look at the passport and started a discussion among themselves.

They told my client the picture in the passport looked far more mature than he appeared to be. My client was about 7 to 8 years younger than the person in the passport picture. In general, a passport picture usually looks younger than the real person. My client insisted that it was his passport and was able to answer all questions because he had memorized all the information in the passport. Later the airline clerk asked the airport security staff over to interrogate my client. They asked him for his ticket and boarding pass from Sichuan. This is when my client knew he couldn't get away anymore. So he admitted that he was using someone else's passport. He made up a story and told the airport security that he had met a stranger at the airport who asked him if he would like to go to the U.S. and then provided him with this passport.

I was sitting nearby and overheard the entire interrogation. When I saw the airport security escorting my client away, I stood up and exited the airport as quickly as my legs could carry me. When I exited the airport immigration checkpoint, I was asked why it took me so long to leave the airport since my flight had arrived a long time ago. I told the immigration officer that I was shopping for some duty-free products and got carried away. It was really nerve wrecking.

Later my client had to request to have his own passport returned before the Hong Kong authorities would let him return to Fuzhou. Upon his arrival in Fuzhou, he was detained by the Chinese border patrol and fined. I had to pay 10,000 yuan for his fine. It was a disaster and I almost got caught myself.

METHODS USED IN TRANSIT

Snakeheads usually transport their clients through transit countries by sea, land, or air. Sea-based operations often become an endurance test. One of the subjects in this study, who owned a leisure boating company in Taiwan and later quit to be a full-time human smuggler, explained that his responsibility in the operations was to get the boat close to the U.S. shore and while still in international waters unload passengers onto speedboats:

> I was responsible for leasing and piloting the boat. There were many headaches during these operations, since I was responsible for navigation, insuring clients' safety, and overseeing their daily activities onboard the ship.
> I had to deal with clients' seasickness and physical ailments, as well as to distribute food and water and other daily supplies. I normally divided the clients into several groups, each with an appointed group leader. There was a lot of pressure because I had to look after these clients while operating the boat. Once, two clients started a fight that almost caused a riot on the ship. They were later subdued by my crewmen. I think some of the group leaders were to blame for the incident because they were rude and unreasonable to other people. I found that it was really important to keep open and frequent communications with my clients, so I always dealt strictly with group leaders and separated them from the clients if needed.

For immigrants who travel inside cargo containers or as stowaways, the journey seems even longer. They often hide at the bottom of the freighter or inside containers for the entire trip. One snakehead in New York, who was working for his group as an escort for such transoceanic trips, explained the ordeal:

> The captain is usually bribed and knows that we are on board. But what I am most afraid of is being discovered by other crewmen on the ship. The number of clients on each trip ranges from ten to twenty. I have to keep them at the bottom of the container ship. We have air ventilation down there and we bring water, food, and other supplies. But we have to stay down there for up to one month before we reach the U.S. port. I am in charge of distributing food and water. After we arrive in the U.S., our local contacts come at night time when it is quiet to get us off the ship .

Four weeks on the sea seems like a short trip compared with being loaded on a freighter that has to make a few stops before arriving at an American seaport. Some clients are shipped to several transit countries and then flown to the United States. One snakehead in New York, who at one time was active in arranging maritime smuggling operations out of Hong Kong, complained about never being certain of the exact time of arrival of his clients:

> The worst headache was when the captain and his ship did not arrive in the U.S. as scheduled. Instead, the ship would sail for two to three months to different countries, loading and unloading cargoes. If the ship could arrive in the U.S. within a month after departure, it was considered a fast trip. Unfortunately, the captain had to follow the shipping company's schedule decisions and pick up goods along the way.

In comparison, by-air smuggling operations occur during a much shorter period. Snakeheads and their clients typically meet at an international airport where they swap travel documents and continue to the next point in their journey. As discussed earlier, one common strategy is that of *duirentou*, in which human smugglers provide passports with photos that look like their clients. They also hand over other travel documents, including airline tickets, at the transit airport. Gambling that "all Chinese look alike" to Western inspectors, snakeheads for years have successfully used this scheme to smuggle illegal migrants to North America and Europe. With some preparation and training, the fraudulent passport holders frequently are able to pass immigration inspections.

A variation of this *duirentou* strategy is the so-called "boarding-pass swap" scheme, which for years has been widely exploited at international airports throughout Southeast Asia. As one snakehead in Fuzhou explained:

> This method is actually quite easy. You and your client both arrive at the international airport from wherever, and switch boarding passes once you are inside the boarding areas. This is really a big loophole for airport security. Few will check your passports or identifications after you enter the boarding area. Although in some places, such as in Hong Kong, you may still be questioned by airport security, you can travel at a similar time to different countries, and switch your boarding passes right before boarding. The client gets the U.S. boarding pass to enter the plane, and the collaborator uses the client's boarding pass to return to China. I may waste portions of the unused tickets in such a transition. Doing a transfer this way, my client must destroy all documents, flush them down the toilet before arrival, and then turn himself in to U.S. Immigration and apply for asylum. Because all seats are accounted for before departure, airline representatives and immigration officials don't check if all boarding passes are actually held by the same passengers who checked through security earlier. It will be hard for immigration officials to determine, after all passengers have left the destination airport, whose boarding passes have been swapped. Even if the real boarding pass holder can somehow be tracked down and questioned, he can always claim that he changed his mind at the last minute and left the airport to return home. There is no way to link the collaborator to my client.

Boarding pass swapping has been familiar to many airlines and airport security personnel for years. Many U.S.-bound airlines now check passports against boarding passes before boarding, but one can still find many flights heading to the United States that do not require passengers to undergo a careful verification process. Even with such an inspection, human smugglers can still use the passport substitution (*duirentou*) scheme. When passengers line up to board the plane, most airline staff have neither the time nor adequate training to thoroughly inspect travel documents and engage in interrogations to weed out passport imposters. According to Chang Tseng-liang, deputy director of the C.K.S. Airport in Taipei, variations of this swapping scheme have been employed at his airport by Taiwanese snakeheads. He explained:

> Mainly two methods are used here at the C.K.S. Airport by human smugglers. First, two Taiwanese with fake Taiwanese passports and American visas will check in at the C.K.S. Airport and head for the gate. Two would-

be migrants from Mainland China will arrive in Taipei from Hong Kong at the same time. The two Taiwanese will hand over the Taiwanese passports and boarding passes to the two Mainlanders, who will board the plane heading for the U.S. The two Taiwanese will either check out of the airport or take the passports and boarding passes from the two Mainlanders and fly to the two Mainlanders' alleged destination. Second, two escorts from Hong Kong (mostly Taiwanese) arrive in Taipei from Hong Kong on their way to the U.S. In the meantime, two Mainlanders also arrive in Taipei from Hong Kong, supposedly to enter Taiwan. However, the two escorts will hand over their passports and boarding passes to the two Mainlanders, so that they can board the plane to the U.S.

Land-based operations in transit countries involve more steps and collaborators than either by-sea or by-air operations. As discussed earlier in this chapter, human smugglers in transit countries must provide room and board and a means of transportation, and must rely on other local partners who know the terrain well enough to identify each border crossing. Despite widespread news reports of international collaboration, the core smuggling infrastructure is still overseas Chinese. They have been settled in these transit regions for some time and have developed the wherewithal to facilitate smuggling activities. For instance, in a recent investigation in the Netherlands code-named Operation Lotus, the alleged female ringleader was accused of having smuggled 572 people in a two-year period, netting more than 8.7 million euros (Bulsing 2004). Her base of operation was her barbershop, where she gave newly arrived clients a haircut to make them look like Japanese. She then would give her clients Japanese passports she had acquired earlier. These illegal migrants would travel as Japanese visitors from the Netherlands to another European country or to the United States; they did not have to worry about visa problems because Japan has visa exemption agreements with most European countries (Bulsing 2004). Using police investigation and wire-tapping records, Soudijn (2006) made the same finding: that Chinese snakeheads employed Dutch-based or other foreign document forgers to acquire Japanese, Korean, and Taiwanese passports because of their visa-waiver status. These fraudulent documents are often sent through regular courier services, such as DHL, UPS, or FedEx.

In recent years, European authorities have also noticed an increase in the use of cargo trucks by Chinese human smugglers to hide illegal migrants in harbor areas where cargo ships are docked and loaded for destinations in

England. The cargo trucks are often parked along freeways leading to seaports in the Netherlands, where drivers are known to spend the night and leave their vehicles unattended for extended periods. Snakeheads allegedly determine if a truck is England-bound from the lettering on the vehicle. In the past, many Chinese migrants used this method to cross illegally into England. Nowadays, migrants of other nationalities, including Sri Lankans, Indians, and Nepalese, increasingly use the cargo-truck method (Bulsing 2004). In the major Netherlands port city of Rotterdam, shipping companies these days routinely use dogs and carbon dioxide sensors to check container trucks for hidden human cargo. The Dutch police, in collaboration with other European law enforcement agencies, have found many illegal Chinese migrants who arrived by way of the Czech Republic; they believe that a well-established human smuggling network has been established from China, through Moscow, the Czech Republic, the Netherlands, Belgium, and Spain. Although most of these migrants may be headed for European countries, it is fair to speculate that many seek entry into the United States or Canada.

CHAPTER 5

Arrival and Payment Collection in America

Most Americans never see behind the bustling storefronts or jostling street vendors in U.S. Chinatowns and are therefore oblivious to the vital role illegal immigrants play in the Chinese enclave economy. The rapid economic expansion of Chinese communities in the United States in recent decades has been made possible by the influx of illegal immigrants, who provide the cheap labor necessary to maintain such pillar businesses as garment factories and restaurants. Chinese human smuggling activities contribute to this economic expansion by providing the burgeoning Chinese communities with a continuous supply of cheap labor, thus creating incentives for illegal immigration. The influx of illegal immigrants again fuels further expansion of the enclave economy, in turn furthering opportunities for the snakeheads.

It is generally not difficult to get people in Chinese immigrant communities in America to discuss channels of irregular migration (human smuggling, for example). They are usually willing to discuss the type of documents they had when they arrived in the United States and whether they have "helped" friends and relatives come to this country. Some even admit that they are doing it for a profit. People of varied backgrounds and occupations have been found taking part in arranging, coordinating, and helping their countrymen enter the United States, legally or illegally.

Snakeheads in the United States

Nearly all U.S.-based human smugglers in this study were either self-employed business owners or hourly wage earners who worked in places such as take-out restaurants and garment factories. Many snakeheads (one-third of all U.S.-based subjects) simply called themselves "unemployed," because they found it hard to place their economic activities in any single occupation. Nonetheless, a few subjects were not afraid to admit that they operated massage parlors, ran gambling dens, or worked as debt-collection musclemen. Many of them had themselves entered the country illegally. Therefore, none were strangers to the smuggling business. Their personal experiences only proved that helping others come to the United States is worth a lot of money.

Smuggling operations in America involve a wide range of activities. At first sight, the activities of snakeheads in America and their counterparts in China seem very similar. Many activities that take place in China's sending communities also occur in American receiving communities, such as recruiting prospective immigrants, securing a financial guaranty, arranging fraudulent documents, and coordinating transportation. A 44-year-old smuggler in New York City's Chinatown described how his group set about recruiting eligible immigrants:

> First, our people in Fuzhou seek out those who want to come to the U.S., including our own relatives, friends, and even referrals that we don't personally know. Once we have a list of prospective clients, we will find out about their financial situations. These people, in general, don't have the money to pay the smuggling fees, and their relatives here usually frontload the costs, so we must get in touch with their relatives here in the U.S. and confirm their telephone numbers and residence addresses. Then we must verify if these people have the funds to pay the smuggling fees.

Although similar in procedures, fundamental differences exist between U.S.-based smuggling activities and those taking place in China. For instance, recruiters in the United States not only enlist prospective immigrants but also seek out people whose legal documents, immigration status, or business entities can be used to finance or facilitate smuggling operations. For instance, in one common smuggling scheme in the 1990s, snakeheads would target new legal immigrants, because their passports contained temporary green card stamps that could be used to smuggle other people. These new arrivals, once recruited, would return to China and sell their passports to local smugglers, who immediately matched them with prospective clients of similar appearance. After the substituted immigrants entered the United States, the real passport holders would go to a nearby U.S. consulate to report that their passports had been stolen. A temporary travel document would then be issued to allow them to return to the United States.

Although snakeheads in China also conduct similar recruitment drives, often in collaboration with their U.S. partners, it is usually the American-based snakeheads who initiate the smuggling process. They play a vital role in human smuggling, holding the beachhead and signaling to their partners in China and other parts of the world whether to forward more or fewer migrants. Without the collaboration of associates in America, few smuggling operations could materialize. Like their counterparts in China, U.S.-based snakeheads enter the smuggling business mostly through contacts in their own social circles and often under fortuitous circumstances. One waiter-turned-snakehead in New York's Chinatown told the story of how he became involved in this business:

> I was walking on the street one day and ran into the snakehead who smuggled me into the U.S. a year ago. He asked what I was doing, and I told him I was working in a restaurant. He then asked if I would like to help him recruit newly arrived legal immigrants as a side job. I agreed. My role is to find immigrants who have just arrived in the U.S. (within three or four months). These people have Chinese passports with temporary green card stamps. I look for these clients myself or ask a friend of mine to help. As soon as I find these people, I will ask them if they are willing to sell their passports to me for $2,000. I then sell these passports to my snakehead partner for $3,500 apiece. I also ask my relatives and friends in China to look for anyone who has obtained legal immigration papers, so I will know where to locate these people ahead of time. I usually meet the prospective clients in a quiet location and discuss the deal with them for about thirty minutes. There is no risk in what I am doing. If they want to sell their passports to me, great. If not, we just walk away.

Besides soliciting new arrivals for their immigration documents, recruiters in the United States also seek eligible candidates for marriage fraud and businesses willing to invite or sponsor "official delegations" from China. One Los Angeles–based snakehead who specialized in arranging fraudulent marriages described where she acquired her bachelors:

> Both male and female "bachelors" are recruited in the U.S. There can be several middle persons who make referrals from one to another to reach the eventual candidate. For my cases, I have a few contacts in the Vietnamese community who maintain a list of eligible bachelors ready for referrals. I think some of these referral sources are probably connected with the black society (the underworld). Many of these so-called bachelors are actually married and have families, but their marriages are not registered with any government agencies, so they can claim to be single and make some money. Another main source of bachelors are heavy gamblers who are in a lot of debt and desperate for money.

In general, the range of U.S.-based snakehead activities appeared to be much wider than those reported by their counterparts in mainland China. This is most likely because the majority of these snakeheads are permanent residents or U.S. citizens, a legal status that affords them greater freedom to travel and makes them better able to gather and deploy resources. For example, all trans-Pacific escorts in this study and all those who got them through transit countries were U.S.-based smugglers. Many subjects in China claimed to have either met or worked with U.S.-based partners or someone from outside China. It seems logical that overseas Chinese would be better suited for coordinating and planning transnational activities. The U.S.-based snakeheads probably assume leadership in the majority of smuggling operations, creating opportunities and collaborating with their contacts in mainland China. Their ability to travel freely certainly broadens their range of activities and increases their efficiency when carrying out tasks that require trust building and face-to-face interaction with snakeheads in China and transit countries.

It should be noted, however, that U.S.-based snakeheads depend on their collaborators in China to screen and recruit prospective clients, to collect down payments or payment in full, and to secure passage through various border checkpoints in China. Furthermore, depending on their roles, many U.S.-based snakeheads are happy not to have to travel overseas and choose instead to focus on exploiting opportunities close to home. This is particularly true for part-time smugglers who must also tend to their own businesses. A 44-year-old payment collector in New York's Chinatown explained that he had been smuggled by boat to Germany and then entered the United States with a photo-substituted passport. The man said he operated several other businesses, including a gambling den, a nightclub, and a karaoke bar, while running his smuggling fee collection service. He claimed to have no desire to expand his human smuggling business overseas:

> I mostly ask my people to collect money from the relatives, family members, or friends of the smuggled clients. When clients don't have the money to pay their smuggling fees, we have to lock them up until their families and relatives give us the money, but these are very rare cases. In some situations, when families and relatives of the smuggled immigrants don't have enough money to pay right away, we will arrange a schedule and give them some time to pay off the balance. Although I am a U.S. citizen, I don't travel to China or any other countries. I am busy enough with what I have here. I must stay put in the U.S. to take care of business here.

Arrival and Payment Collection

Some smuggling activities (e.g., receiving clients and extorting payments) are carried out solely by U.S.-based smugglers. Arrival is probably the most vital step in most smuggling operations. Illegal immigrants often do not even care if they are caught while crossing into the United States, as long as they can set their feet on U.S. soil. Because of the nature of deportation procedures, by far the majority of detained illegal immigrants are allowed to go through formal court hearings, during which most, if not all, can find someone to bail them out.

Historically, the majority of immigrants from Fujian Province have headed to New York City or Los Angeles. U.S. government intelligence reports have identified at least two other "redistribution centers" for Chinese immigrants once they enter the United States: Houston and Chicago. After reaching these major relocation cities, illegal migrants fan out across the country, finding jobs in two main industries: construction and restaurants (Thompson 2000).

Collecting the final payment represents the formal conclusion of a smuggling operation. Previous research findings (see Chin 1999) and news reports have established that many immigrants are held in safe houses, where they are beaten and tortured by the smugglers themselves or by gangsters hired by smugglers because they are unable to pay the smuggling fees. Findings from this study suggest, however, that payment problems are actually uncommon in this business. Either through family members already in the United States or through a mutual aid system consisting mainly of people from the same ancestral descent or the same village, most illegal immigrants are able to secure sufficient funds to pay for their journey. The practice of borrowing money from friends and relatives to pay for one's voyage can be traced back to the credit-ticket arrangement used by the early Chinese immigrants in the mid-1800s (Wong 1998).[1] Like those early immigrants, today's newcomers often rely on the collective financial resources of relatives and friends to pay for the journey and usually pay off the loans in a few years. In fact, paying off these seemingly enormous smuggling debts has never been a major concern for most illegal Chinese immigrants. As one illegal immigrant in a Chinese buffet restaurant in Sacramento, California, explained:

> I make about $2,000 a month here. Because I work in a restaurant, the owner provides food and lodging free of charge. This is a standard practice in most Chinese restaurants. I practically spend no money of my own, so I can save all my income each month and send it home.

Most snakeheads in this study reported that their clients paid off the fees soon after arrival. Contrary to the common perception conjured up by news reports, many snakeheads claimed that their clients and clients' families paid the smuggling fees gladly and gratefully. One snakehead in Queens, New York, who was in the photo substitution business with her husband, said they rarely had any payment problems with their clients. Acting as the debt collector in this husband-and-wife team, she said:

> Our clients know that we also have to pay a lot of money to get them to America. When a client arrives, I will get a call from our partner. I then call and instruct the client's family members to bring the money to a specific location. I will decide where to meet for the payment handover. When we meet, we will count the money and once everything is cleared, my partner

and I will leave, and the client and his relatives will go their way. In this business, I am least concerned about whether my clients will pay me. I am far more concerned about whether my clients can get through immigration inspections at the airport. We teach these clients about life in Chinatown in New York City and train them to believe that they were actually living here, but occasionally some clients are still caught as imposters. All of us lose a lot of money when our clients are caught.

Though infrequent, when payment problems do occur they often produce grim consequences for all parties involved. According to the subjects in this study, payment problems occur mainly for two reasons. First, clients lie about their financial means and have no intention of paying the fees upon arrival. Second, the U.S.-based relatives or friends of prospective clients fail to come up with the fees, either because of their own financial problems or as a result of a conspiracy to defraud the snakehead. In any event, not getting paid after braving all the challenges and risks to smuggle people into the United States is simply unacceptable to any snakehead. This is why "safe" houses often instead imprison clients who cannot make payment arrangements as soon as they arrive.

When the final payment becomes an issue, snakeheads usually resort to hiring Chinatown gangsters. In most cases, families and relatives of the clients involved know that bad things will happen and usually find ways to gather enough money to pay off the fees quickly. Violence becomes inevitable when, in a few cases, clients repeatedly put off making the payment or cannot provide an acceptable installment plan. Most beatings and tortures go unnoticed even when clients suffer horrendous treatment by their captors (Chin 1999). A 39-year-old snakehead in New York City, who was responsible for escorting clients on container ships and for collecting final payments upon arrival, justified the beatings in the few cases that involved him:

> I risked my life and risked being imprisoned to help these people to come to the U.S. Why shouldn't I get paid? These clients should understand this basic rule. We take great risks in this business and work hard in getting these people over. They have no reason not to pay us. If any clients don't pay up immediately, I will pay them a visit with a muscleman. We either beat them up or threaten to use violence if the balance is not paid in a short period of time. They know that this payment problem will not be good for

their families in China either, because we know who they are and where they live. We also know who their siblings are and where we can find a backup person to pay the fees. There is nothing wrong with beating them up. In this business, we always make it clear that upon arrival in the U.S., all fees must be settled right away.

Snakeheads in most cases refer only their delinquent clients to gangsters for payment because the collector's fee cuts into the snakehead's profit. One of the snakeheads in this study, who claimed to be the retired former boss of a well-known street gang in New York's Chinatown, said that his *mazai* (foot soldiers) got involved only when the smuggled immigrants could not pay:

> My snakehead contacts would provide me a list of delinquent clients. I wouldn't go out to collect money myself but sent my *mazai*. Once the money was collected, I'd split with my snakehead clients 40/60. My share was 40 percent of whatever I collected. At first I thought it was strange that these snakeheads would ask us to collect the payment. Since they were all illegal immigrants and would not dare to call the police, any Chinatown gangs could do the job. Later I learned that it was because we were a Fuzhounese gang and could speak the clients' dialect.

Over the past two decades, payment practices in the smuggling business have changed somewhat. More and more, smuggling fees are settled in China. China's rapid economic development and lax banking regulations have made financial transactions easy. Furthermore, financial transactions among individuals and even among businesses are still mostly made in cash, making them difficult for authorities to monitor and trace. With many overseas Chinese remitting money to China each year, an increasing number of families in Fuzhou and elsewhere in China maintain foreign currency bank accounts and therefore can easily pool their resources to sponsor prospective immigrants. Even when someone needs actual money from overseas to sponsor an immigrant, members of a family can easily convince a relative or friend to serve as a guarantor. When the trip is completed, a so-called "mirror transfer" can be arranged quickly with a few phone calls.[2] It is rare these days for anyone to actually wire smuggling fees back and forth between China and the United States or to use carriers to transmit large sums of cash.

According to a few subjects in this study who had experiences with some of these "problematic cases," the financial guarantors still pay the snakeheads. The guarantors then must work through local thugs or gangsters to exact payments, sometimes for years to come, assuming they are able to maintain control over the indebted immigrants' movements in the United States. In some cases, both snakeheads and their hired gangsters know that their deadbeat immigrants are a lost cause because they simply cannot monitor their movements over time, and there is little chance to secure the remaining payments. These gangsters or snakeheads usually exert continued pressure on the deadbeat's family in China until the debt is repaid. In such instances, the obligations imposed by the cultural expectations of the sending community often force these immigrants or their families to pay the fees owed. Many gangsters know well how to use cultural expectations as a coercive measure to exact payments.

It should be noted, however, that payment problems are the exception, not the norm, in the Chinese human smuggling business. The reports of kidnappings or hostage holding in the news indicate serious lapses in the screening process and poor judgment by the recruiters. The recruiters involved not only will not be paid, but they are often held responsible for compensating some of the losses. When asked how she was going to get the recruiter's commission back in the case of a delinquent client, a female snakehead in Los Angeles described her practice:

> I usually keep a receipt from her, showing in her handwriting how much she has received from me as commissions for her referrals. If her referred clients ever fail to live up to their end of the contract, I will ask her to return the money. I don't worry a bit as long as I know where she and her husband live. I can hire a Vietnamese gangster to pay a visit to her husband's store and spread word about his wife owing me money. I believe she will pay me back quickly.

The common perception, created by the news media, of large numbers of illegal immigrants being brought into the United States or other Western countries to be indentured labor is neither true nor logical. For instance, it was reported that in February 2004 some twenty Chinese immigrants drowned in a fast-rising tide while harvesting cockles at Morecambe Bay in northwest England. Many media stories directly pointed to snakeheads and local gangsters as the parties responsible for these deaths or insinuated, using quotes from British government officials, that those behind the scenes had totally disregarded safety precautions while paying only one pound sterling for a nine-hour shift (Johnston 2004). Similarly, other stories of hostage taking, beating, and torture of illegal immigrants conjure up images of a modern day slave trade (Associated Press 2004). However, according to the subjects in this study, no snakeheads work with clients on the mere promise of being paid in installments for years after the clients arrive in America. Most human smugglers will become discouraged from further involvement or even go bankrupt if they encounter frequent payment problems.

As later chapters will illustrate, human smuggling is an enterprise in which participating individuals realize their profits by completing specific tasks. Smugglers have expenses to cover and expect to make a profit at the end of an operation. Snakeheads are not philanthropists, as they sometimes purport to be, nor are they money lenders. Long-term payment plans, if they do exist, are the exception rather than the norm.

When resorting to actually holding clients hostage or using violence, snakeheads are always anxious to resolve the payment problem quickly; all measures available to them are usually applied either at once or in short intervals, including threatening the non-paying client's family members in China. Time is of the essence to these snakeheads and their hired muscle-men, because every extra day of delay increases the likelihood of attracting police attention. Sometimes these cases are resolved when the snakehead takes whatever money he can recover and absorbs the rest as a loss. There are, however, limits to how effective violence can be in securing payments, as one thirty-two-year-old debt collector in Brooklyn stated:

> If these clients cannot pay us, we will beat them up. But honestly, we can't beat them to death. This is the U.S. There is law. If someone dies, the police will come. Then we will all be in trouble. That's why even violence has its limits. Occasionally, I will encounter some clients who know the law in the U.S. They know how to call the police. In most cases, these illegal immigrants are afraid of being caught by immigration officials, so even if we beat them up, they won't dare to report it to the authorities, so we use this weakness toward our advantage.

Not all safe houses are run by street thugs bent on taking advantage of new arrivals or beating up clients at will. One subject in Los Angeles, who came to the United States as part of a fraudulent business delegation, begged to differ with some widely held perceptions about the horrendous conditions and abuses at these safe houses. This snakehead claimed that he was working for an associate of the infamous Sister Ping in New York.[3] When Chinese immigrants crossed the border from Mexico into the United States, they were sent to his safe house in Los Angeles. There he provided them with food and water and other supplies while they waited for the next segment of their journey. He noted:

> I would bring groceries and other daily items to keep these clients comfortable.
>
> We never beat our clients. These people were very happy to be in the U.S., and they were waiting to be transported to other parts of the country, mostly to the New York or New Jersey area. I was in charge of providing groceries because I was in the restaurant business and knew where to buy cheap groceries. I also brought them videotapes and magazines for entertainment purposes.

The above snakehead's involvement in the smuggling business was short-lived because his safe house was exposed eventually to the police. He described how his smuggling career came to an abrupt end:

> One night, somehow our neighbors tipped off the police. The neighbors probably noticed that we drove so many cars and vans to this house and many people went inside the house but never came out. Our clients stayed inside the house all day long because we told them not to show their faces in the neighborhood. But one night, the police came by and there were helicopters flying over the house. Our clients were scared and they ran out of the house and into the streets. Some went hiding in the nearby hills. I was running errands at that time. When I returned, I saw the entire neighborhood was in chaos. I didn't go to the house fearing the cops may be waiting for me. The next day, I was driving all over town and the nearby hills looking for our clients. Some of them were still hiding in bushes. I only found a few of them the next day. It was a disaster.

In the early years of Chinese human smuggling, both snakeheads and their clients would gamble on a journey in which both might lose money (mostly for transportation and document procurement). In recent years, however, more and more would-be immigrants have demanded that snakeheads guarantee successful arrival or return all down payments. Many smuggling operations have failed either inside China or somewhere in transit countries, with the bulk of the detained migrants repatriated. In these cases snakeheads must pay all of their clients' costs in exchange for their own protection. Most of the expenses are not recoverable (such as the money paid to the original passport holder and the bribes for border security personnel).

When clients are repatriated, they simply tell the authorities that they were approached randomly by anonymous snakeheads in their hometown and asked if they wanted to go to the United States. However, if the snakeheads do not cover the repatriation costs, their clients may retaliate by telling the police who organized the trip. Such a trade-off is a fairly standard practice these days in Fuzhou. In a few cases, however, the snakeheads have lost so much money to arrest and repatriation fees that they simply ran away.

Two factors have contributed to this new development in payment arrangements. First, ever-increasing smuggling fees appear to have gradually forced prospective immigrants and their families to think carefully about which snakehead they can trust with the investment. To woo clients, snakeheads not only show off their smuggling experiences, backed up with stories and references from successful cases, but also demonstrate their capability with a "money-back" guarantee. Second, paying all the costs, in the event of a failed operation, is not only effective but necessary for ensuring self-protection. As one subject in Fuzhou explained:

> If any of my clients are caught and returned, I always pay their fines. I have to. Otherwise, my clients will turn in my recruiter, who may also expose me. Clients are the safest in terms of financial risks. Those of us who spend money on bribes and transportation will lose our money for good. In this business, there is a clear expectation that snakeheads pay clients' fines if they are caught, and in return, clients must not tell the police where to find the snakeheads.

Smuggling activities in the United States follow similar patterns to those in China, except the snakeheads have greater opportunities because of their freedom to travel in and out of the country. Liberty to travel is no trivial matter in transnational human smuggling operations. It is a key asset that allows U.S.-based snakeheads to garner greater influence in smuggling operations than their counterparts in China. Because of their location, U.S.-based snakeheads also face the additional problem of having to settle final payments; in a handful of cases, doing so can lead to unpleasant consequences involving hostage taking and violence. In most cases, though, snakeheads receive their agreed-upon smuggling fees with no problems. Illegal migrants and their families are glad to pay the fees upon successful completion of the journey. Most snakeheads also take precautions to prevent payment problems in the first place through careful screening and background verification.

CHAPTER 6

Making Money from Human Smuggling

Transnational human smuggling is big business, but no one knows just how big it is. Although fees paid to human smugglers have been widely reported and verified by a few empirical studies, the biggest unknown is the actual number of people being smuggled into the country each year. If the number of apprehensions at the nation's borders is any indication, one can multiply commonly quoted smuggling fees by the number of arrests to arrive at a rough estimate of the size of this underground economy. The U.S. Border Patrol estimates that for more than a decade, the number of illegal immigrants apprehended at the border has consistently exceeded one million each year. The only exceptions were for the two years immediately following the 9/11 events, 2001 and 2002, when the number dropped slightly below one million.[1] By far, most of these arrests occurred along the southern border, where Mexican nationals have historically represented the vast majority of illegal border crossers.

Mexican smugglers usually charge their countrymen around $1,000 for the journey into the United States (Cornelius 2000). The price goes up to $2,000 or more if migrants want to be transported farther north instead of simply being dropped off across the border. In a more recent investigation, federal agents arrested two U.S. Navy petty officers on charges of smuggling illegal Mexican immigrants through an old port building at San Ysidro in San Diego. The smuggling fees were reportedly $3,000 a person (Soto 2006). Using $2,000 as the average per migrant from Mexico and other Latin American countries, from apprehension of illegal border crossers alone we can project a business in the billions of dollars annually.

Fees charged for smuggling Latin Americans are still considered inexpensive. The same cannot be said about those from Asia (mainly China and Korea). Based on the available reports, illegal Chinese migrants pay higher smuggling fees than those from any other country. Even Mexican human smugglers have learned to charge their Asian clients higher fees for help crossing the border than others (Castillo 2004). According to the subjects in this study as well as law enforcement intelligence, Mexican human smugglers charge up to $6,000 per person to help Chinese migrants cross into the United States. In comparison, migrants from the interior of Mexico or from other South American countries pay only a few hundred to a few thousand dollars for help entering the United States.[2] Because the net costs of human smuggling activities are low, the profits in this business are impressive. One of the objectives of this study was to gauge just how much snakeheads make from their activities.

Subjects in this study were asked about four main features of the money issue: (1) how much money they invested in this enterprise; (2) what prices they charged for their services; (3) how much they typically made for each specific service rendered to their clients; and (4) how much money they typically made in a year from the smuggling business. As expected, these questions numbered among the most difficult areas of inquiry in this study, for obvious reasons. Many subjects declined to report the amount of money they invested or what they made from the smuggling business; others skirted direct questions but hinted at how much money they made, or told how much money their partners or other snakeheads made. In some cases, snakeheads declined to report their income but went into detail about how much they spent and what kind of businesses they purchased with the smuggling proceeds. In one such case, a snakehead in his early thirties who had recently arrived in the United States refused to reveal how much he was

Table 6.1. Smuggling fees and earnings

	Median	*Mode*	*Range*
Investment in smuggling business (N = 71)	$3,000	$0	$0–$500,000
Smuggling fees (N = 81)	$50,000	$60,000	$1,000–$70,000
Profit per client (N = 69)	$10,000	$10,000	$117–$40,000
Annual income from smuggling business (N = 82)	$50,000	$50,000	$0–$2,000,000

making but was quite open about what he was doing after arriving in Los Angeles. He was looking for a restaurant to buy. At the time of the interview, he claimed:

> I have hired a real estate agent to look for potential restaurants. We just found one place that I really like. I have already signed the lease. The monthly rent is $12,000. I am remodeling it now, which will probably cost me another $200,000 to $300,000. I had flown back and forth seven times from Louisiana to Los Angeles to find a good restaurant to buy. Each time I stayed in a cheap motel and tried to be frugal. I have stayed in this motel for two months. I am worried about how soon I can open the restaurant for business. No matter how frugal I try to be, I spend at least $2,000 dollars each month. I need to start making money soon.

It was clear that this snakehead must have accumulated a sizable fortune to be able to start a restaurant business on such a scale. Several other snakeheads also told stories of their spending but declined to report how much money they made. Still, many subjects provided some figures. The effective sample sizes in Table 6.1 reflect the number of subjects who answered these questions. By no means do these figures represent the potential profits and annual income of the Chinese human smuggling trade in general, because the interviews in this study were obtained through personal contacts and their referrals. Nevertheless, these figures provide some idea of the enormous financial incentives for becoming involved in this business.

Expenses and Earnings

Because anyone who actively participates in coordinating and arranging the transportation of illegal migrants is considered a snakehead in the Chinese context, the expenses required to enter this business can vary widely, depending on one's role and responsibilities. Most low-level recruiters and transporters who received fees for their services said that they did not have to invest anything. Others reported investing tens of thousands, some even hundreds of thousands, of yuan, depending on what they wanted to accomplish or whether their clients were caught and repatriated. Maritime smugglers, who had to acquire transoceanic ships and supplies for the long voyage, made the biggest up-front investments. Depending on the payment arrangements with the captain and his crew, a smuggling organization could easily spend hundreds of thousands of yuan before the journey even began. The return corresponds well with the initial capital outlay, however. One maritime smuggler, though a captain himself, had to lease a ship. He described his income situation:

> I had to invest more than 400,000 yuan (about $50,000) in each operation. Other than leasing the ship, the most expensive item was fuel, followed by wages paid to the crew, then food, and other daily supplies. I could make about 750,000 yuan (about $91,000) per voyage if the boat reached the U.S. I made about three million yuan each year (about $370,000).

The different types of smuggling activities included in this study reflect significant variation in pricing structure. The subjects in this study quoted two types of prices, one for the snakehead's specific services and one for the going market price for the entire journey. The most quoted smuggling fee for an entire case was $60,000; the median price was $50,000. Depending again on the method of transportation, the prices varied somewhat. Fraudulent marriages, which were considered to be the most reliable and almost guaranteed method of entry into the United States with a valid immigration status, appeared to garner the highest price, $70,000 a person on average.

The question of profits per client was difficult for most subjects to answer because snakeheads could only guess the net costs for other members of a smuggling operation. It was clear, though, that because recruiters usually did not invest any of their own money, they also profited the least. Some recruiters made as little as 1,000 yuan for each successful referral (about $120), while others were able to make more. Recruiters who found eligible bachelors for fraudulent marriages, for instance, could earn $2,000 or more for each successful referral. Payment collectors on the tail end of the smuggling business also seemed to make rather small profits because of the sporadic need for their services. One 38-year-old payment collector in

New York's Chinatown complained about his meager income from assisting snakeheads:

> I only get paid each time I collect something. On average I make about $2,400 a month. I love to gamble and have women (prostitutes), so I spend a lot. Also, I send my parents (in China) $300 a month. I don't have a lot of money because I spend my money fast. I have not invested money in anything else, nor have I bought any real estate.

By and large, the profit-earning pattern in the smuggling business is clear. Those who invest the largest sums of money in smuggling operations also tend to make the most. Based on the reported earnings, profits among the subjects in this study were substantial—a median of $10,000, and up to $40,000 per client. Some snakeheads claimed to have made two million U.S. dollars a year. However, a few subjects reported that they had not made any money from smuggling. The median annual income for the subjects in this study was $50,000, which was also the most frequently quoted figure (i.e., the mode).

This study has uncovered a range of prices for the most common smuggling services, as shown in Table 6.2. The list, although limited in its scope, provides some indication that the cost of human smuggling is as unpredictable and varied as the transportation strategies are.[3] It is difficult to say exactly how much each successive stage of a smuggling operation costs, because no subjects know what others in the group charge and because they typically set their own fees for the portions of the operation under their direct control.

Over time, snakeheads also develop different smuggling methods and routes, which often involve partners at various transit locations. Many subjects in this study claimed that a change in itinerary or transit country could

Table 6.2. prices of specific smuggling services

Services	Most Quoted Price Range
Passport purchase	$10,000–$25,000
Expenses for passport seller in China	$5,000
Photo substitution (passport photo alteration)	$3,000–$5,000
Maiguan (bribery at border check point)	$8,000
Client recruitment	$500–$1,000
Escort (through transit points)	$4,000–$5,000
Bribery of port inspector (to allow stowaway)	$1,000–$5,000
Smuggling boat captain payoff(per trip)	$200,000
Debt collection fee (per client)	$500–half of recovered fees
Eligible bachelors (for fraudulent marriages)	$5,000–$30,000

lead to significant changes in costs. The true cost of a typical smuggling operation, if there is one, may never be known. This is so because factors such as the route and the mode of transportation have a significant bearing on the eventual profits, and they vary from operation to operation. As a general rule, direct flights and smuggling methods involving few transit points tend to garner higher profits.

Distributing and Spending the Money

Although money often goes through many hands, no smuggling organization has ever required a financier or banker to manage or monitor its financial transactions. Most snakeheads are independent contractors and work within their own network of contacts and resources rather than for a mutual boss.

Some simple principles govern financial transactions among smugglers. Money passes from one snakehead to the next, mostly in the form of cash on delivery, and fees are paid for specific services rendered. In other words, snakeheads do not turn to a mutual source, such as an escrow company or a mafia boss, for payment for their services. Some members of a smuggling unit—those in charge of acquiring travel documents, arranging transportation, or bribing border checkpoint personnel, for example—receive payment quickly. Others must wait until their clients complete the journey. In any case, all members of a smuggling group expect to get paid in full as soon as clients arrive in the destination country, often within days. Thus, money in human smuggling appears to flow in a serial manner, first through the key players and then outward to auxiliary contacts or service providers connected to the key snakeheads. A financier does not appear necessary in any of the smuggling transactions.

The diverse backgrounds and circumstances of snakeheads are reflected in the ways they chose to dispose of their profits. By far, the majority of the snakeheads in this study spent their profits in three ways: (1) on personal and family expenditures (such as buying houses or luxury items, or increasing daily living expenses); (2) on legitimate businesses (such as expanding existing businesses or purchasing new ones); and (3) on gambling and prostitution or other thrill-seeking activities. Most low-level operatives, such as recruiters and payment collectors, claimed to use the money earned from smuggling to augment their daily living expenses. These people often mentioned that with the extra income they could have a more comfortable life. A few snakeheads used the money to pay back the debt they had incurred smuggling their own family members abroad. A good number of other subjects invested much of their profits in legitimate businesses. A 38-year-old snakehead in Philadelphia, who generally was provided documents and escorted clients from China to the United States, described how he spent his smuggling profits:

> The money from this business mostly has been diverted into legitimate businesses, such as buying restaurants and real estate properties. My relatives and I are running restaurants, including buffets and fast-food takeouts. The cost of living is also quite high in the city.

Some snakeheads' spending habits were quite eclectic, as one 44-year-old snakehead in New York reported:

> The money from the smuggling business is spent in the following manner: I spend a lot of time in Atlantic City and certainly lose a lot of money there. Then I invest in legitimate businesses like fast-food takeout restaurants. I also buy blue chip stocks, real estate, and cars. I only put a small amount in the bank, because the IRS may get suspicious if I put a lot of money there. Of course, I also send some money back to China.

Some spent their profits as quickly as they earned them. One 39-year-old smuggler in Brooklyn, who served as an escort for his snakehead boss on smuggling ships, said that he was single and spent his money as fast as he made it:

> I go to Atlantic City a lot and I like to play blackjack, but I have lost a lot of money in gambling. I haven't bought a house, nor have I invested in other businesses. I am single and don't have any responsibilities. I want to emphasize that although I have lost a lot of money in gambling, it doesn't mean I have no money. I just haven't made a good saving plan to set aside money to buy businesses or real estate or stocks.

Not all snakeheads make money from the business. In the event that authorities in the United States or China apprehend their clients, smugglers typically pay all repatriation expenses and fines. One subject in Fuzhou's Mawei claimed to have smuggled more than a hundred clients, mainly through maritime operations by way of Argentina and Canada, and estimated that he had made two to three million yuan (about $244,000 to

$365,000) a year. When asked if he had ever lost money in the smuggling business, he was quick to respond:

> Yes! When my clients were arrested, not only did I lose all the money I fronted to cover the transportation, but also the fines my clients had to pay to the border police when they were repatriated. The most I had paid out of my pocket in one case was more than one million yuan (about $120,000). I had to swallow these losses when I ran out of luck. There were times I simply could not cover the losses, then I would go into hiding.

In addition to reporting how much they made and how they spent the money, many snakeheads complained about the expenditures required to remain in the game, because they had to spend lavishly to maintain their contacts in China. One snakehead in Fuzhou said:

> There are many fixed expenditures in this business. If you are only doing the *taitou* operations, the costs tend to be less. But the risk for your clients is also the highest. In this case, the most expensive part is bribing the security checkpoint staff. Another major expense is purchasing passports. You can buy a stolen passport for about $8,000 to $10,000. But any altered passport will do as long as you can bribe the security checkpoint inspector properly. I have been in this business for about six to seven years. You may think I have made a lot of money. But the expense is enormous and the risk is high. I didn't do any cases last year because two of my clients were caught and sent back. I lost a lot of money on these two clients. I really felt nervous about the whole business. Especially after the Dover incident, I completely stopped my activities for some time. I've only begun to slowly pick up the business recently.

The money made in human smuggling business is good by any Chinese standard, regardless of how the snakeheads in this study chose to qualify or downplay their earnings. The immense profits have kept many in the business for years, as long as they managed to keep their contacts and network in operation. It is clear, however, that most of the subjects in this study realized that human smuggling was neither a career nor a "real" business. Many invested smuggling proceeds in legitimate businesses. Others used their sporadic earnings to improve daily life. Even the most successful ones wanted to leave the business as soon as they made enough money, but, when pressed for a clarification, few could say just how much they thought was enough.

Many shared the view of one 36-year-old snakehead in New York, who came to America by way of Russia:

> When I was first involved in the smuggling business through my friends, I thought this was a much easier way to make a living than working in a restaurant. I helped my clients to arrange false documents to get passports and visas, something that relied on my brain and intelligence rather than my manual labor. But I did not quit my regular job, and later I started my own business. This immigration business is not legal and not something you can count on in the long run. I am only doing it part time and don't expect it to last very long. But the money is so good. Every time a client arrives in the U.S., I get to make a lot of money. I know it is illegal, but there is so much money to be made.

In sum, although media and government reports cite enormous profits as the driving force behind human smuggling activities, the reality is far more complex, as the pricing conventions of the market and the particular service rendered determine one's share of the illegal proceeds. Like their clients, who search for better fortune for themselves and their families, human smugglers also seek to improve their own families' economic situation. Thus, like their clients, human smugglers use their earnings mainly to elevate their standard of living, with only a handful making enough to expand into other (often legitimate) businesses.

PART TWO

The Human Smuggling Organization

CHAPTER 7

Organizational and Operational Characteristics

Reports from news media and government agencies often portray Chinese human smugglers as well organized and connected to sophisticated global networks. Accordingly, one main objective of this study was to explore how Chinese human smuggling groups are organized and how they make their operational and other decisions. Of the study's two sets of inquiries, one focused on organizational arrangements (i.e., the size of a group, the decision-making process, and smugglers' collaborations with other individuals), and the other examined operational styles (i.e., variation in means of transportation and in financial transactions among snakeheads).

There are several unique patterns in the business transactions and group dynamics of Chinese smuggling organizations. As Table 7.1 shows, more than one-third of the subjects claimed that the core members of their group numbered from two to five individuals. Another 17 percent claimed six or more core members. Most surprisingly, 40 percent of the subjects did not consider themselves part of any organization and did not regard their smuggling partners as organized in any way. These subjects had no problem admitting that they worked with friends or business associates, but they did not consider themselves involved in any formally organized business arrangements, because in their minds an organization had to have a name, a leader, formally listed members, and a regular meeting location. These subjects truly believed that the casual and sporadic nature of their business activities and their gatherings and private "conversations" in restaurants or teahouses were not organizational activities. These were the same activities that they would engage in with their friends anyway,

Table 7.1. Characteristics of smuggling organizations

	Frequency	Percent
Number of core members		
Denied any group identity	45	40.9
2–3 core members	30	27.3
4–5 core members	18	16.4
6–7 core members	6	5.5
8–10 core members	4	3.6
11–20 core members	3	2.7
More than 20 members	4	3.6
Total	110	100.0
Decision makers		
Independent decision	18	16.5
Collective decision	21	19.3
Snakehead in charge	50	45.9
Follow boss's instruction	10	9.2
Depends on contribution/ability	3	2.8
No idea	7	6.4
Total	109	100.0
Clarity in Division of Labor		
Clear division of labor	76	72.4
Somewhat clear division of labor	5	4.8
Unclear division of labor	14	13.3
Difficult to describe	2	1.9
No idea	8	7.6
Total	105	100.0
Collaboration with Other Smuggling Groups		
Yes	30	28.8
No	74	71.2
Total	104	100.0
Partners		
Stable Partners	70	63.6
Unstable Partners	40	36.4
Total	110	100.0

NOTE: Percentages are rounded.

with or without any business being transacted. One female snakehead in Fuzhou stated:

> Most of us in this business do not deal with each other like a formal business. When I get together with my (snakehead) friends, we typically eat out and we take turns to treat one another. When I am with my girl friends [female snakeheads], we sometimes go to a sauna, take a hot bath, get a massage, and then we play cards or drink tea and chat. It is very relaxing that way. We don't always do business. If we have business, we will take care of it.

When I asked the subjects who had the authority to make decisions in a smuggling operation, the responses became somewhat mixed. Only a small number of the subjects (16 percent) claimed that they made all their own decisions. Another 19 percent stated that they usually worked with their partners to reach collective decisions. Almost half of the subjects, about 46 percent, claimed that the snakeheads behind the scene were in charge of the operation. When pressed for details, few were able to tell what roles and responsibilities these behind-the-scene snakeheads had or whether they were working for even bigger snakeheads, suggesting that most human smugglers know little about what the other members of the smuggling ring are doing. On the other hand, low-level operatives (i.e., recruiters, whose rewards in the business were no more than small referral fees) responded primarily to requests for clients from other snakeheads. These low-level recruiters seemed to have little say in how an operation was to be carried out. Their lack of decision-making power was not the result of a deliberate organizational arrangement or a command structure, but primarily due to their limited connections and resources in the smuggling scheme. A snakehead in Fuzhou described his decision-making role in his smuggling organization:

> I work closely with two to three individuals, some in charge of coordinating with our contacts in the U.S., and some in charge of client recruitment. They are either my relatives or reputable people I have done business with in the past. We have people in charge of coordinating with foreign contacts, and some are in charge of recruiting clients. I am mainly responsible for arranging transportation. In general, we just get together, discuss our work and agree on what to do. It is really hard to say who has the most power in our group. The decision makers are usually the ones who have invested the most money or have the most connections.

Despite the fact that many illegal immigrants put snakeheads into two broad categories ("big" and "small") (Chin 1999), few subjects in this study drew any connection between the size of their smuggling business and their power to command. The authority structure was clear to most: there was none. One snakehead explained why snakeheads needed no leadership but still appeared as if they knew what they were doing:

> I can tell you that few people have control over the entire smuggling process. If anyone claims he knows everyone in the entire process, he is lying. There are a lot of mind games here. A client will not take you seriously if you sound like you have no idea about the entire smuggling process and about the capability of your partners at transit locations. So in order to convince the client, a snakehead must tell you what you want to hear so that he can get you to Vietnam or Thailand. But once you get here, you are basically sold to the snakeheads at those transit locations. Each snakehead does only one part of the deal and forwards the client to the next level.

Hierarchical Structures

Media reports, government documents, and even academic studies have portrayed Chinese human smugglers as highly organized, with complex and far-reaching global networks. However, there is no empirical evidence to suggest any clear hierarchical order resembling that of any traditional Chinese criminal societies. The best way to describe the structure of smuggling organizations is "amorphous." With few exceptions, none of the subjects in this study were working for a "godfather" somewhere behind the scenes. There were a few "big" snakeheads in this study, but none considered themselves in a dominant position in their smuggling network. Most subjects described others in their network as their friends or business partners.

It does appear that the more valuable the resources one brings to a smuggling operation, the more influence one will have over the direction and pace of it. Human smuggling organizations appear to have multiple layers of operatives, with an inner core consisting of only a few close associates. These business partners all seem to have their own networks of contacts, who in turn may have other contacts. Because transnational human smuggling involves several distinct stages—recruitment, travel preparation, departure, transit, arrival, and payment collection—each is coordinated and managed by snakeheads who are supported by additional networks of friends and partners. They all contribute to the eventual goal of landing clients in the United States and collecting their respective fees.

An example of this lack of hierarchical structure involves a female subject in Los Angeles, who specialized in marriage fraud and claimed to move thirty to forty clients into the United States each year. In the course of two months of field observations, she appeared to have little control over whether and when her partners would deliver the promised services, even though she claimed to know all the parties involved in the marriage fraud business and was the central coordinator. At one point, one of her snakehead partners was supposed to send an eligible bachelor to Fuzhou for a phony marriage ceremony on a mutually agreed-upon date; but the partner changed travel plans without even informing her. A few days later, her partner re-emerged and claimed that he had been sick. After he missed the first scheduled delivery date, she negotiated another and urged him to carry out his part of the deal as soon as possible, because her contact in China had already made all the wedding arrangements with the would-be bride and her relatives. The wedding plans included hiring a photographer, arranging a banquet, and making an appointment at the local government agency for official registration. Three days after the re-scheduled date, her partner again missed the appointment. This time, he claimed to have gone on a vacation. After his vacation came Memorial Day (a national holiday in the United States), which he used as another excuse for not being able to deliver the promised service. Throughout this seemingly endless waiting period, the female snakehead made numerous phone calls, looking for updates from her partner while she frantically informed her contact in Fuzhou of the many changes in plans and delays. When asked about the progress of the case weeks later, she described these delays in a rather matter-of-fact manner, as if these hitches were a normal part of the business. Although everything eventually worked out, it was clear that she had no control over how and when her partner would do his job.

A similar lack of control over the timing of each transaction was evident in many other smuggling operations reported by the subjects in this study. It was clear that these snakeheads had high levels of tolerance for unscheduled changes. Most of them appeared surprisingly flexible and accommodating in their dealings with one another. They were also experts at making up stories to explain why their services could not be delivered on time or as promised. Although timelines in terms of how long one part of a smuggling operation would take were frequently mentioned, unexpected delays seemed to occur often in most cases tracked in this study. Most snakeheads and their clients seemed rather understanding and patient, almost to the point of being fatalistic. This finding strongly suggests that snakeheads typically do not have control over each other's work and are thus at their partner's mercy when it comes to the delivery of promised services. A partner may be late or even fail to deliver a promised service as previously scheduled. As long as the promised service remains crucial to the smuggling operation and cannot be replaced, others have to adapt to this snakehead's unreliability.

Surprisingly, despite the lack of a hierarchical order and the absence of a godfather, most smuggling activities are successful. Other than the frequent changes and delays in plans, most operations seem to proceed uneventfully. Smuggling tasks appear to be carried out solely in pursuit of the eventual financial reward owed to the individual snakeheads at each level, rather than out of deference to any hierarchy or organizational need.

Horizontal Differentiation and Role Imperatives

Although smuggling groups demonstrate little hierarchical differentiation, their members seem to know each person's role. The division of labor in a smuggling operation is never ambiguous, as one 36-year-old snakehead, who specialized in acquiring U.S. passports from naturalized citizens, explained:

> It is difficult to describe the organization of human smuggling activities, because I can't tell who the members of the group are. I know someone is responsible for sending off clients and receiving clients, and someone is responsible for escorting clients through security checkpoints. I only know the person I am working with in Changle County and I have a few recruiters working for me. My role is to gather information in local townships on who is returning with a valid U.S. passport. Then I approach this person and propose to buy his passport. Once I obtain a passport, I notify my recruiters to find a prospective client who matches the passport holder in gender, age, and appearance. I will work with anyone willing to sell his passport. But the recruiters I work with are stable. It is easy to do business this way. We rely on mutual trust.

The majority of the subjects in this study worked with stable partners. Trust is a key element that binds these enterprising agents together. In addition, however, there are few alternatives for snakeheads to acquire the necessary services elsewhere. It is, after all, an illicit enterprise in which all involved try to hide from the authorities. There is no market mechanism for snakeheads to compete and there are no vendors from which to pick and choose.

Human smuggling operations involve detailed and highly specialized tasks and procedures, such as screening prospective clients for their ability to pay, collecting down payments, procuring necessary travel documents, arranging transportation, meeting clients and delivering them to safe houses, notifying relatives, and collecting payments. As one subject in Los Angeles explained:

> The division of labor is really clear. Everyone involved is useful in his own way and does his own thing only. There is no leadership in any smuggling rings. Leadership will not emerge because the work involved is so specialized.

Many specialized roles have emerged in response to the highly differentiated tasks involved in smuggling operations. Depending on the complexity of the transportation plan, some smuggling operations involve more specialized tasks than others. In general, smugglers specializing in direct by-air routes to the United States operate at the low end of organizational complexity. Smugglers who must send their clients to other countries for transit purposes make use of a combination of by-land, by-air, and even by-sea methods that require multiple stopovers, and thus operate at the high end of organizational complexity.

Because of the various business arrangements and the different roles involved in smuggling, it is difficult to group snakeheads into meaningful categories. One method of classifying them is to examine the stages at which they are involved, such as recruitment, transit, or arrival. Some stages involve more tasks than others, however, depending on the mode of transportation. Such a classification strategy oversimplifies the unique characteristics of the roles played by a particular snakehead in the smuggling process. For instance, one of the subjects in Fuzhou acted as a recruiter, but he also provided transportation for his clients to meet with his partner. When the parties reached an agreement, he collected the down payments. At the end of a smuggling operation, he was also responsible for collecting the remaining balance from the clients' relatives in China. Thus he played multiple roles—recruiter, payment collector, and transporter. Others are responsible for only one task, such as procuring travel documents or bribing security personnel at an exit checkpoint. To avoid glossing over crucial details of the many specific tasks snakeheads undertake, subjects in this study were grouped by their primary responsibilities in Table 7.2.

The three largest categories were recruiters, document vendors, and payment collectors, and those roles can be further divided into more specific groups of tasks. One cannot assume that all recruiters are the same, as they tend to target different clients and use varying methods of recruitment. Some only approach would-be clients, while others recruit U.S. passport or green card holders in order to procure their legal documents. Still others only look for eligible bachelors willing to enter into fraudulent marriages. Some of the document vendors specialize in preparing documents for busi-

Table 7.2. Roles in smuggling business

	Frequency	Percent
Primary role in smuggling business		
Recruiter	29	22.5
Document vendor	16	12.4
Payment collector	15	11.6
Coordinator	11	8.5
Transporter	8	6.2
Arranger of fraudulent business delegation	5	3.9
Securer of deposits	5	3.9
Escort	4	3.1
Fraudulent marriage arranger	4	3.1
Guard	3	2.3
Arranger of travel	2	1.6
Guarantor	2	1.6
Leaser of boats	2	1.6
Receiver of clients	2	1.6
Corrupt official	1	0.8
Arranger of stowaways	1	0.8
Student visa fraud organizer	1	0.8
Unable to determine role	18	14.0
Total	129	100.0
Roles change over time		
Yes	47	36.6
No	45	34.9
No longer in business	13	10.1
Unable to determine	24	18.6
Total	129	100.0
Role complexity		
Single role	83	64.3
Multiple roles	28	21.7
Unable to determine	18	14.0
Total	129	100.0

NOTE: Percentages are rounded.

ness delegations or securing certificates for fraudulent marriages. Others produce paperwork for various student or trainee visa applications or arrange for photo-substitutions. Irrespective of their specific tasks, recruiters generally perform either of two functions—enlisting fee-paying clients or acquiring legal papers that enable clients to travel. Document vendors likewise have different specializations, depending on their connections and the type of legal papers required for each smuggling operation. Because many government agencies and commercial entities produce legal documents that can be used to facilitate smuggling activities (e.g., passports, birth certificates, marriage licenses, business letters, financial affidavits), document vendors are truly a mixed bunch. Some are only tangentially involved, because the value of the documents they provide is limited (such as business letters and company descriptions), but others play a more influential role in smuggling operations, supplying birth certificates and passports. Then there are counterfeit artists, who either alter authentic legal documents or produce entirely bogus ones. Document vendors command an essential position in the smuggling business and are also the most diverse in their specialties. Payment collectors also fall into different categories. Some collect down payments when clients sign up with their smugglers, and others collect the remaining fees at the end of an operation.

In sum, not all snakeheads engage in identical activities. Most carry out activities determined by the resources at their disposal. The categorization of snakehead roles as presented in Table 7.2 is by no means exhaustive. At times during the course of this study, it was impossible to classify or even identify the responsibilities of some of the subjects, either because they refused to discuss them or because the interview setting was inappropriate for making specific inquiries. The following sections discuss some of the major role imperatives in smuggling operations.

Recruiters These are often the would-be migrants' relatives or close friends, who somehow know the smugglers. They may or may not have any involvement in subsequent smuggling operations. For each referral they receive a payment of up to $2,000. As one recruiter in a village near Fuzhou noted:

> The local snakeheads all have bosses behind them. They are responsible for recruiting people in China, and I don't think they play any role in the

operations outside of China. I mean these local snakeheads have very little education, have never traveled abroad, and do not speak any English. That's why it's hard to imagine that they play any role in overseas operations. There are a lot of these middlemen who are recruiters. They make $2,000 per recruit. If there are two middlemen involved, the $2,000 will be split between them. The middleman who knows the big snakehead will get the $2,000 from the big snakehead and it will be up to that person to decide how much he/she wants to pay the lower middleman.

Coordinators   These are the central figures in smuggling operations. However, they have nothing more to offer than the right connections to the necessary services, for a fee. Their survival depends on one-on-one relationships with other partners who are able to provide them with specific services. One such coordinator in Fuzhou described his operations:

> I do only direct flights. My customers fly from China to New York City or Vancouver using photo-sub foreign passports. They do not need to spend any time in transit points. I charge $55,000 per person, and I use about $15,000 for bribery. Otherwise, it wouldn't be that easy to have my clients pass through various customs and checkpoints.

Transporters   When an immigrant is to leave China by land or by sea, a domestic transporter helps him or her get to the border or to the smuggling ship. Transporters based in the United States are responsible for taking smuggled immigrants from airports or seaports to pre-arranged safe houses. Some U.S.-based transporters are also responsible for ferrying clients from Canada over the U.S. border or for coordinating with Mexican smugglers to help clients cross the southern border. A subject in Los Angeles described his early role in the smuggling business as a transporter:

> After a boat reached the U.S. shore, I would move the illegal migrants to an apartment that I had already rented. I would provide them with food and clothing, then get in touch with the snakeheads in New York to find out if any of the migrants had paid their smuggling fees. As soon as the fees were paid, I would drive them to the airport in Los Angeles to fly to New York. What happened after they got to New York was not my business.

Document vendors   Well connected with government officials or legitimate businesses, these individuals are able to produce the different types of documents necessary to facilitate the transportation of illegal immigrants. Some of these papers are authentic and go through official or irregular channels. Others are outright fraudulent. As one document vendor in New York's Chinatown described:

> I help my partners in China to prepare documents and certificates as well as invitation letters to enable them to apply for passports and visas. It is easy money, but I have to be very careful in every step to make sure all written materials are coherent and well prepared. If any of my clients get rejected by the U.S. consulates in China, I usually re-examine documents I prepared and learn from my mistakes. I am doing documents mostly for business delegations, family visitations, and professional artists.

Corrupt public officials   Law enforcement authorities in China and many transit countries are paid to aid illegal Chinese immigrants entering and exiting their countries. As one subject in New York noted:

> I used to be a customs inspector in China. I had a good job and a comfortable life. But I wanted to make big money and got involved with snakeheads. I became acquainted with a snakehead in 1995, and he asked me to help him with his smuggling business. Each time, he would tell me which boat contained his clients and I would choose to "inspect" that boat. After I completed the "inspection," I would write a report confirming that everything was okay.

Some corrupt government officials act not only as facilitators but also as core members or partners of a smuggling organization. Many subjects in this study insinuated or even openly admitted that government officials were among the key members of their smuggling groups.

Guides and crew members   A guide is responsible for moving illegal immigrants from one transit point to another or for helping immigrants enter the United States by land or air. Snakeheads hire crew members to charter smuggling ships or to work on them. One subject in New York noted:

> My contact (the snakehead) gives me instructions to fly to Fuzhou to meet with his clients. I go there and fly with his clients to the U.S. and sometimes to France. We usually leave China from Guangzhou Airport. When we go through the Chinese border control, we stand in the same line. I take the lead and the clients will follow me.

Enforcers   Enforcers, usually illegal immigrants themselves, are hired by snakeheads to work on smuggling ships for a reduction in their own smuggling fees. They are responsible for maintaining order and for distributing food and drinking water. One subject in New York described his job as an enforcer:

> I only do smuggling part time. My snakehead partners need me because I am a U.S. citizen. It is easy for me to go in and out of China. I fly to China twice a year, usually around February or December. They usually make all the arrangements for me and two or three other enforcers to go to Fuzhou and meet the clients at a certain seaport to board the ship. After we board the ship, we send all the clients down to the cargo hold at the bottom of the ship, where we watch them throughout the journey, which usually takes about a month. Once the ship arrives in the U.S., I get paid and go home. The snakeheads pay me $5,000 per trip.

Debt collectors   U.S.-based debt collectors are responsible for locking up illegal immigrants in safe houses until their smuggling fees are paid. China-based debt collectors harass the families and relatives of smuggled clients for prompt payment of the fees. One subject in New York noted:

> I do what my snakehead boss tells me to do. That is, I will call the people on a list he gives me. The list contains the clients' names, phone numbers, and addresses, and dates when they are supposed to make their payments. I usually give them a phone call first to notify them when and where to make their payment. If some clients fail to show up as they are told, I will wait for them near their residence. When they leave their apartments, I will threaten them or beat them up. I usually go with two or three other people. It is not hard to do. They are illegal immigrants and dare not call the police.

The specific players needed in a smuggling operation vary, depending on its complexity and the method of transportation. These roles usually play out sequentially in successive stages of the smuggling operation, with the recruiter working up front and the debt collector coming in at the destination. Not all operations require all roles, and some snakeheads will assume more than one role. Most smuggling tasks are specialized, and snakeheads deal with each other mostly on a one-on-one basis. These exclusive working relationships and their clear division of labor do not preclude snakeheads from assuming as many roles as they desire, as long as they have the necessary connections and resources. Many of the subjects in this study were able to manage multiple tasks within their smuggling groups, most of which complemented their primary role. A few even claimed to have complete control over their smuggling activities. As a 45-year-old businessman in New York described his practice:

> Because I have done business for many years between the U.S. and China, I travel extensively and have made many friends. Many of these people in China want to come to the U.S., so I started out by sending invitations and arranging travel documents to help them apply for temporary business visas. Many of the documents were fraudulent. Once I made a few successful cases, I realized that this could also be a money-making opportunity. Now I am doing this immigration business along with my regular business. Since I am using all my own resources and connections, I negotiate with my clients directly, preparing the necessary documents for them to apply for visas, meeting them at the airport, and collecting payments. I don't need anyone else. This is a serious business, and I have to be responsible for my clients. If I mess up anyone's case, it will ruin my reputation.

Many of the subjects also reported that their roles changed over time. As they became more familiar with the business and more established in it, their tasks and responsibilities also seemed to shift. Mostly their roles appeared to evolve from low-level activities, such as making referrals and recruiting clients, to more complex tasks, such as coordinating several partners and making arrangements for transportation and payment guaranty. The snakeheads' gradual accumulation of experience and contacts in the smuggling business appeared to be the main impetus behind the shift in roles. Naturally, snakeheads usually want to progress from simple and low-level tasks to more profitable ones that enable them to have more control over pricing. A 36-year-old snakehead in Lianjian County, who also owned and operated a brick factory, told about the evolution of his roles in the smuggling business:

> At first I was merely looking for would-be clients for other snakeheads. I don't recruit anymore. Instead, I gather information in my village or neighboring villages about villagers who have already obtained U.S. citizenship, and find out if any of them are about to come home for a visit from the U.S. As soon as they return, I approach them and try to buy their passports. Once I obtain a passport, I inform my recruiters, who will in turn look for a client whose appearance and age will best match those in the passport.

Characteristics of the Human Smuggling Business

Transnational human smuggling, at the least in the Chinese context, tends to be haphazard in its formation, irregular in its planning and execution, and uncertain in its outcome. The manner in which each segment of a smuggling operation is carried out largely reflects the personality and work habits of the individuals involved.

INFORMAL PROCEDURES AND SPECIALIZED SERVICE

Despite its enormous profits, human smuggling remains an informal business, with most, if not all, transactions conducted in conversations among small groups of individuals standing or sitting close to each other. Although news stories have reported on written contracts between snakeheads and their clients, none of the subjects in this study used such documents to formalize their business transactions.

Payment between and among smuggling partners is mostly made in cash or cash equivalent. Prices for agreed-upon services are seldom disputed. Despite lurid news reports of botched smuggling operations or torture of illegal immigrants, by far the majority of the subjects in this study reported being able to complete their operations. In most cases, their transactions with partners were smooth, albeit frequently delayed. As one subject said:

> We never draft any written contract with anyone. You are doing business with your own relatives or people you know. If you cheat me once, it will be the end of your reputation. The circle (of smugglers) is not big, and people in this town will know about you, because they will hear from me.

Despite the informality of transactions in the smuggling business, a snakehead's services are well protected, and smugglers typically develop their own specialties within the business. Some specialize in fraudulent marriages, while others prefer arranging business delegations to the United States. A smuggler once said, "The business of human smuggling is like the old Chinese fable of eight gods crossing the sea—everyone has his own heavenly capacity to accomplish the goal." Another snakehead in Fuzhou bragged about his proven method:

> The best method nowadays is the *peidu* (accompanying someone to study abroad) route. If you can obtain the cooperation of Chinese students in the

U.S., I can find clients to apply for F-2 visas in China (i.e., visas for spouses of foreign students, who typically hold F-1 student visas).[1] These Chinese students only need to send us their personal information. It won't cause any problem. Staff at the American consulates won't bother these applicants, even though these "spouses" cannot speak a word of English. We are willing to pay the collaborating students $10,000 to $30,000, and they don't even have to come back to China.

CORRUPTION AND BRIBERY

Research on transnational human smuggling has rarely mentioned official corruption, although it is widely reported by the news media and snakeheads alike. There has been no systematic data collection on the part played by corrupt officials in the smuggling business. This study has attempted to explore the connections between government officials, either direct or indirect, and other members of the smuggling group.

In China, illegal migration (whether immigration or emigration) is called *tousidu*, which literally means "clandestine and private trespass." For practical purposes, the term denotes two types of covert migration: "clandestine trespass" (*toudu*) and "private trespass" (*sidu*). It is considered clandestine trespass when people cross into any of China's neighbors, such as Myanmar, Vietnam, or Russia, without any official travel documents. Official corruption is limited in the context of clandestine trespass, because the snakehead only needs a guide who is familiar with local terrain. For instance, entrepreneurs (who are mostly farmers) from many villages along the Chinese-Myanmar border have been known for years to provide illegal border-crossing services to fee-paying customers. Occasionally, bribery ensures a safe passage at a border crossing point. Private trespass, however, is the use of fraudulently obtained documents to leave China for a destination or transit country (Fujian Ribao 1993). The official corruption that allows private trespass is considered an integral part of the smuggling business. Chinese government officials have long been implicated in both practices (Burdman 1993c; Engelberg 1994; World Journal 1993).

U.S. officials believe that because China is a tightly controlled society, it is difficult for Chinese smugglers to move large numbers of people out of the country without their being noticed by the authorities (U.S. Senate 1992). Indeed, during the years of my field work, illegal immigrants and snakeheads alike told stories about how common official collaboration in smuggling activities was. For instance, an illegal immigrant who was deported to China from Mexico claimed that she and a group of people from Fuzhou were transported by a military truck to the seaport where they boarded a freighter.

In private trespass, migrants leaving the country need to obtain travel documents from the authorities. Here, human smugglers often exploit legitimate channels to get their "documented" clients into transit countries. Some of the most popular channels they make use of to leave the country include (1) leaving China as a foreign guest laborer; (2) participating in a business delegation; (3) visiting relatives living abroad; and (4) joining a sightseeing tour to Hong Kong and Macau or Singapore and Thailand. Smugglers take advantage of corrupt officials within the officially sanctioned channels to secure assistance from their agency contacts, thereby facilitating their clients' exit from the country.

Although contact with corrupt officials is most likely restricted to the innermost circle of a smuggling organization, acknowledgment of such connections seems to be pervasive. About one-third of the subjects in this study claimed to be well connected with government officials, and more than half claimed at least some government connections. Regardless of whether they personally had connections with any government officials, the majority of the subjects observed that systematic bribery is an essential part of the smuggling business because, without such collusion, very few people could leave China. As for their connections with public security officials, customs agents, and border control officials, the same was true. More than half of the subjects claimed to have at least some contacts within law enforcement agencies, and more than one-third said that officials provided assistance to their smuggling business. The nature of the corruption varied widely, depending on the type of services desired. As a snakehead in Changle County noted:

> Every day, I spend a lot of money "buying hours" (bar girls in nightclubs and karaoke clubs are paid by their customers by the hour). On some nights, I spend more than 10,000 yuan (about $1,250). Every day, I am building up my connections, and they are my "assets." Not everybody can invite officials to a dinner party, because they don't just accept anybody's invitation. Sometimes they come out because they have no choice but to give face to a host.

Once they accept your invitation to have dinner together, bribing them with money and gifts after dinner becomes a lot easier. When I entertain them, it's normally a lavish dinner, followed by a trip to a karaoke club, where I encourage them to have a good time with the girls, and then take these girls to a hotel.

Interestingly, the officials involved tend to occupy low-level but crucial government positions, such as passport inspectors at border checkpoints, clerical staff dealing with passport applications, and officials issuing residential registrations or marriage certificates. Smugglers eagerly pursue such officials. For instance, because the vast majority of illegal Chinese immigrants to the United States have for decades come from Fujian, any form of identification or travel document issued in this province invites increased scrutiny at immigration checkpoints. Human smugglers often send their clients to other provinces to apply for travel documents. However, before anyone can apply for any travel document, one must first establish a record of residence with the local public security agency. As one snakehead in Fuzhou explained:

> If you have a Fuzhou passport, you are not going to get an American visa. As soon as the embassy people see the first four or five digits of your passport number, they will recognize that it was issued in Fujian Province. Your application will go into a trash can. They know that most smuggled Chinese are from the Fuzhou area. One should get a passport issued by other provinces, such the three provinces in northeast China or Hebei or Henan. That's where official connections are useful.

It makes sense that human smugglers pursue only low-level government officials for their pragmatic purposes. High-ranking officials have rarely been implicated in any smuggling operations, although some subjects in this study did claim that in a few cases family members of ranking public security officials in regional governments were involved in providing referrals and financial guaranties. This occurred is mostly because ranking government officials, who are removed from detailed government operations, are of little use to snakeheads.

Some snakeheads report being able to cultivate connections with government officials to secure necessary documents for overseas travel purposes, but others are more inclined to develop connections at border checkpoints.

One snakehead in Fuzhou explained how she worked her official contacts in border security at a major airport:

> The soldiers who inspect travel documents are rotated frequently, but not their supervisors. We have people who are in charge of bribing these super-visors (or *maiguan*). They spend a lot of time and money to build relation-ships. They work with these management people mostly because they don't sit at the security booths, and therefore tend to rotate less frequently. So the relationship, once developed, tends to remain stable for some time. When it comes to helping my clients through security, these contacts usually ask their subordinates for a favor to take care of a few "friends" of theirs who are on a business trip to the U.S. or some other country. Most soldiers know what that favor implies. Even the slow ones will get the idea once they see stacks of cash being slipped into their pockets by their supervisors or other mutual friends after the favor has been provided. To these soldiers, tens of thousands of yuan in a day's work is a fortune. Knowing they won't be manning the booth for long, because of frequent rotations, it becomes a race against time to make as much money and as quickly as possible. Besides, they don't care whether the illegal immigrants will make it to the U.S. or be repatriated the next day.

Bribery is a necessary but expensive component in this business. The snakeheads who pay to secure and maintain official connections often have mixed feelings about these corrupt officials. One of the subjects in Fuzhou complained:

> You think the snakeheads are criminals? It's the government officials who are the real criminals! You bribe them, and they allow you to move a few people out, but you'll never know when they are going to arrest you. They take our money and arrest us whenever they feel like it. Why? Because they have to prove to their superiors that they are doing their job and deserve to be pro-moted. We work hard to make money in this business but these government officials easily take the money out of our pockets. Some officials do not ask for bribes; they demand a share of our profit. They act like our shareholders but they do not invest any money in the business and take no risks at all.

On the other hand, many snakeheads consider bribery a standard pro-tocol in this business and gladly share their profits with their government contacts. To them, this is a two-way street, as one subject explained:

> We need to know all kinds of people and that's why our expenses are so high. Whenever we go out to eat, drink, and have fun with women, we

always pay the bills. Otherwise, how else are you going to establish a good relationship with government officials? We cannot put all the profits in our own pockets. Nobody can move clients by himself through various checkpoints. We need help from officials who are capable of acquiring passports quickly, and we need people who can help us pass through border security checkpoints. At any rate, it is a business where everybody makes money.

Although official corruption in China is widely acknowledged in the smuggling community, talk of corrupt U.S. government or immigration officials is not common. This somewhat asymmetrical pattern of official corruption (China but not the United States) is difficult to miss in any conversations with snakeheads. On the one hand, smugglers in China routinely obtain legal travel documents and arrange "official" escorts for their clients. Document vendors and their government contacts seem to have established a widely recognized symbiotic relationship. On the other hand, rarely have any snakeheads in the United States or China claimed to have connections within U.S. law enforcement agencies that allow easy passage of their clients. It is entirely possible that corrupt officials exist in the United States but are so well insulated by multiple tiers of operatives in smuggling operations that they are inaccessible to outsiders. It is also likely that the limited range of subjects in this study simply failed to include any smugglers with solid contacts within U.S. government agencies.

Still, U.S. officials are not immune to corruption. The news media have occasionally reported on corrupt U.S. immigration inspectors assisting human smugglers at ports of entry. The media have also carried accounts of overseas consulates issuing visas or green cards for personal gain. But in this study, reports of corrupt U.S. officials were rare. Furthermore, few subjects in this study seemed to have any idea of how one would go about cultivating contacts within U.S. federal or local governments for smuggling purposes. One subject in Queens, New York, noted:

> As far as I know, none of our partners have all the connections needed, especially contacts within the U.S. consulates in China or the INS. I don't think it is possible to establish a relationship with these people. At the most, our group can work out some deals with the Chinese customs agents, and for these contacts we have already spent a lot of money.

Chinese snakeheads tend to stick to themselves and operate within their own ethnic enclaves in the United States or else work with collaborators and corrupt officials in China or transit countries. Most snakeheads seem to share the perception that U.S. law enforcement officials are among the most difficult to corrupt. As one of the subjects in Flushing, New York, noted:

> For those of us in the smuggling business, the main target is to buy off border control officials in China. Authorities in the U.S. such as the police, the U.S. consulates or immigration officers are of little use to us. They are also very difficult to corrupt. No snakeheads have this part worked out. Overall, I think the U.S. Immigration Service is the most challenging agency to deal with, and in comparison the Chinese border control officials are the easiest.

TEMPORARY ALLIANCES AND SPORADIC ENGAGEMENT

Unlike traditional organized crime, in which continuity is often a key organizational goal (Kenney and Finckenauer 1995; Abadinsky 1990), human smuggling organizations involve only temporary business alliances. The purpose of a smuggling partnership is clearly defined and understood, and it often dissolves quickly after an operation is completed. Each snakehead appears to operate within a limited, albeit well-connected, circle of associates or friends. As one full-time snakehead in Fuzhou noted:

> People in this business know one another fairly well. Most of them are active in the same place. I go back and forth between China and the U.S. all the time. I've been in China this time for more than a year. Everybody has his smuggling strategies. We (the snakeheads in Fuzhou) sometimes work together; while at other times we just help out one another.

Although some snakeheads spend most of their time involved in smuggling-related activities, most also engage in conventional business activities, such as selling fruit, organizing tours, running restaurants, or working at construction sites. Oftentimes these mundane businesses are their only source of stable income. Smuggling opportunities occur irregularly, and snakeheads remain mostly dormant between operations. Some snakeheads even decline opportunities because of safety concerns. One subject in Los Angeles said that she stopped her business for almost a year because of increased crackdowns by law enforcement agencies in China and the United States:

> Whenever I hear that someone that I know is arrested or sent to jail, I get nervous. I also read these things in newspapers. I stopped for a year because

my instinct told me to stop. It was just a gut feeling. I trusted my instinct and did not do any cases for a year. Now I am beginning to feel safe enough to resume my business.

Most snakeheads recognize the illicit nature of their activities and do not plan to be involved in the smuggling business for long, despite the enormous profits. Balancing the risks involved, one smuggler in Fuzhou noted:

If I had the money, I wouldn't want to be in this business. I'd rather do something else. This is a high-risk business, even though it is very lucrative. For every person we smuggle out, we make more than 150,000 yuan (about $18,000). If we can help four to five people out, we can make about 800,000 to 900,000 yuan (about $100,000). But many customers also owe my brother-in-law, who is also a snakehead, a lot of money, about a million yuan. Some clients, after arriving in the U.S., said they didn't have the money. You have to know that many of our clients are friends and relatives. It's not appropriate to force them to pay right away.

Because smuggling operations are mostly carried out in secrecy, few snakeheads know any details of how other partners plan and execute their assigned tasks; hence smuggling organizations are highly susceptible to changes in membership. Any removal of a link along the smuggling chain can lead to an overall breakdown. As one former snakehead in Fuzhou recalled:

I used to be a recruiter for my brother-in-law. At the very beginning, before we became red hot, we had to go out to recruit customers. Once we established our reputation, customers came looking for us. At that time, my brother-in-law was a "brother" to the head of the Fuzhou Public Security Bureau (PSB, the police), and that's why we were able to get our applications for travel documents approved quickly. Altogether we made about a million yuan. Later, the PSB head stepped down, and that's when we stopped smuggling and started a seafood business.

The breakdown of an organization due to the loss of a crucial link may end the flow of easy money; moreover, an organizational breakdown during an operation can lead to a disastrous outcome, even tragedy. Occasionally in news outlets there are stories about illegal immigrants being left to fend for themselves in the Arizona desert or about abandoned immigrants found wandering along the road in strange neighborhoods, begging for food and water. One subject in this study, a self-employed electrical appliance repairman, worked as a part-time recruiter in the business. He told the story of his own failed voyage to America:

> It was back in 1995, when I was being smuggled on a boat to the U.S. We spent more than four months at sea. The snakehead in the U.S. ran into trouble. He was arrested and failed to send people to meet us in international waters. We ran out of water and food. Finally we staged a mutiny and tied up the crew. We set off emergency signals and even set the boat on fire to alert U.S. authorities. We were all detained and repatriated, and I was fined 17,000 yuan when I came home.

Of the fifty-one subjects (46 percent of the sample) who claimed to have stopped their smuggling activities, more than half had been in the business for a year or less. Only four subjects in this study claimed to have stayed in the business for ten years or more. When asked why the smuggling business is so precarious and so unreliable as a stable source of income, one Los Angeles subject in his late thirties described the factors that put him out of the business:

> This is a temporary business. I had a very good friend working in the government agency that reviewed and approved applications for a guest labor program. I did a lot of business through him, but he and his family were in a car accident a few years ago and he died. I lost him as my inside contact, and accordingly a lot of my business. In another case a close friend of mine who was my partner left Fuzhou and now lives in Europe. Because of these losses, I basically stopped smuggling. It is all about connections. If you don't know the right people, you can never get into this business.

Another, a 50-year-old snakehead in Brooklyn, New York, once used passports purchased from the Dominican Republic to bring clients out of mainland China for the journey to Hong Kong. He then hid them as stowaways in cargo ships bound for the United States, but he had to quit the business when his partner in Hong Kong died of cancer. He was a U.S. citizen when he began smuggling:

> I was doing business steadily with Ah Zhou (his partner) in Hong Kong. He made all the arrangements to get the passports and arrange for the clients to be hidden in a container ship. I would go to mainland China to recruit clients, usually three to five clients in a group, and escort them to Hong Kong. Things went really well, and I made a lot of money and closed my

previous electronic watch export business. In the three years we were in this business, I made about $420,000. I only dealt with Ah Zhou and had never asked him about his captain friend. He had never introduced him to me, either. After Ah Zhou died, there was no way for me to continue. I wish I had known his contacts so I could have continued the business on my own.

These subjects' short careers as snakeheads suggest that human smuggling is not a lasting occupation for most. This finding also supports the argument that most smuggling organizations are made up of persons whose involvement with each other is only temporary.

VIOLENCE AND INTIMIDATION

Since transactions in illicit businesses are not legally recognized and therefore cannot be legally protected, violence and intimidation have traditionally served important functions in organized crime syndicates (Gambetta 1993). Violence is mainly used to (1) maintain order and discipline members within the group, (2) settle disputes with rival organizations, thus eliminating competition, and (3) silence witnesses (Martin 1992; Stille 1995).

Chinese human smuggling organizations do not fit this traditional model, however. Smugglers rely on violence mostly to exact payments from delinquent clients (Chin 1999). However, they rarely use violence against other snakeheads. Most subjects in this study were aware of the problem of collecting payments for services delivered, but few ever resorted to violence or intimidation as a means of retaliating against unscrupulous partners. Business conduct and individual behavior in Chinese human smuggling seem to be regulated mainly by smugglers' mutual desire for making the eventual profit and maintaining a clean reputation to attract future clients. Perhaps their collective fear of negative consequences arising from the breach of their obligations has kept most snakeheads committed to carrying out their part of the deal. The ability to build and maintain a trustworthy image thus becomes a crucial benchmark of success in this business. A self-proclaimed full-time snakehead in Fuzhou explained:

> Everybody has his or her own smuggling routes, and sometimes we need to help one another get things done. Those of us in Fuzhou sometimes work on our own and sometimes together. We sometimes get into conflicts but we do not end up having to solve them by force. We are all friends. No one

dares to cheat or defraud anyone else. If you dare to do it once, you'd better leave town for good.

In a few rare cases, however, two subjects did report using violence against other partners, but the dispute was almost always about how to split the profits fairly. A 44-year-old payment collector in New York's Chinatown told of his experience:

> The key members in my payment collection crew often have quarrels over how to divide the profits. Sometimes there are even physical fights. In such situations, I will step in and try to resolve them. I always try to emphasize that it is important to keep harmony, and then I will ask them to let me decide how to divide up the profits. I try to keep these people from holding grudges against each other. It is not good for the business.

If a snakehead does want to use violence to retaliate against unscrupulous partners, there may be logistical obstacles. Because human smuggling activities often involve working relationships over different regions or countries, a snakehead may have to travel great distances or hire thugs to beat up a dishonest partner, assuming that he can even leave China or the United States freely to do so. Generally, the logistics and expenses required probably discourage most snakeheads from carrying out violent acts against other snakeheads—not to mention the risk of attracting unwanted attention from law enforcement agencies.

ABSENCE OF MONOPOLY

No empirical evidence thus far suggests that transnational human smuggling is moving toward a monopoly or is being consolidated by a decreasing number of smuggling organizations. Nor did I find evidence of overt competition among snakeheads in any geographical region. On the contrary— snakeheads seem happy to collaborate with friends, relatives, and business associates. Although many claim to be working only with specific partners, they do not hesitate to develop working relationships with other smugglers. As one successful snakehead in Fuzhou noted:

> Nobody can monopolize the human smuggling market. That's because we all have our own method of transportation. Occasionally, when I run into problems such as not being able to move clients from one transit point to another, I will find another snakehead to work with me in that particular deal.

Another snakehead, based in Los Angeles, who claimed to have engaged in smuggling activities on and off for ten years, expressed the same opinion. "I don't think anyone can control another person's network," he said. "If you can deliver the service and I have the clients, we work together. No one is the boss here."

Another indication of the absence of monopoly in this illicit enterprise is that thus far no snakeheads have been able to describe the boundaries of their business territories. Most only point to one or two villages where they have the most clients or report working with someone from this township or another. Snakeheads generally cannot tell who else might be working in the area outside of their own particular network. In traditional racketeering, most criminal organizations know exactly who controls what business (e.g., waste management, construction, or gambling) and in which neighborhood. Although U.S. law enforcement agencies have for years been pursuing a list of so-called "big" snakeheads (Thompson 2000), there have been no reports of any kind about any big snakeheads driving away their competitors from any particular village or township.

THE TASK FORCE AS AN ORGANIZATIONAL PATTERN

There appear to be three basic prerequisites for forming a transnational Chinese human smuggling organization: (1) an existing market demand, (2) membership in a tight social network, and (3) an opportunity to build a relationship with snakeheads. Figure 7.1 depicts and conceptualizes the basic elements of the smuggling process.

The human smuggling enterprise requires flexible networks of individuals who are strategically located in different parts of the world and are capable of pooling resources (i.e., time, energy, expertise, and capital to generate profits). The following list summarizes the main features associated with Chinese human smuggling organizations and their operational styles:

- Smuggling groups consist of mostly small peer groups (often three to four core individuals) arranged in simple hierarchies.
- Snakeheads typically participate in smuggling activities on a part-time basis, but most have legitimate businesses on the side (e.g., import/export, restaurants, immigration services, and travel agencies).
- Authority within a smuggling organization is mostly derived from one's

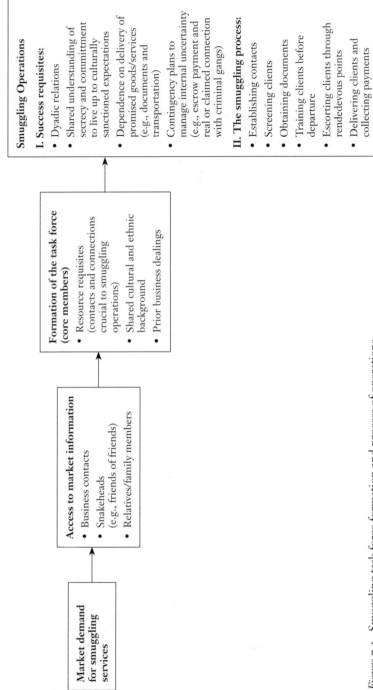

Smuggling Operations

I. Success requisites:

- Dyadic relations
- Shared understanding of secrecy and commitment to live up to culturally sanctioned expectations
- Dependence on delivery of promised goods/services (e.g., documents and transportation)
- Contingency plans to manage internal uncertainty (e.g., escrow payment and real or claimed connection with criminal gangs)

II. The smuggling process:

- Establishing contacts
- Screening clients
- Obtaining documents
- Training clients before departure
- Escorting clients through rendedevous points
- Delivering clients and collecting payments

Formation of the task force (core members)

- Resource requisites (contacts and connections crucial to smuggling operations)
- Shared cultural and ethnic background
- Prior business dealings

Access to market information

- Business contacts
- Snakeheads (e.g., friends of friends)
- Relatives/family members

Market demand for smuggling services

Figure 7.1. Smuggling task force formation and process of operations

control over resources crucial to an operation. That is, the more vital resources one has, the more one influences the direction and pace of the smuggling operation.

- Smuggling operations involve highly differentiated and specialized roles that are neither easily eliminated nor easily duplicated.

- Transactions among snakeheads are mostly one-on-one (i.e., dyadic). Redundancy in assigned tasks and contingency plans is rarely possible because most smugglers carefully guard their own resources as trade secrets.

- Official corruption is widely acknowledged by snakeheads in China.

- Smuggling organizations are mostly fluid and temporary. Their continued existence depends on the availability of clients and the socio-legal conditions of the market.

These features point to a pattern of mixed organizational attributes. On the one hand, groups of entrepreneurs meet through familial networks and fortuitous social contacts, form flexible international networks, and supply services to move fee-paying clients to their desired destinations. These smuggling organizations are made up of loosely affiliated individuals with diverse backgrounds, and the relationships among core members are mostly horizontal, with no clear structure of leadership. These small groups of enterprising agents appear to have kept the smuggling industry vibrant by being highly adaptable to market constraints and uncertainties. Some groups may break up over the loss of key members or a lack of opportunities, but others quickly fill the void and continue to provide services to meet the market demand.

On the other hand, while vertical differentiation might be limited, most smuggling operations seem to involve discrete individuals performing limited and highly specialized tasks. The flow of information is highly restricted, and responsibilities along each successive stage of an operation are clearly defined. Relationships among snakeheads are mostly serially linked. Most smugglers maintain additional layers of contacts of their own.

The result of these unique organizational patterns and operational norms is a distinctive task force orientation among entrepreneurs participating in this enterprise. These organizational structures and business practices have emerged as a result of the unique socio-legal challenges and operational requisites in the market.

CHAPTER 8

The Dyadic Cartwheel Network

The previous chapter provides only a descriptive analysis of the organizational characteristics and various role imperatives in Chinese human smuggling organizations. This chapter presents a conceptual framework to explain these unique structural attributes and their resultant operational patterns.[1]

Approaches to Studying Organized Crime

All criminal organizations share some common attributes, such as secrecy and conspiracy to profit from providing illicit goods and services. However, opinions diverge on whether most criminal organizations are hierarchically arranged, monopolistic, and governed by rules and regulations, or are merely loose associations of entrepreneurs who share nothing more than a desire to make money through illicit means. Although many studies have tried to define the essential elements that constitute organized crime, it remains a challenge to assess the extent to which a criminal activity is *organized*.

Various theories have been proposed to explain organized criminal activities. Kenney and Finckenauer (1995, 25) argued that organized crime is sufficiently varied and complex that one explanation or one theory cannot cover all forms of it. Mainstream criminology offers two traditional perspectives on criminal organizations. One, shared by many scholars and law enforcement agencies and perhaps articulated best by Donald Cressey, describes crime syndicates, such as the Italian mafia, as hierarchical, centralized, and bureaucratic structures similar to those of a modern corporation (Cressey 1969; Abadinsky 1990). Like their legitimate counterparts, these criminal organizations seek to monopolize certain enterprises by expanding in size and forming large cartels of national and international scope. They operate gambling casinos, prostitution rings, drug trafficking networks, and offshore banks (Block and Scarpitti 1986). In some cases, such as in Italy and the republics of the former Soviet Union, it is alleged that crime syndicates have developed a symbiotic relationship with the government to the point that they assume political and administrative functions (Nikiforov 1993; Jennings 1993; Marotta 1997). These criminal organizations run like normal corporations, operating with clear divisions of labor and chains of command. Although the mafia boss may rely on an inner council consisting of close friends and family members, most organizational tasks and responsibilities are carried out by a specially designated "staff" with specific skills and abilities. Rules and regulations govern members' activities, and membership is restricted.

Much of the discourse on Chinese crime organizations follows this traditional school of thought and describes criminal organizations such as the triads in Hong Kong and the gangsters in Taiwan as corporate-like entities. Like the Italian crime families (Jacobs and Gouldin 1999), triad societies, although operating independently of each other, often share a common and stable internal composition—a hierarchical structure enveloped in secrecy. "Godfathers" at the top of the organizational structure delegate responsibilities to their lieutenants, who in turn direct local and overseas branches to engage in a variety of criminal activities (Booth 1990; Black 1992; Chu 2000). Although today's triad societies are said to be far more fragmented than their forefathers were, they still possess well-defined organizational structures with at least five levels of hierarchy and clearly assigned roles and responsibilities at each level (see Chu 2000, 27–28). To gain formal membership in these groups, potential recruits pass through a certain period of probation and are inducted through ritualized procedures.

On the opposite side of this corporate perspective is an argument that the traditional concept of organized crime should be abandoned in favor of an "enterprise model" (Block and Chambliss 1981; Passas and Nelken 1993; Van-Duyne 1997). The enterprise model suggests that organized crime is mostly made up of flexible and adaptive networks of enterprising individuals that can easily expand and contract to deal with the uncertainties of the criminal enterprise. These entrepreneurs are organized only to the extent that they can effectively carry out profit-generating activities, which, some economists have argued, are utilitarian and rational (Reuter 1983; Savona 1990).

Reuter (1983), for instance, has argued that illegal enterprises are relatively small and short-lived; and, like their legal counterparts, illegal markets are characterized by competition and not by collusion. Several empirical studies have focused on the entrepreneurial nature of organized crime and described the transitory alliances of bold risk takers who seize opportunities to make profits on their investments (Dobinson 1993; Potter 1994). Apart from a relatively small group of core members, most associates work as needed to provide special services.

Much of the recent research on the structure of organized crime has been organized around the enterprise model. However, this approach is not without its critics. Liddick (1999), through his analysis of the numbers gambling industry in New York City in the 1960s, found little evidence to support Reuter's enterprise model (Reuter 1983). As an alternative to these two perspectives on the structure of organized crime, Dwight Smith (1975, 336) provides a continuum perspective and argued that "entrepreneurial transactions can be ranked on a scale that reflects levels of legitimacy within a specific marketplace." Illegitimate markets exist beyond the boundaries of legitimate markets and should be examined in their specific industries to understand the "spectrum of legitimacy" (Smith 1980).

The spectrum perspective offers alternatives to the dichotomous perspective, which classifies criminal enterprises as either formal organizations or informal entities. Criminal organizations respond to varying market demands by contracting or expanding in size. They assume a variety of organizational structures shaped passively by external social-legal factors rather than actively by design. On the one hand, some crime groups, such as those involved in construction or gambling businesses, may require an elaborate hierarchy and a clear division of labor, necessary organizational prerequisites for remaining viable in these illicit businesses. On the other hand, crime groups such as those involved in loan sharking and fencing of stolen goods must respond rapidly to changing consumer demands in the street, and therefore require little or no formal organizational structure. It is clear that these two major schools of thought on the nature of organized crime describe realities that stand at opposite ends of a spectrum.

Although the continuum perspective offers greater flexibility in explaining different types of racketeering activities, most empirical studies seem to support one or the other of the two dominant perspectives. Other than Smith's application of systems theory, few studies have made empirical efforts to apply theories of formal legal organizations and markets to the study of illegal enterprises (Liddick 1999).

These different conceptualizations lead to different understandings of criminal organizations, describe different trajectories in the patterns of their criminal activities, and carry different policy implications. Therefore, the development of an empirically based theoretical framework is not merely an academic exercise. It can provide great insight into the phenomenon under investigation and predict its trajectories and possible outcomes, as well as determine how law enforcement strategies can be devised, implemented, and improved upon.

For the most part anti-smuggling policies in the United States have for years been guided by the assumption that large crime organizations are behind transnational human smuggling operations (Zhang and Chin 2002b). Therefore, most U.S. efforts and resources have been devoted to in-depth and long-term investigations aimed at netting the big fish—the godfather and his or her entire organization. On the whole, such a strategy has produced remarkable results in much of the U.S. government's effort in fighting organized crime in the past few decades. *Gotham Unbound*, by Jacobs, Friel, and Radick (1999), provides a detailed account of how government agencies effectively applied strategies, based on the corporate model, to break up criminal organizations in New York City.

Chinese human smuggling, however, is vastly different from traditional racketeering activities in New York City or Chicago. Neither the corporate model nor the enterprise model adequately explains the patterns of transactions among Chinese human smugglers. A unique set of socio-cultural factors, market conditions, and operational requisites combines to produce a set of organizational attributes and operational styles that requires the development of a new conceptual framework.

Market Conditions as a Determinant of Organizational Attributes

Oliver Williamson (1975), in his analysis of markets and hierarchies, emphasized the importance of examining the interplay of human and environmental factors, and argued that the hierarchical structure of a business entity takes the form most conducive to facilitating optimal exchange relations under existing market conditions. Similarly, transnational human smuggling as an illicit business faces many challenges. Successful transactions, therefore, require snakeheads to arrange and deploy their resources in a manner most suitable for overcoming these obstacles and for helping illegal migrants reach their destinations. To achieve successful smuggling operations, snakeheads must effectively circumvent a series of obstacles.

PERMANENT FEAR OF ARREST AND ASSET FORFEITURE

Pervasive in the psyche of all smugglers is the fear of arrest and the possible forfeiture of their assets and/or heavy fines imposed by authorities. Soon after the *Golden Venture* incident, the U.S. government recognized the inadequacy and leniency of its existing laws and took significant steps to increase the penalties for human smuggling. Previously, snakeheads caught smuggling illegal immigrants generally served six to eighteen months in prison. Then Congress passed the Violent Crime Control and Law Enforcement Act of 1994, which stipulates that "persons who knowingly bring illegals into the U.S. are subject to a possible imprisonment term of ten years (and/or fines). The maximum penalty is increased to twenty years per illegal immigrant when bodily injury occurs or life is placed in jeopardy in connection with the smuggling offense. Additionally, when death results, the death penalty or life imprisonment is allowed" (U.S. Commission on Immigration Reform 1994, 48). To further raise the financial stakes, the Senate in 1995 introduced legislation to allow law enforcement agencies to use the RICO (Racketeering-Influenced and Corrupt Organizations) procedures, which provide wiretap and asset forfeiture authority, to combat human smuggling and related crimes.[2] The RICO legislation has for decades been reserved mostly for fighting mafia families in New York, Chicago, and other cities.

This increased attention from law enforcement agencies forced snakeheads to go further underground. Smugglers typically conduct clandestine transactions and seek as little attention as possible, thus eliminating the possibility of any active and open recruitment of prospective clients.[3] When authorities in China and the United States launch campaigns to crack down on human smuggling activities, snakeheads usually take precautions and keep a low profile even among their own kind. Some have decided to leave the business. One snakehead who was operating a travel agency in Los Angeles said:

> After Sister Ping was arrested, I didn't feel safe anymore, so I stopped the smuggling business for a long time and didn't even want to talk to anyone. I pretty much kept it to myself and ran my regular business quietly for a year without taking any immigration cases.

Although most Chinese, both in the United States and China, do not consider illegal immigration a criminal activity in the traditional sense, few snakeheads plan to make a career out of it. For instance, there was a pervasive nervousness among the subjects that I encountered in this study, who feared that they might one day run into trouble with the law. Most wanted to leave the business soon. Several used an old Chinese proverb to describe their state of mind: "When you walk at night long enough, you are bound to run into ghosts."

UNSTABLE AND LIMITED CLIENTELE

As a business, human smuggling has an inherently unstable and restricted clientele that offers poor prospects for growth. Although this assertion appears counter-intuitive at first glance, since most people consider China to be a country where millions are eager to improve their lot by coming to America, the reality is that only a handful qualify as clients worthy to be recruited and smuggled. First of all, a prospective client must have the financial wherewithal in order to even begin looking for a snakehead to explore his or her smuggling options.

As described in Chapter 3, snakeheads usually have elaborate procedures to investigate and verify whether their prospective clients can pay the smuggling fees. The most common way to prove one's financial means is to provide evidence that one has close relatives in the United States with enough savings to pay the fee. Otherwise, one must find a relative or friend of significant social standing in the community to convince the snakehead that enough money can be raised from friends and relatives. Without verifiable proof of their financial means, few can become eligible clients. One subject in New York described the ordeal his family had to go through to convince the snakehead to smuggle him into the United States:

> The snakehead who smuggled me was the same guy who earlier had smuggled a friend of mine. After my friend arrived in the U.S., he called and told me the trip took only two weeks. My parents then went to his parents and asked them to contact the snakehead for me. The snakehead at first refused to take me. He did not believe my family could afford the expenses. He wanted a guarantor, but my parents couldn't find one. Later my parents appealed to a relative of ours in the U.S. for assistance, who in turn asked his relatives and friends in the U.S. for help. Eventually, these people agreed to loan me one to two thousands dollars each, which amounted to about half of the fees required. At home, my parents begged their neighbors, relatives, and friends to come up with the rest of the money. A lot of the money was on loan to us with a 2 percent interest a month. So my parents finally gathered enough money, and they approached the little snakehead and even showed him the bank deposits. But the little snakehead said the money was still insufficient and he refused to consider me. My parents then told the snakehead that their relatives in the U.S. could put up more money. The snakehead asked for the telephone numbers of our relatives in the U.S. and said he would call them to verify. After the snakehead called and found out that our relatives in the U.S. mostly owned restaurants, he felt assured. But he still wanted my parents to find a guarantor. Finally, my parents found a relative who worked in a government agency and was quite well-off. He also happened to know this snakehead. This relative acted as a guarantor and charged me $2,000 for his "service." I gave him the bank deposit certificates. The snakehead promised that he would smuggle me into the U.S. within a month, for $60,000.

Financial screening is only one aspect of this unstable business. A snakehead must first identify "worthy" clients, a different task, because they are not immediately visible. Most illegal Chinese immigrants thus far have come from just a few geographical locations in China, thus limiting the smuggling business to these regions.

The fact that transnational Chinese human smuggling is not a widespread phenomenon in China is very much in line with the existing literature on international migration. As Massey et al. (2002, 143) have argued, wage differentials do not necessarily cause international migration and the poorest countries "do not yield significant migration streams, even in the absence of formal barriers." International migrants often build their own infrastructure and expand through kinship networks or friendship. A relative or a member from the same home village, as in the Chinese case, can become a contact as well as a source of social capital for other family members or villagers willing to emigrate, but the momentum is always internal and limited to the social networks of migrants already residing overseas, thus restricting the business of human smuggling to only a few regions where such clients can be found. Moreover, transporting human beings over great distances and through illegal channels is an expensive proposition that requires not only capital outlay but also networks of individuals with the right social connections, thus further limiting the number of prospective clients as well as the number of possible snakeheads.

During the 1990s, U.S. law enforcement agencies learned that most illegal Chinese immigrants came from Fujian Province. Chin and Kelly (1997) found, in their survey of illegal Chinese immigrants in New York City, that almost 90 percent of the subjects were from an even more concentrated region: Changle City, Tingjiang Township, and Mawei District, all within fifty kilometers of Fuzhou (the capital of Fujian province). Although more recently illegal immigrants have arrived from other parts of China, eligible clients have so far remained geographically isolated. As one snakehead in Los Angeles noted:

> I don't know how this business got started in Fujian. It is only natural for me to go to Fujian because that's where most clients are from. In Changle, almost everyone you meet in the street these days has relatives in the U.S. That means their relatives most likely have the ability to pay for the trip.

The clandestine nature of the business, the need to select prospective clients carefully, and the small and concentrated regions from which eligible clients may be recruited, combine to determine that the smuggling business can only afford a small number of enterprising agents with a restricted range of territories where they can peddle their services.

OPERATIONAL COMPLEXITIES

Illegal movement of undocumented immigrants across borders introduces many logistical challenges that range from arranging transportation and providing meals and lodging to safeguarding clients and evading attention from authorities. To launch an operation, snakeheads must plan their trips, acquire proper documents, and coordinate schedules with their partners at successive stages. This process does not take into account interference by law enforcement activities, which can greatly slow down or even put an operation on hold for an extended time.

Although most clients would rather pay the high price required for being transported via direct flights to the United States, this smuggling method is rarely available and finding snakeheads capable of arranging such trips is difficult. Chin and Kelly (1997), after interviewing 300 smuggled Chinese immigrants in New York, found that only seven flew directly from China to America. The rest had to be transported in other ways, using different transportation methods and routes.

One of the few findings on which news accounts, government reports, and academic studies all seem to agree is that snakeheads use elaborate transportation routes to avoid detection and exploit inadequacies in international border control. These routes extend around the world, often involving ethnic Chinese enclaves in various nations as providers of logistical support. These networks of ethnic enclaves consisting of other immigrants provide the most important component of the infrastructure required to sustain international migration, whether legal or illegal (Massey and Zenteno 1999). Chinese communities scattered across the world thus provide shelter, cultural and culinary comfort, and technical know-how to move their countrymen through multiple transit points to their eventual destination.

Reports from U.S. and European intelligence communities have plotted Chinese human smuggling routes practically all over the world. Because of their geographic proximity to the United States and relatively lax immigration control, Canada and Mexico rank the highest as transit countries. In Europe, snakeheads increasingly use former Eastern Bloc countries as way stations to forward their clients to Western Europe, which has also become a major destination for illegal Chinese migrants. Major smuggling hubs have appeared in Milan, Madrid, Frankfurt, and Amsterdam. The U.S. government has participated in or supported several successful investigations in European cities. However, when run out of one location, smugglers resurface in another (Thompson 2000). Such Latin and South American countries as Brazil, Panama, and Surinam have also become major way stations, where ethnic Chinese collaborate with local smugglers, government officials, and police to forward illegal migrants to the United States. In Asia, Thailand and the Philippines have long been major staging areas. Vietnam and Cambodia are gaining prominence as transit countries because of their proximity to China. As one female subject in Fuzhou noted:

> I have a friend who specializes in third country transfer. He told me a few months ago that he had 400 to 500 clients waiting in Thailand, Vietnam, and Cambodia. He asked if I could help him absorb some of his clients. I don't do this type of business. I can't imagine how he could manage all these people. They all need a place to eat and sleep. I know it is cheap to live in those countries, but we are talking about hundreds of people.

HAZARDOUS BUSINESS ENVIRONMENT

Inherent in all cross-border human smuggling activity is the clear and present danger of accidents and mishaps. Although all would-be clients are concerned about their safety and snakeheads usually try to safeguard their precious "cargo," because of the clandestine and illicit nature of the business it is destined to suffer accidents. The death in 1999 of fifty-eight illegal Chinese immigrants inside a refrigerator truck while it tried to cross into Dover, England, from France is an example. All victims were allegedly from Fujian province, and the transfer locations were traced back to the Netherlands and Belgium (Woods 2000). In another case reported by McCarthy (2000), during a long sea journey to the United States, when illegal immigrants fell ill and died their bodies were simply pushed overboard.

Stories like these appear from time to time in the media, and most likely they represent just a small percentage of the actual accidents. No one will ever know what has happened to individuals who left their villages but never showed up in their destination countries. In this study subjects and would-be migrants often told stories about people in their villages whose whereabouts remained unknown years after they left home. During an interview in Fuzhou, a smuggler told this story:

> A guy from my village crossed the border into Vietnam with the help of a snakehead and stayed there for weeks, waiting to start the next leg of the

journey. The group he was traveling with walked for many days in thickly wooded areas. Many of them fell ill, throwing up and having fevers. One man in the group later died, supposedly bitten to death by a swarm of mosquitoes in the jungle. People back at home couldn't believe what they heard. Have you ever heard of anyone eaten alive by mosquitoes?

These tragic events happen occasionally. Some are reported in the news, but many go unnoticed. Small and non-fatal incidents happen even more frequently. Often a simple glitch (e.g., failing to pick up clients at a pre-arranged location, unexpected staff changes at the border checkpoint, or engine trouble with a smuggling vessel) can disrupt the planned sequence of events and cause the entire operation to fall apart. For instance, in August 1999, a group of eighty-two Chinese nationals were taken into custody in Ensenada, Mexico, by local authorities after the police found them wandering around near a highway (Lau and Dibble 1999). The group had arrived by boat five days earlier and had been without food for four days. Because the local collaborator failed to show up, they had to leave their hideout and venture out on their own.

SEQUENTIAL UNCERTAINTIES

All human smuggling operations involve a series or stages of sequential activities, all of which are vital to their eventual success. Chin (1999, 33) quoted a snakehead who characterized a Chinese smuggling network as a dragon: " . . . although it's a lengthy creature, various organic parts (of the body) are tightly linked." This lengthy creature winds from China through various countries all the way to the United States. If any joint of this lengthy being were to become dislodged, the entire operation would be paralyzed, stranding clients in foreign countries. Ironically, the precautions and measures snakeheads use to minimize risks and protect themselves can actually increase the likelihood of operational disruption. As a result, when a joint in this dragon does become dislocated, it will take a long time to heal—that is, if it heals at all.

According to the subjects in this study, most snakeheads dread two stages in a smuggling operation in particular, the stages during which they or their clients are most likely to be caught: (1) when clients are waiting to board the smuggling ship in large numbers in seaport villages, a process that often attracts attention from passers-by, who may alert border patrol authorities;

and (2) when clients actually enter the United States. If they are arrested and held in immigration detention centers, the operation does not count as being successful, and their families in China can refuse to pay the smuggling fees. In other cases, illegal immigrants may conspire with friends and relatives in America to defraud the snakehead, and upon arrival simply disappear at the airport during a bathroom break.

These two critical stages represent the beginning (i.e., leaving China) and the ending (i.e., arriving in the United States) of a smuggling operation. The large majority of migrants, who do not have the luxury of a direct flight to the United States, will make many stopovers during the journey. Although some snakeheads work to develop new contacts and cultivate alternative routes over time, most have only a restricted set of transportation options. If their partners at the next stop fail to deliver, their clients will find themselves stranded in a transit country or arrested and repatriated. Many Chinese migrants are indeed caught in various countries along the way and repatriated.

SPORADIC SMUGGLING OPPORTUNITIES

Human smuggling is a business of opportunities. Eligible clients are not always available, even when a snakehead has the proper contacts to launch a smuggling operation. It takes time for prospective clients to gather financial backing. The snakehead must then verify whether the client indeed has financial backup or relatives in the United States. It also takes time to acquire travel documents, such as a passport appropriate for photo substitution. The number of stages involved creates long waiting periods between operations, thus making the business protracted in operation as well as unpredictable in outcome. Such an unstable business environment helps explain why most of the subjects in this study had other jobs or ran other businesses, and why few wanted to depend on smuggling for their livelihood. It also explains why most smuggling organizations are nothing more than temporary alliances oriented towards one operation at a time, and why snakeheads usually focus on carrying out one operation or one set of related tasks at a time.

The Dyadic Cartwheel Network Perspective

The market conditions described above illustrate the kind of challenges and obstacles snakeheads must overcome to complete their business transactions. Human smugglers operate similarly to many other entrepreneurs—that is, using a network of social contacts and personal resources to engage in a profit-seeking activity. Their task-force orientation helps these entrepreneurs focus on their assigned jobs and encourages the individuals involved to perform their specific roles.

In accordance with Williamson's analysis of peer groups in economic activities (1975), human smuggling operations can be perceived as exchanges among peers. Activities among these peers require minimal organizational structure and a limited hierarchy. However, unlike peer groups in legal and normal economic activities, members of a smuggling organization rarely engage in teamwork (i.e., collective engagement in similar tasks and resource sharing). Their relations with each other are usually secretive and entail mostly one-on-one, or dyadic, transactions. Each individual snakehead develops and maintains an additional circle of contacts and resources that are also clandestine in nature and dyadic in format. Figure 8.1 illustrates the dyadic cartwheel network perspective on the multiple levels of one-on-one relationships characteristic of Chinese human smuggling organizations.

Such an organizational structure, containing members of one's close social network and oriented toward specific tasks, appears to have many advantages. First of all, in a business environment in which contractual re-

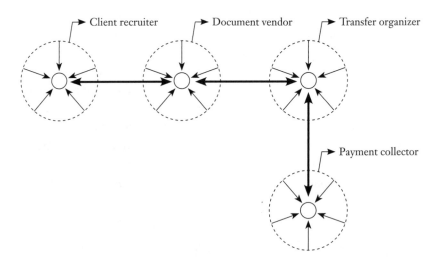

Figure 8.1. The dyadic cartwheel network—a conceptual diagram of Chinese human smuggling organizations

lationships consist of mere spoken agreements (and are thus without formal legal protection), interactions within a small group of friends and relatives serve to increase shared understanding of the tasks that need to be completed. Two parties must reach an agreement that spells out service and financial requirements or the dyadic transaction will not occur. The dyadic cartwheel network effectively minimizes interpersonal tension and increases personal accountability. A clear trading atmosphere, therefore, is easy to achieve and maintain because only individuals who can perform and deliver agreed-upon services are likely to join and stay in a certain network. Those who cannot perform will be excluded from the task force because there won't be any meaningful roles for them to play. Shared expectations are easily promoted in these small groups. The resultant mutual understanding reduces uncertainty, increases collective commitment, and produces smooth transactions. This is particularly true when the core members of a smuggling organization speak the same dialect and share the same ancestral township.

Second, small group interactions expedite information gathering and forwarding, improve communication, and facilitate decision making, particularly when most transactions take place on a dyadic basis. Almost by definition, the one-on-one transactions common to most smuggling operations prevent any large, complex organizations from emerging. In a deliberate effort to evade the attention of law enforcement, snakeheads often plan complex transportation routes and rendezvous points. Completion of each stage of a smuggling operation relies solely on successfully getting through the previous stage. Small group interactions can reduce sequential complexity in smuggling operations. Each cluster of individuals (or task force) focuses on completing one phase or one set of tasks, such as obtaining fraudulent documents, arranging transportation, or securing the cooperation of corrupt officials at border checkpoints. When there are only a small number of individuals involved in a limited number of immediate tasks, timely adaptation in decision making is possible. Because any transaction or exchange occurs over the shortest distance—between two individuals—maximum efficiency is possible, with a minimal number of players.

Third, the dyadic cartwheel network can achieve maximum security with minimal exposure to law enforcement personnel or other operational hazards. Because of the restricted flow of information and the limited contact with other members along the smuggling chain, individuals or clusters of individuals in a smuggling ring are insulated from one another. When one snakehead is arrested or one stage falls apart, the remaining members of the smuggling group do not likely face any imminent danger. Therefore, the survival of the human smuggling business does not hinge upon the success of one specific organization, but on the collective entrepreneurial efforts of the many groups of individuals involved in the process.

Additionally, the dyadic cartwheel network increases the security of transactions against unscrupulous snakeheads. When any pair of snakeheads engages in a transaction, one of them expresses what service she needs and the other indicates whether he and only he can supply the service. If he cannot provide the requested service, a snakehead most likely will withhold information about others who might be able to supply the needed service. Instead, he will often act as a go-between and charge a fee to acquire the needed service from someone else. This way he can control the source of service for as long as possible.

Services or goods vital to smuggling activities are exclusively held and carefully guarded by individual snakeheads. There are few opportunities to shop around, although over time a snakehead may expand his or her network of resources. A minimum level of redundancy and one-on-one transactions ensure that the operation reaps the maximum profits for the parties involved. Protection of one's share of the profit relies solely on one's ability to keep his/her resources inaccessible to others.

Fourth, when contingent transactions are the norm and sequential operations are unpredictable and vulnerable to disruption, small groups (or task forces) are capable of expanding and contracting in response to market uncertainties. Small groups of entrepreneurs (as opposed to a specific smuggling organization) can emerge to take advantage of new opportunities and adjust to different client demands and transportation strategies. Most snakeheads also operate other legitimate or illicit businesses and only gather for a viable opportunity. After the operation is complete, the group of snakeheads will disband or remain social friends, going about their daily business as usual. Therefore, small exchange relations (with minimal organizational structure and simple hierarchies) can withstand the scarcity of opportunities in an uncertain market.

Figure 8.2 summarizes this dyadic cartwheel model, and depicts the process of Chinese human smuggling and its various operational requisites.

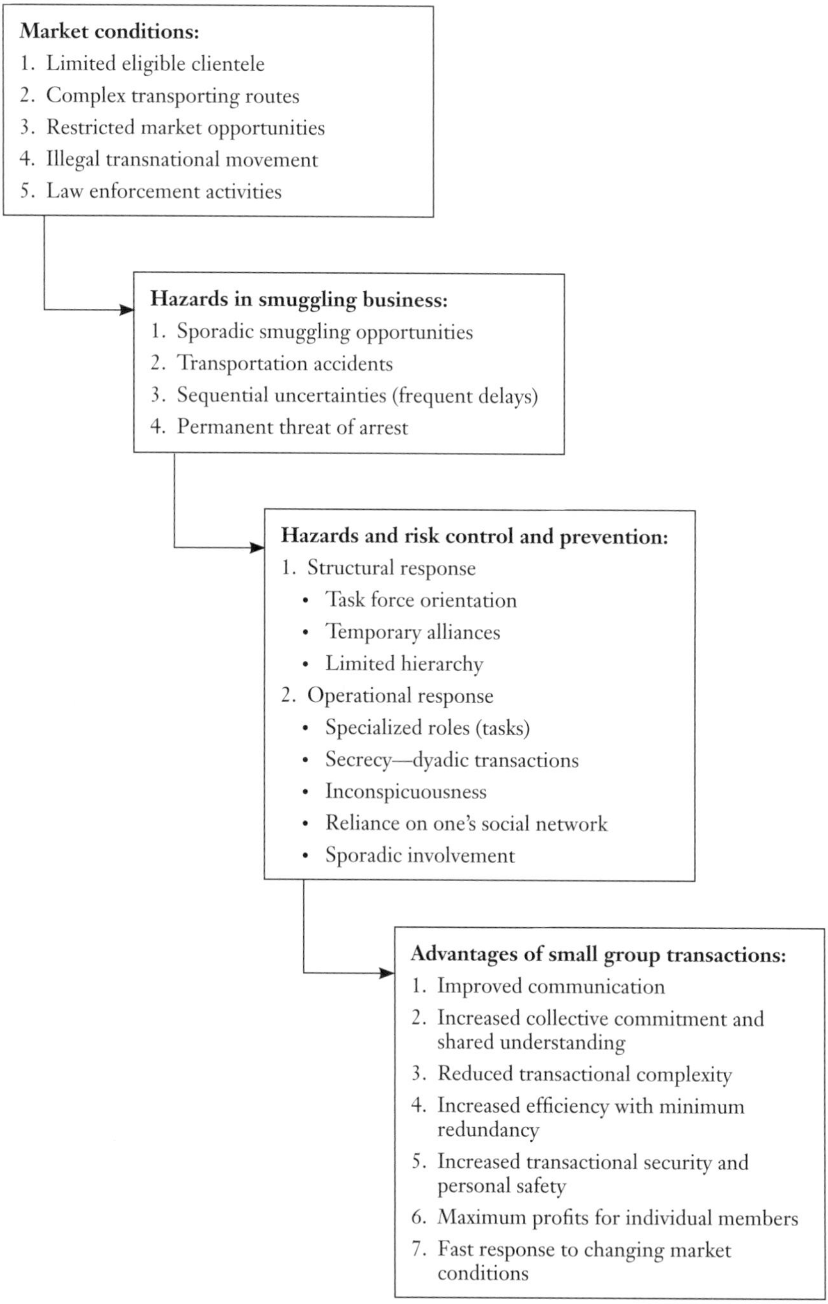

Market conditions:
1. Limited eligible clientele
2. Complex transporting routes
3. Restricted market opportunities
4. Illegal transnational movement
5. Law enforcement activities

Hazards in smuggling business:
1. Sporadic smuggling opportunities
2. Transportation accidents
3. Sequential uncertainties (frequent delays)
4. Permanent threat of arrest

Hazards and risk control and prevention:
1. Structural response
   - Task force orientation
   - Temporary alliances
   - Limited hierarchy
2. Operational response
   - Specialized roles (tasks)
   - Secrecy—dyadic transactions
   - Inconspicuousness
   - Reliance on one's social network
   - Sporadic involvement

Advantages of small group transactions:
1. Improved communication
2. Increased collective commitment and shared understanding
3. Reduced transactional complexity
4. Increased efficiency with minimum redundancy
5. Increased transactional security and personal safety
6. Maximum profits for individual members
7. Fast response to changing market conditions

Figure 8.2. A conceptual diagram of the task-force orientation of Chinese human smuggling organizations

Risk Management in Response to Hazardous Market Conditions

Smith (1980) argued that the study of organized crime should focus on the activities (i.e., the enterprise) rather than the group or groups of individuals undertaking the enterprise. Along the same line, perhaps the best way to understand the organizational attributes of a human smuggling organization is to examine the nature of the business and its varied operational requisites. An important dimension of these requisites is the management of risks pervasive in criminal racketeering activities.

One must examine snakeheads' risk prevention, control, and absorption strategies to fully appreciate the ingenuity of their structure and operations and make sense of the conceptual framework presented in this chapter. The key to understanding the social organization of the smuggling business is to explore snakeheads' perceptions of and responses to various risks in this business. A criminal organization, whether it consists of complex command structures or simple peer groups, must mitigate the risks of the market place in order to achieve a successful business transaction. Accordingly, human smugglers interact with their partners on a one-on-one basis for insurance purposes, because such arrangements create a buffer against the effects of unanticipated events and provide contingency plans during a smuggling operation. One recruitment coordinator in Putian County (a coastal county south of Fuzhou), who specialized in sea-based smuggling operations, explained how he managed the risk of detection by law enforcement agencies:

> What I am most afraid of are two things—one, when some of my clients change their minds and don't want to go anymore, in which case they can expose my action plan; and two, probably the worst, there might be informants among my clients working for the border patrol police. Therefore I never tell my clients in advance when they will leave or where to meet. I always make last-minute announcements to get them to the gathering location, and I do not allow them to contact anyone, not even their families. I usually give out only my pager numbers and use payphones to give instructions.

Because of the illicit nature of the business, the absence of formal legal protection, and the fear of law enforcement activities, people involved in the smuggling business must stay inconspicuous and seek as little attention as possible. Risk management thus becomes the factor that determines their group structure and operational style. It begins at the very front of an operation (i.e., client recruitment and screening) and continues until the very end, when the smuggling fees are collected. Once an opportunity arises, risk management by all snakeheads participating in the operation becomes the focal point at every stage of the smuggling process. To a great extent, risk management becomes a central theme that affects not only the organizational structure but also individual behavior within the organization. Snakeheads use several protective strategies for risk management purposes.

PROTECTIVE STRATEGIES

As in all illegal enterprises, human smugglers must develop strategies to deal with constant safety concerns and to reduce the uncertainties inherent in the business. The defense mechanisms that they rely on include ethnic exclusivity (same hometown dialect, ancestral lineage, and familial relationship), one-on-one business relations, underground banking, frequent change of cell phone and pager numbers, and spontaneous meeting locations. Many of their business transactions are innovative as well as unique.

An example is the way large sums of money are exchanged. Direct cash transactions remain the predominant payment method. But in addition, there are two common methods involving formal business procedures to handle payment issues. Both methods reportedly have emerged in response to occasional fraud or fraudulent representation in the smuggling business—a con artist may portray himself as a snakehead and request a down payment from his or her clients, and then disappear. In one protection method, to ensure service provision and payment receipt, the client and the snakehead go to a bank to open a joint account requiring both signatures to withdraw money. When the smuggling operation is completed or the agreed-upon tasks are fulfilled, both parties return to the bank to settle the payment. In the second method, the client (usually a relative of the smuggled client) opens a bank account, deposits the agreed-upon sum of money, and gives the passbook—but not the password—to the snakehead. Without the password, the snakehead cannot make a withdrawal, but without the passbook, neither can the client. When the smuggling operation is completed, the client will supply the password to the snakehead, who can then withdraw the money. Because of China's expanding economy and plethora of banking activities, such financial transactions rarely arouse suspicion from the authorities. Furthermore, because most smuggling operations take months, if not years (in the case of fraudulent marriage) to complete, these bank deposits are usually long-term and hence even less visible to official scrutiny.

Despite the huge profit potential, most subjects in this study remained extremely cautious and conservative in their business approach. Many seemed to have developed certain profiles with which to scrutinize prospective clients; others had a particular style of carrying out their smuggling activities. As one smuggler in Fuzhou described:

> I only do a small-scale smuggling business because I am not greedy. Some people, after they've succeeded in few cases, become so carried away that they drastically increase the number of clients in subsequent operations. That's how they get into trouble. These aggressive snakeheads are mostly young guys. I am more conservative. I don't get involved if I am not 100 percent sure, nor do I do business with strangers. That's why I've been able to stay in this business for such a long time. Of course, after I have saved enough money, I will quit. Come to think of it, why do we have to have so much money? All my children have their own restaurants in the U.S. I don't need to work so hard.

Secrecy in this business is an absolute necessity. The snakeheads in this study mostly used mobile phones and pagers to communicate with their clients and partners. Some snakeheads even avoided dealing with clients in the townships where they lived. They would arrange to meet in a public place first, such as a restaurant or hotel lobby in Fuzhou, and then proceed to a mutually comfortable location to discuss the details. Since there are no venues for public announcement or open advertising of this business, snakeheads' networking and self-promotion take place only under circumstances in which trust can be easily built—among members of a family clan or people from the same village, for instance. Secrecy is also ensured when snakeheads deal with their partners or clients only on a one-on-one basis. Even partners in the same group withhold details from one another, for self-protection and out of fear of being cut out of the profits. One document vendor in Fuzhou described an interaction with his higher-up partner like this:

> Whenever I want to see my "big brother," I always call his cell phone. He never tells me where he is except right before he wants to meet me. He calls me and tells me where to meet him and at what time. When I deliver my documents (photo-substituted passports) to him, he usually drops them into his briefcase, where I often see dozens of other different passports bundled

together. There have been a few times when I asked about his other contacts, and he would snap at me, "Why are you asking? It is none of your business." In this business, as long as you can provide the service as promised, no one will ask about how things come about.

Such one-on-one interactions, although conducive to protecting individual smugglers, have also ensured that the human smuggling business remains secretive as well as fragmented. Few snakeheads know anyone above or below their direct contacts. Smuggling organizations or networks generally consist of a tight inner circle that few outsiders are able to infiltrate. Smugglers who are well known in one village are usually strangers in neighboring townships. They operate mostly within their own circles of contacts and seldom know what other snakeheads are doing. One's reputation as a snakehead typically goes only as far as his or her social networks.[4]

Another defensive measure taken by snakeheads and their operatives is to temporarily suspend all activities, a typical response to a crackdown by Chinese or U.S. authorities on human smuggling activities. It reduces their visibility in the community and deflects attention from their social networks. For example, soon after the Dover incident, Chinese authorities learned that most of the illegal immigrants who died inside the sealed refrigeration truck came from Fujian Province. A massive manhunt was launched to catch those responsible for the smuggling operation. Word of the crackdown immediately spread to the smuggling communities and sent most, if not all, snakeheads into hiding. Almost all of the community contacts in this study, in China as well as in the United States, disappeared. Attempts to reach these people went nowhere. Their cell phones were canceled and pagers turned off. Previously scheduled interviews and meetings were canceled without notice. Would-be migrants who were in the middle of their smuggling preparation felt the impact, too, as one such client in Fuzhou complained:

> I am really disappointed after [name of a snakehead] told me today what has happened in Dover, England. I mean my plan to go to the U.S. is in limbo now. I have called my snakehead several times today and I have not been able to get through to him. His wife answered the phone when I called his home and she said: "I am not his wife. The family has already moved and I've just moved in. I don't know where they are." I knew that it was his wife, but she would not acknowledge it. I tried his mobile phone but it's been turned off. You see, he has my passport, but I can't find him. It's really

frustrating. What am I going to do now? I thought I was going to America soon. Now I don't know when I will ever be going to the U.S.

Because most snakeheads have other sources of income, a temporary shutdown of their operations does not seem to have a great financial effect on them. One subject said that she stopped her business for almost a year because both China and the United States were cracking down hard on smuggling activities. This 43-year-old snakehead, who specialized in photo substitution and also owned a Chinese fast food restaurant in the Bronx, noted:

> It is not that easy these days. The Chinese government has finally figured out that many people use the method of swapping green card holders' passports to be smuggled out. I have not done any cases since January 2000. But this is only temporary. Right now the inspection in Fuzhou [international airport] is really tight. But I am waiting for an opportunity to start again.

Finally, being a member of a unique cultural group still provides people with one of the best assurances about who can be trusted within a cooperative but illicit economic activity (Smith 1980). Although some scholars have questioned the notion of ethnic ties as a key component of organized crime (Potter 1994), in the context of Chinese human smuggling, having a common ancestral lineage or hometown carries considerable weight among snakeheads in determining whose clients are trustworthy. Speaking the same dialect and knowing each other's social circles can greatly strengthen the expectations of mutual interests and commitment to the illicit activities. It is also the best way to prevent the intrusion or infiltration of outsiders.

Reconciling the Two Theoretical Models: A Proposal for a Diagonal Relationship

In an illicit enterprise such as transnational Chinese human smuggling, the exchange terms in small group transactions are far superior to those that any traditional criminal organization can provided. When members of small exchange relationships are closely linked to one another, continued cooperation is possible and the interests of all parties are protected. This can produce a satisfactory trading experience against the backdrop of an unpredictable and precarious business environment.

With their temporary alliances and dyadic interactions, Chinese smuggling organizations can respond effectively to uncertain market conditions, reduce exposure to law enforcement activities, and offer favorable financial terms to individual snakeheads. However, such organizational patterns also have drawbacks. Because of the restricted flow of information and the absence of a clear hierarchy, human smugglers do not enjoy the benefits that come from established crime syndicates, such as control over members of a group, coordinated operations, efficient deployment of operational resources, increased organizational continuity, and a monopoly within certain markets. As a result, snakehead groups suffer from several organizational deficiencies. First, enforcement of contracts must rely heavily on informal social control and a cultural environment that promotes an understanding of human smuggling and related tasks. Familial relations and sharing the same dialect and the same ancestral township thus become important elements of the informal social control. One's social position and membership in a network hinge heavily on the delivery of promised services. As a result, such a social and economic environment promotes conformity and is regulated mainly by the snakehead's sense of obligation to his or her social network. In other words, there are few real consequences or penalties for a transgression against a group's expectations. Second, without a hierarchy and clear chain of command, accountability and disciplinary actions are impossible. Because snakeheads often find group loyalty an insufficient protection of their safety and profit, unique business practices have emerged in the smuggling business. These practices, such as dyadic transactions and special bank deposit arrangements, ensure individual members' commitment to the shared goal.

The peculiar tension between trust and suspicion in a market full of uncertainties seems to explain why the business of human smuggling is best suited for freelance operators who are transient in their commitment to the criminal enterprise. Adler and Adler (1983) describe how drug smugglers and dealers oscillate in and out of their illicit businesses, depending upon the rise and fall of perceived social and legal costs. In the same way, human smugglers venture into the business by taking on specific roles only when the "climate" is right, then returning to their conventional activities when the perceived risk rises. Two factors seem to influence interactively a person's further involvement in the smuggling business: (1) the level of law enforcement activities and (2) maintenance of one's social network. When official anti-smuggling activities fluctuate according to the political atmosphere of the sending and receiving countries, maintaining a dyadic smuggling network can be challenging.

Since dyadic relationships prevent the sharing of resources, a smuggling operation can only be carried out by individuals who fulfill specific roles. Their need for secrecy and self-preservation thus makes individual smuggling rings vulnerable to changes in external conditions. Because transnational human smuggling takes place over vast distances and through mostly one-on-one transactions, the loss of a key player or any mishap during any of the stages will severely weaken the entire smuggling group, or even cause its demise.

The dyadic cartwheel network model presented in this chapter is intended to address two issues. First, we need a conceptual framework that makes sense of how these organizations deal with varied and uncertain market conditions. Their capacity to expand and contract amid many challenges demands a systematic conceptualization.

Second, the mixed nature of the organizational features uncovered in this study requires us to synthesize the two dominant theoretical perspectives on the structure of organized crime in mainstream criminology. Without godfathers commanding from the top and with limited vertical differentiation within smuggling groups, human smuggling seems to best fit the enterprise model of organized crime. However, the business of human smuggling still requires clear assignments of responsibilities with highly specialized tasks and specific roles, and here the corporate model provides a better fit. In other words, the corporate model and the enterprise model need not be seen as existing on two parallel continua. Instead, as the paths of the two models crisscross one another, a diagonal relationship between the two perspectives seems to make better sense.

Although it is not my intention in this book to integrate the two theoretical models or to resolve their differences, the dyadic cartwheel network perspective seems to best explain how and why Chinese human smuggling groups take on these special organizational attributes and operational styles. Further empirical research is needed, however, to validate and refine this theory.

CHAPTER 9

Human Smuggling and Traditional Chinese Organized Crime

For decades, the literature on Chinese organized crime has largely been dominated by research on triad-type secret societies.[1] Chinese triad societies are alleged to be the largest, most dangerous, and most globally organized crime groups (Morgan 1960; Bresler 1981; Black 1992; Booth 1999; Chu 2000). More than a decade ago, Posner quoted a police chief in California as saying that Chinese triads were well on their way to dominating the underworld in both Europe and America and that "they will make the Sicilian Mafia look like a bunch of Sunday-school kids" (1988, 261). Other scholars and law enforcement agencies, in anticipation of the transfer of the former British colony of Hong Kong to China, predicted a massive influx of organized crime groups of all sizes and types (Kenney and Finckenauer 1995). Black (1992) envisioned that the Chinese triads, the world's most ruthless criminal cartel, would spread like a cancer within the culture of the West.

Triad societies have gained much notoriety in recent decades for their transnational criminal activities, such as extortion, gambling, prostitution, heroin trafficking, counterfeiting, immigrant smuggling, and money laundering. Their reported successes in bona fide business operations like restaurants, night clubs, and shipping companies have caused great concern to law enforcement and government officials in the United States, Canada, Australia, and much of Europe (Chin 1990; Black 1992; Dubro 1992; Chin 1996; Kleinknecht 1996; Booth 1999; Chu 2000). American law enforcement authorities consider Chinese crime groups one of the most serious organized crime problems in America and speculate that they may surpass the extent of Italian organized crime in the near future (U.S. Senate 1992).

Although little research exists to verify that triad societies have indeed achieved global dominance in the underworld, the people who have come to dominate the business of transnational human smuggling have thus far turned out to be mostly ordinary citizens. Entrepreneurial and resourceful, these individuals have caused grave concern to law enforcement agencies around the world with their apparent success in moving large numbers of illegal migrants from country to country and raking in billions of dollars in profit. Chinese snakeheads in particular have gained notoriety in this illegal enterprise, with their ability to transport illegal migrants over vast distances to any country of their choice. Despite wide speculation that traditional Chinese organized crime groups, such as the triad societies in Hong Kong, are behind most smuggling activity, there has been little evidence to substantiate these contentions. Time and again, those who have been arrested for human smuggling have turned out to be freelance entrepreneurs. This chapter will compare and contrast traditional Chinese organized crime groups with human smuggling organizations and attempt to build a conceptual framework to explain how human smugglers have managed to establish themselves successfully without much assistance from traditional crime syndicates.

The "Chinese Mafia"

Many adolescent and adult Chinese groups are involved in racketeering (Chin 1990, 1996). Although these groups are unique in terms of their structures and criminal activities, the law enforcement community tends to view all of them as part of a Chinese mafia (Chin et al. 1998). Lacking precision, the term "Chinese mafia" invites misunderstanding and obscures the particular historical, cultural, social, and economic conditions and antecedents that gave rise to various Chinese crime groups. Traditional Chinese crime groups generally fall in four main categories: Hong Kong–based triads, Taiwan-based organized gangs, U.S.-based tongs, and Chinatown street gangs (Chin et al. 1998). Although Chinese crime groups share consistent cultural and transnational characteristics, it is perhaps still best to examine them according to their geographical locations.

HONG KONG–BASED TRIADS

The triad societies in Hong Kong are alleged to be the largest, most dangerous, and best organized crime groups in the world (Booth 1990). The word "triad" refers to the unity of three essential elements of existence in traditional Chinese philosophy—heaven, earth, and humanity. The triads originated in patriotic secret societies three centuries ago that fought against the oppressive and corrupt Qing dynasty (Chin 1990; Chin et al. 1998). When the Qing dynasty (1644–1911) collapsed in 1911 and the Republic of China was established, some of these societies began to engage in criminal activities (Morgan 1960). Questioning this explanation, Chu (2000) describes the origin of Hong Kong triads as an informal social network of disenfranchised laborers, who later formalized their fraternal organizations with rules and rituals.

Regardless of their origin, triad societies are believed to control most illegal enterprises and many legitimate businesses in Hong Kong. The roughly 160,000 triad members belong to some fifty factions (Chang 1991). For a densely populated Hong Kong filled with migratory laborers, triad membership provides job opportunities, protection, and social support—a powerful attraction for the powerless, the uneducated, and the illegal (Chu 2000).

Some of the societies are believed to be well organized, with highly disciplined members ruled by leaders who are among the most influential figures in Hong Kong society (Booth 1990). Chu (2000), however, has argued that although Hong Kong triads share similar organizational structures and rituals that bind their members together, they are actually loose cartels made up of numerous autonomous gangs, whose primary interest is to extend mutual aid to their members by selling protection and monopolizing job opportunities in a particular trade.

Triad activities are not limited to Hong Kong and its adjacent regions, such as Macau. Law enforcement agencies in China, North America, Europe, and

Southeast Asia have reported that triad activities such as extortion, gambling, heroin trafficking, and immigrant smuggling are on the rise (Dubro 1992).

Taiwan-Based Organized Gangs

According to Willard Myers (1996), the Taiwanese are the most powerful and important ethnic group in transnational Chinese organized crime. The emergence of criminal organizations in Taiwan can be traced back to the mid-1940s, following China's recovery of Taiwan from Japan. Many of these gangs, such as the United Bamboo, originally emerged as self-protection groups to fend off other street gangs, but they gradually developed into powerful criminal organizations (Kwong 1987; Chin 2003). Criminal organizations in Taiwan were once mainly involved in vice, operating or protecting illegal gambling dens and brothels, collecting debts, and extorting protection money from business owners. However, since the mid-1980s there are allegations that these criminal organizations have become active in drug trafficking, human smuggling, arms trafficking, collusive bidding for government projects, and other sophisticated crimes (Chin 2003).

The Taiwan connection has long been thought to be at the core of the worldwide clandestine migration of illegal Chinese nationals. At least in maritime smuggling activities, the Taiwan connection has been well established. The majority of the smuggling vessels (mostly fishing trawlers and small freighters) seized in maritime smuggling activities by U.S. authorities in the 1990s were either owned or leased by Taiwanese (Hood 1994; Chin 1999). Aside from their dominance in seafaring smuggling, Taiwanese gangs have also allegedly controlled the majority of the hubs and way stations for immigrant smuggling in Latin America. Oceangoing vessels have never accounted for more than 10 percent of total smuggling traffic and maritime smuggling activities have drastically decreased since the mid-1990s (Hood 1997, 78).

In recent years, members of criminal organizations are widely believed to have infiltrated legitimate businesses in Taiwan to become owners of restaurants, coffee shops, nightclubs, movie companies, cable television companies, magazine publishers, and construction firms (Chi 1985). Some gang members are involved in futures trading, the stock market, and other commercial activities (Chen 1986). In the early 1980s gangsters were reported to be heavily involved in manipulating the outcomes of local elections in Taiwan (Chin 2003). Intimidation and vote buying assured the election of political candidates of their choice. In the late 1980s, to protect themselves from frequent crackdowns by the authorities, gang members themselves ran for public office (Liu 1995). According to a former minister of justice of Taiwan, many legislators, assemblymen, and local representatives are believed to be current or former members or associates of organized crime groups. Chin (2003), through in-depth fieldwork, revealed the intricate relationships between the Taiwanese political system and the underworld, leaving people to wonder whether Taiwan is actually ruled by mobsters.

U.S.-BASED TONGS

Tongs in the United States were first established in San Francisco in the 1850s, following the first wave of Chinese immigration. The word "tong" simply means "hall" or "gathering place." Before the emergence of tongs, Chinese communities in the United States were controlled by dominant families or associations of immigrants sharing the same ancestral lineage. Immigrants with uncommon last names or from small villages were not accepted into these established associations, and therefore they often found solace and support among their own kind. To better fend for themselves, they banded together and established the tongs. Because there were no special qualifications to join a tong, tongs expanded rapidly. Rival tongs were soon drawn into street battles known as the "tong wars" (Dillon 1962). More than thirty tongs formed in the United States, mostly in cities with concentrated populations of Chinese immigrants such as New York and San Francisco. Like the family and district associations, the tongs provided many benefits, including job referrals and housing assistance to immigrants who could not otherwise find the help they needed. The tongs also acted as power brokers who mediated individual and group conflicts within the community.

Much of tong culture has continued today. Most tong members are gainfully employed or have their own businesses. They pay dues to their associations and congregate occasionally at these tongs to meet friends, socialize, or to gamble. Tongs also hold banquets and picnics a few times a year. However, the leaders of the tongs make the important decisions and control the groups' daily affairs. These leaders usually maintain connections with youth gangs, who act as their street soldiers in illegal activities.

Historically, tongs have been active in operating or providing protection for opium dens, gambling houses, and brothels (U.S. Senate 1978; McIllwain 2003). Over the past three decades some tong members have been arrested for narcotics trafficking or immigrant smuggling. Although a tong as an organization has never been indicted for its involvement in transnational crime, U.S. authorities generally consider tongs to be organized crime groups that are heavily involved in transnational operations. In the 1990s, tongs in New York City, San Francisco, Chicago, Houston, and Atlanta were indicted for racketeering (Chin 1999).

McIllwain (2003) has provided a historical analysis of the evolution of tongs and their participation in organized crime in the United States. Contrary to the assumption that the history of organized crime in America is the history of Italian and Jewish gangsters, and that other ethnic groups failed to muster syndicates of any real substance, power, or sophistication before the 1980s, McIllwain (2003, 2) argues that Chinese organized crime, mostly in the form of the tongs, was deeply involved in such classic organized criminal enterprises as gambling, prostitution, and the importation, distribution, and sale of narcotics between 1870 and 1910. Tong members were also known to engage in violent crime (extortion, protection rackets, and murder) and corruption. Using the case study of a conflict between the Hip Sing Tong and the On Leong Tong, McIllwain (1997) demonstrated that these nineteenth-century overseas Chinese societies demonstrated sophisticated structural and organizational characteristics that predated criminal organizations of other ethnic origins that were later labeled as "modern" organized crime by academics, the media, and the government.

U.S.-BASED STREET GANGS

There are more Chinese street gangs in New York City than in any other American city (Chin 1996). As a result, New York is considered the center of Chinese organized crime in the United States. The first Chinese street gang, the Continentals, was formed in 1961 by native-born Chinese high school students. Their primary objective was self-protection. Subsequently, new gangs such as the White Eagles, Black Eagles, Ghost Shadows, and Flying Dragons began to emerge. During the early years, Chinese gangs were, in essence, martial arts clubs headed by tong members who were masters of martial arts.

During the late 1960s and early 1970s, these clubs transformed themselves completely from self-help groups to predatory gangs. They terrorized the Chinese community, demanding food and money from businesses and robbing illegal gambling establishments. When these youth gangs began to shake down merchants and gamblers who were themselves tong members, the tongs decided to hire other gang members as their street soldiers to protect themselves from robbery and extortion and to solidify their position within the community.

In the 1980s, new gangs such as the Fuk Ching, White Tigers, Tung On, Green Dragons, Golden Star, and Born-to-Kill emerged on the periphery of New York's Chinatown and in the outer boroughs of Queens and Brooklyn, following the expansion of Chinese businesses and neighborhoods. Beyond the major Chinese communities in New York, San Francisco, and Los Angeles, Chinese gangs have also become active in Oakland, Dallas, Houston, Boston, Philadelphia, Chicago, and Falls Church, Virginia. American authorities consider Chinese street gangs to be organized crime groups. In the 1990s, almost all major Chinese gangs in the United States were indicted at one time or another for racketeering (Chin 1999).

In summary, these four types of criminal organizations (Hong Kong-based triads, Taiwan-based organized gangs, U.S.-based tongs, and U.S. Chinatown gangs) differ significantly from each other in their historical and cultural backgrounds as well as their geographical origins. However, these crime groups do share many organizational similarities, such as hierarchical structure, restricted membership, monopolistic practices in their commercial activities, use of violence to eliminate competition or resolve inter-group conflicts, and rituals for strengthening group identity and self-perpetuation. These crime groups are territorial, and cross-group collaborations are rare.

The Missing Link

As soon as Chinese were found to be active in smuggling illegal immigrants into the United States, authorities charged that gang members, along with members of tongs and triads, were the main culprits (Zhang 1997). For many years, U.S. anti-human-smuggling efforts have operated under two assumptions. First, they assume that an elaborate international network exists to facilitate the transport of Chinese nationals through various transit points and that people of prominent backgrounds, including ranking government officials, are involved in the business. Second, they take for granted that Chinese human smugglers are connected with traditional crime organizations such as Hong Kong–based triads and U.S.-based tongs and gangs (U.S. Senate 1992; Bolz 1995; Myers 1996). Interpol for years has also pointed to the Chinese triad societies as the masterminds (together with Japanese yakuza, Albanian mafia-style organizations, and Mexican coyote groups) behind most transnational human smuggling activities in the world (Interpol 2004). Despite their clear policy implications, these assumptions were largely made with little empirical evidence.

In the early years after the *Golden Venture* incident, Taiwanese crime groups were presumed to have secured the majority of the fishing trawlers used to transport illegal Chinese migrants across the Pacific (Hood 1994). This presumption received a major boost in credence when street gang members were found to be involved in debt collection and safeguarding safe houses while smugglers awaited their final payments (Chin 1999).

Despite these claims, no researchers who have engaged in primary data collection have yet produced convincing evidence to substantiate any systematic participation by traditional Chinese criminal organizations in human smuggling. Instead, most Chinese human smugglers caught by authorities or interviewed by researchers and journalists alike have turned out to be ordinary people, whose entry into the smuggling trade was made possible by their familial networks and fortuitous social contacts. When members of traditional Chinese criminal societies were implicated in some court cases, their membership in a particular crime group was found to be an incidental factor, rather than a qualification for participation into the smuggling operations. Furthermore, few smugglers who have claimed membership in traditional Chinese crime groups have played dominant roles in any smuggling organizations. On the contrary, most snakeheads typically make efforts not to entangle themselves with gangsters or other crime groups in the Chinese community. As one female snakehead in Los Angeles explained:

> You know the old Chinese proverb: it is easy to invite a god into your house, but difficult to ask him to leave. You never want to entangle yourself with people from the underworld. Once they know you, your business, and even where you live, you will never be able to get rid of them.

Interestingly, before their own involvement in the business, a sizable number of the subjects in this study also thought that the human smuggling trade must be controlled by organized crime. They were surprised to find out later that they were wrong. Other subjects were quick to point out why traditional crime syndicates have largely been absent in human smuggling activities. One snakehead explained:

> What advantage will a known gangster have in recruiting customers? Why would any families want to entrust their money and family members to known gangsters? Gangsters will have a big problem building social networks. No government officials or police officers will want to have dinner with gangsters. The underworld scares people. No clients or even snakeheads would want to deal with known gangsters.

With the possibility of such immense profits, one would assume that established criminal organizations would want to expand into this new enterprise. After all, any transportation of illicit goods across nations (whether undocumented immigrants or drugs) requires significant planning and coordination, which well-established criminal organizations seem best suited for. The reality seems counter-intuitive. The findings of this study suggest that Chinese human smuggling is largely dominated by groups of freelance entrepreneurs who build their own networks and deploy their own smuggling resources, independent of any traditional triad-type crime group.

A Structural Deficiency Perspective

The question remains: why has an enterprise with immense profits been largely dominated by freelance operators? For more than two decades, the bulk of the evidence has failed to suggest that the market is moving toward consolidation, with fewer but bigger players dominating the business. Several factors may account for why traditional Chinese crime syndicates have not availed themselves of the opportunity to engage in not only human smuggling but also most transnational criminal activities.

A *structural deficiency perspective* may explain why traditional triad societies are ill-equipped to take advantage of emerging transnational criminal opportunities. The market conditions and operational requirements of human smuggling are vastly different from those of such traditional and established racketeering activities as protection, extortion, gambling, loan sharking, and prostitution. The absence of widespread participation by triads and other traditional criminal organizations in transnational human smuggling activities is no coincidence. It is caused by the deficiencies inherent in their organizational structures.

CONTINUITY AS AN ORGANIZATIONAL OBJECTIVE

As discussed earlier, success in the business of transnational human smuggling entails meeting a set of unique challenges—a scattered and limited eligible clientele, complex transport routes, and illegal cross-border movements. Smuggling opportunities are mostly sporadic and unpredictable, transnational operations are hazardous, and snakeheads operate under constant fear of arrest and asset forfeiture. These market constraints and operational challenges have given rise to such trademark characteristics of the smuggling business as task force orientation, dyadic exchange relations, and temporary alliances.

In contrast, traditional criminal organizations, such as the Hong Kong–based triads or the Taiwan-based crime groups, have historically focused on a different set of organizational priorities. In addition to vying for control of traditional vice industries, criminal organizations are mainly interested in infiltrating and dominating legitimate businesses for stable, predictable, and long-term financial gains. Like the Italian mafia (Jacobs and Gouldin 1999), many triad societies, although operating independently, share a common structure consisting of a rigid hierarchy surrounded by secrecy. This very structure, which has served these crime syndicates well for decades or even centuries, appears handicapped in a transnational environment. The pursuit of stable and predictable revenues creates an institutional reluctance to expand into territories where contingency and situational fluidity are the norm rather than the exception. The hazards of unreliable service providers, the difficulties in developing and maintaining stable official collusion, and the risk of being detected in foreign territories are conditions unfavorable to maintaining a business environment that consistently and reliably generates profits. Moreover, traditional Chinese crime groups have evolved historically in specific geographical areas and specialize in one or more regional vice industries (e.g., gambling, prostitution). Their organizational structure, chain of command, and secretive operations work effectively only in places where patron-client relationships are stable, police-community relationships cozy, and long-term revenues sustainable. Their business agreements and obligations, built upon specialized role expectations, serve well enough to guarantee stable and predictable organizational outcomes.

ADAPTATION AND RESULTANT ORGANIZATIONAL ATTRIBUTES

Human smugglers must adapt to a different set of market conditions and socio-legal constraints, none of which are conducive to long-term planning and sustainable profits. In this unstable international market environment, few of the characteristics of human smuggling organizations promote either organizational continuity or permanency. Instead, smuggling alliances have evolved to be present-oriented in order to reduce exposure and uncertainty and to secure fast profits. As a result, the organizational attributes of human smuggling groups are unique and far different from those of their traditional counterparts.

First, human smuggling organizations are typically small, involving only individuals with valuable resources to contribute, and the formation of a smuggling group is mostly haphazard, developing out of coincidental social meetings, as opposed to the traditional Chinese crime groups' deliberate expansion and systematic screening of potential members. An alliance among snakeheads is only a temporary business arrangement.

Second, there are no godfathers in human smuggling organizations, even though the schemes employed by participating brokers may be complicated. As a result, few snakeheads have absolute control over an entire smuggling operation or even over other smugglers within their group. Human smuggling groups and traditional triad societies do share one common organizational trait, however: a clear division of labor. Operational tasks are performed by specific individuals, or role imperatives. These role imperatives have emerged as a result not only of concerns about safety and profit protection but also the predominant practice of one-on-one transactions. In comparison, in traditional triad societies the division of labor emerges as a result of organizational hierarchy. The specific needs of an enterprise dictate the assignment of different roles. As Chu (2000) illustrates in his study of Hong Kong triad societies, the members of a crime group earn or are assigned their roles, and roles may elevate over time. In human smuggling, roles are self-assumed. No snakeheads are promoted for either seniority or merit.

Third, in human smuggling groups alliances are temporary, and gatherings are sporadic. In contrast to traditional criminal rackets, smuggling organizations dissolve as quickly as they are formed. Once an operation is completed and there are no immediate opportunities on the horizon, there is no reason for a group of snakeheads to stick around. Most return to their regular jobs or businesses. Any future operation depends solely on the availability of suitable clients and the suitability of transportation strategies. Although they may continue to interact socially, snakeheads have neither the mechanism nor the rituals to maintain an organization in the long run. In fact, in this study most snakeheads considered human smuggling a temporary business and wanted to quit as soon as they made enough money. In contrast, members of traditional Chinese organized crime rarely quit their organizations, especially those in triad societies. Loyalty is expected and reinforced with rites and rituals. As a result, members often spend a significant portion of their adult years contributing to and relying on the welfare of their crime families.

Fourth, traditional Chinese crime groups have developed multiple-leveled command structures for assigning tasks and building in redundancy to ensure reliable operations, with protocols for passing information between the boss, his lieutenants, and street soldiers. Such complex arrangements provide strong group support to individual members as they carry out their tasks and deploy organizational resources in a reliable and predictable manner. Human smugglers, on the other hand, deal with each other mostly on a one-on-one basis. The dyadic cartwheel network, although lean and efficient in many ways, can function properly only if every individual performs his or her promised tasks. Without contingency plans and organizational support from others, unanticipated glitches in smuggling operations often prove fatal. Human smugglers have few resources for pursuing organizational continuity. Their one-on-one organization often falls apart over the loss of a key player. Many snakeheads are forced to quit the business because gaps that develop in their serial network cannot easily be bridged (Zhang and Chin 2002).

PRESERVATION OF CONVENTIONAL STAKES

Triad societies have long penetrated legitimate businesses in which profits are not only predictable but also legally protected. Some of these criminal syndicates have also shown interest in entering the political arena to seek and obtain further protection and preservation of their achievements. As discussed earlier, gangsters in Taiwan are widely believed to have infiltrated the political system and manipulated local elections since the early 1980s through vote buying and voter intimidation (Chi 1985; Chin 2003). These organized crime groups have allegedly set up their own members to run for public office. Some have been successful, becoming legislators, assemblymen, and representatives in different levels of the government (Chin 2003). With stakes mounting in the legitimate world, well-established criminal organizations may be less tempted to venture into emerging illegitimate markets, however lucrative they may be.

For crime groups that are not so well established in the legitimate world, participation in a high-profile transnational racket such as human smuggling or drug trafficking may attract unwanted attention from authorities, thus threatening their more stable revenue-generating activities. It seems logical, then, to hypothesize that the more established a criminal organization is in conventional racketeering activities, the less likely it is to venture into unconventional enterprises.

THE PRECARIOUS MARKET CONDITIONS OF HUMAN SMUGGLING

In human smuggling, market demand is as unpredictable as the illicit "cargo" being transported. Unlike gambling or extortion, in which the clientele remains stable and the "business" activities are tied to specific neighborhoods, human smuggling typically involves one-time transactions. Once a client has been smuggled into the United States, he or she will not be a customer again. Even when a transaction involves multiple members of the same family, the prospect of sustained profits for any smuggling organization is limited by the length of time it takes to save enough money to smuggle them all out of China. With a limited and scattered pool of eligible clients, the smuggling enterprise has limited growth potential. Furthermore, transactions mostly take place between the snakeheads and their clients, thus providing few opportunities for competition from or infiltration by other players. The actual transportation of illegal migrants involves arrangements that are secretive, idiosyncratic, and known only to those directly involved. In sum, because of unstable clientele, fragmented market locations, and ever-changing transportation schemes, human smuggling as a business seems best suited for freelance entrepreneurs. Traditional triad societies may see this market situation as too precarious to manage, and its profits too volatile to sustain.

As Chinese communities have expanded in the United States, the demand for cheap labor has followed, but in fragmented and unpredictable patterns. Two decades ago, the vast majority of Chinese immigrants settled in and around a few major metropolitan areas, such as New York, San Francisco, Los Angeles, and Houston. A look at any Chinese language newspapers published in America today reveals job openings in Kentucky, Illinois, and Utah. These job ads often offer one-way bus tickets to successful candidates. As the demand for illegal migrant labor expands to different locations, smugglers cannot help but adapt and accommodate these new opportunities. Therefore, only those who have the connections and resources can stay in the game.

So long as its patron-client relationships remain short-lived and business opportunities remain unpredictable, the business of human smuggling is unlikely to consolidate; nor is a monopoly or an oligopoly likely to emerge. Furthermore, in the absence of a clearly defined neighborhood, violence, the most powerful tool of old-fashioned organized crime, is of little use, because there is no turf to protect, and few stable targets to shake down.

GROUP IDENTITY VERSUS PERSONAL NETWORKS

In all organized criminal activities, conspiracy is the most common method of protecting and furthering control of illicit services or goods. Clandestine economic activities are carried out within specific geographical and social circles. Members of a criminal organization are typically recruited from people of similar social backgrounds, who live in the same or nearby communities. Snakeheads, however, follow a different path when they establish contact with one another and form business alliances. There are few geographical restrictions in an era of low-cost air fare and widespread telecommunication, so human smugglers can meet and forge partnerships over vast distances. Free from any institutionalized culture, these entrepreneurs can engage in collaborative work after a brief interaction without undergoing any kind of formal initiation or screening. They are able to bond quickly and carry out smuggling operations on their own terms and at their own leisure.

In comparison, traditional triad organizations follow time-honored membership recruitment procedures that reinforce or affirm the group's identity. For instance, membership in a triad is granted through highly developed organizational procedures and symbolic rituals. Not everyone who desires the comfort and protection of a fraternal organization can take the blood oath. Prospective members must prove their "worthiness" and be sponsored by others already in the organization. Although the rituals vary from one criminal organization to another, and differ from Hong Kong to Taiwan and to New York's Chinatown, in all traditional Chinese criminal organizations membership is restricted and the recruitment process deliberate. Because of their rigid organizational structures, these organizations cannot emulate the freelancer's flexibility that is required in order to take advantage of emerging transnational crime opportunities.

Traditional Chinese criminal organizations rely heavily on such cultural values as group identity, loyalty, and binding relationships to create a sense of belonging and personal commitment. Rules, rituals, oaths, codes of conduct, and chains of command are organizational elements essential to the group's cohesion. These organizational imperatives are not necessary in human smuggling, however. When the market is fragmented and dominated by free-lance operators in temporary arrangements, stable organizational structures and strong group loyalties do not evolve. Rituals and induction ceremonies are unnecessary, because there is no group identity to uphold. Snakeheads are committed to each other only to the extent that they are interested in making money. Once an operation is completed, the group dissolves quickly or continues on to another deal, so long as there is money to be made. This utilitarian mentality is common and pervasive in the smuggling community. While many human smugglers may consider their partners friends and continue to socialize with them after they are no longer active in the business, none do so out of a sense of belonging to a specific organized group.

Comparison of Traditional Criminal Organizations and Human Smuggling Groups

The pattern of differences between triad-type organizations and the emerging criminal organizations involved in transnational human smuggling is summarized in Table 9.1.

The paradigm I presented here argues that the absence of widespread participation in human smuggling activities by traditional Chinese criminal organizations arises from the latter's structural deficiencies. However, this theory is predicated on the assumption that triad societies and other traditional Chinese crime syndicates still exist as they have been described in the

Table 9.1. A comparison of triad-type organizations and
human smuggling groups

	Triad Organizations	*Smuggling Groups*
1. Organizational Structure	• Rigid hierarchy with clear leadership structure • Command driven • Organized through clear division of labor • Membership ranging from dozens to hundreds	• Non-hierarchical • Task force orientation • Collaborative rather than command driven • Organized through clear division of labor • Core membership of 3–5 individuals
2. Identity and Membership	• Membership is exclusive • Recruitment based on connection and capability • Time-honored traditions, rituals, and codes of conduct • Lifetime membership and sense of belonging • Multi-generational	• Casual association through social or family contacts • Membership based on ability to provide specific services • No formalized rituals • No articulated organizational rules or group identity • Membership is short-lived and alliance temporary
3. Operational Characteristics	• Territorial • Emphasis on developing stable patron-client relationship for long-term revenues • Monopolistic • Systematic coordination of various role imperatives • Systematic corruption of local public officials	• Transnational • Non-territorial • Entrepreneurial and short-term operations • Cooperation of individuals with dyadic connection with service providers • Official corruption is done haphazardly, and based on fortuitous personal contacts
4. Use of Violence	• Instrumental • To enforce contract • To achieve domination (by eliminating competitors) • To coerce unwilling participants (e.g., business owners) • To discipline triad members • To settle inter-triad conflicts	• Instrumental • To enforce contract (i.e., payment collection) • To maintain control during smuggling/trafficking operations

literature. One may question the belief that triad societies still represent the most durable agents of Chinese organized crime. There is no doubt about their infamous past, but these crime syndicates have historically been hunted and prosecuted by law enforcement agencies of their various governments in the same way that Italian mafia families have been pursued in United States and Italy. Many believe that persistent American law enforcement attacks over the decades, assisted by new civil and regulatory strategies, have left the survival of the Italian mafia-type families in doubt (Jacobs and Gouldin 1999). The same might be true for traditional Chinese triad societies. It may be that these crime syndicates are much weaker than has been assumed, and that their strength is more mythical than real. Hong Kong law enforcement authorities have repeatedly asserted that triad societies have been turned into mostly loose-knit groups of individuals and no longer major players in regional criminal activities. As one ranking Hong Kong police official stated:

> Of some 50 known criminal organizations, fewer than 15 come to regular police attention and only 5 groups (i.e., Sun Yee On, Wo Shing Wo, 14K, Wo On Lok, and Wo Hop To) are still thought to remain active. While the traditional structure of a triad society can be well organized, nowadays triads are only a collection of loose-knit groups or gangs. Members of these loose criminal groups continue to use triad jargons and rank structure, mostly to impress new recruits of their somewhat dubious relationship with a formal crime society and to instill fear in the public. Of all detected crimes in Hong Kong, only about 5 to 10 percent can be linked to triads. These include gang fights arising from inter-gang conflicts, intimidation, and serious assaults. (Leung 1999, 1–2)

Hong Kong law enforcement authorities attribute the weakening of traditional triads to successful crackdowns that rely heavily on infiltration and organizational sabotage within and between triad factions. Reportedly, a pervasive fear exists among triad gang members that government undercover agents have infiltrated their groups, monitoring and tallying their criminal offenses for an eventual bust. The same is true with Taiwan-based organized gangs and U.S.-based tongs and gangs, as many of the leaders of these crime groups are either serving long prison terms or hiding in foreign countries (Chin 2003).

Triads may well be in a state of flux, trying to survive by extending into mainland China, mostly in Guangdong Province, by investing money in legitimate businesses and presenting themselves as businessmen instead of triad leaders. For instance, Chinese authorities raided a Sun Yee On initiation ceremony and arrested eight members (*World Journal* 2000). However, such incidents may also be seen as desperate measures to keep a fading tradition alive among a few die-hard members yearning to revitalize their brotherhood. If this argument holds any truth, we are facing a different reality—that there is a vacuum in the underworld, with traditional triad societies simply too weak to make serious inroads into emerging criminal opportunities. It is difficult to gauge the degree of triads' involvement in either legitimate or illegitimate businesses in Hong Kong, particularly after the 1997 transfer of sovereignty to a totalitarian regime known for its intolerance of any entity that threatens its authority.

It is safe to claim that the criminal groups responsible for transporting the most Chinese nationals to the United States and other Western countries are non-traditional. There is no evidence to substantiate any systematic involvement by traditional Chinese criminal societies in the smuggling trade. These non-traditional criminal groups consist of an assortment of people—import-export businessmen, community leaders, restaurant owners, ordinary wage earners, gamblers, housewives, and street vendors. Few of them have ties to any triad-type criminal organization. They take advantage of their social connections, official or business positions, and community reputations to provide illicit goods and services for profits. Their participation in illicit enterprises is not limited to human smuggling but also includes money laundering and underground banking.

Because of their diverse backgrounds and extensive involvement in legitimate businesses, human smugglers blend into mainstream society better than traditional Chinese crime groups. Their participation in criminal activities is sporadic rather than continuous. They may participate or invest in one human smuggling operation, collect the profit, and put the money in real estate or other legal businesses such as restaurants. They may not be involved in any illegal activities for a prolonged period, until another opportunity arises. They stop illicit business activities whenever there is a heightened level of law enforcement scrutiny. The overall business environment is therefore determined by the collective entrepreneurial commitment (willingness to engage in illicit business activities) of these snakeheads, and is relatively unaffected by the failure of any one particular smuggling group.

What remains unclear is whether these entrepreneurs will ever move towards consolidation across broad geographical areas and international regions, or whether they will eventually face a challenge by more established and better organized triad-type crime syndicates once the market volatility subsides. At this point, there are no indications that human smugglers are following the traditional path of organizational transformation, because the historical conditions (i.e., mutual aid, protection, and securing employment opportunities) that gave rise to such criminal organizations as 14K and United Bamboo are neither present in nor applicable to the human smuggling trade. Whether these entrepreneurs will eventually gain enough of a shared identity or the market will mature enough to foster the growth of formal criminal organizations also remains to be seen. It is clear, however, that when market conditions are ripe for larger organizations, either the traditional crime groups will venture into this business, or the existing smugglers will evolve into formalized entities.

Questions That Remain

The lack of involvement by traditional Chinese criminal organizations does not mean that they are completely absent from the human smuggling business. Some subjects in this study claimed that they knew maritime-based snakeheads who employed gangsters to maintain order onboard smuggling ships and to collect money afterwards. As one subject described:

> We do not have any connections with gangs. Only those who use boats in smuggling need gangsters to collect money. That's because they usually have a large number of clients of all kinds, including those who can't come up with the smuggling fee. We have our own people in New York City to collect the money, so we don't need the help of gang members. When Sister Ping was in maritime-based smuggling, she worked with the Fuk Ching gang's leader, Ah Kay. Of course, some Fuk Ching members who have fled the U.S. now work as snakeheads in Fuzhou.

Nine of the subjects in this study claimed to be either current or past members of Chinese organized crime groups. Six of them claimed to have entered the smuggling business on behalf of their criminal organizations; the other three were recruited into the business by other snakeheads who were not connected with any criminal organizations. Of these nine subjects, two served as escorts on smuggling ships, two claimed to have organized various smuggling schemes mainly by way of Hong Kong, and the remaining five were all payment collectors. One 39-year-old boat-based smuggler claimed that as a member of the Fuk Ching gang in New York's Chinatown, he was working for his gangster boss–turned-snakehead to escort clients on smuggling boats. However, he was adamant that he got involved in the smuggling business solely for the sake of money, because he was considered the black sheep of his family and wanted to prove otherwise:

> Before I went into this business, my brothers looked down upon me and considered me incapable of making decent money. I often had to borrow money from them. I was furious and decided that I would do anything to make money, except dealing drugs, arms, killing people, or setting houses on fire. Later I began working with this snakehead to escort clients on container ships. I was in a total of eight smuggling operations between 1995 and 1999. I didn't make a lot of money, but it was much better than working in Chinatown.

Of the six who claimed to work for their criminal organization while escorting smuggling ships and collecting payment, all had joined their gangs because they were in serious financial trouble and there was no other way to make money. A 26-year-old gangster, who claimed to have first been a member of the Flying Dragons and later of the Fuk Ching in Flushing, New York, said he followed his boss (or *dailou*) into the collection business because he had a gambling problem and owed a lot of money:

> I had no other motives than making money. After I moved to Flushing, I worked on all sorts of temporary jobs, sometimes in a garment factory and other times in a restaurant. Later I borrowed a lot of money against my credit cards and gambled in Atlantic City. I lost it all. I thought I could make a living just being a professional gambler. I was introduced by a friend to join the Fuk Ching gang. I am doing the collection business only part time. I have not given up the hope of winning back the money I lost in Atlantic City. I spend most time in casinos. When I run out of money, I call my *dailou* to see if there are payment collection opportunities.

News reports of snakeheads employing gangsters to solve payment problems seem to corroborate the data obtained from the organized crime figures in this study. It makes sense that once inside a Chinese community, it is difficult for any newcomer to escape the shadow of local gangsters. As much as ordinary snakeheads want to avoid entanglement with Chinatown gangsters, unscrupulous clients who evade their payment promises must still be dealt with, and the only option available is the underworld. A 38-year-old debt collector, who claimed to be a member of the Fuk Ching gang in New

York's Chinatown, did not think of himself as a snakehead, but he acknowledged that he was collecting money for a snakehead:

> My main task is to collect money from newly smuggled immigrants. I have
> been doing this since 1995, and am not doing much else because noth-
> ing else is as easy or makes as much money as this business. Each week on
> average I'll bring two members of the gang to meet clients or their relatives
> or friends at pre-agreed locations to collect payments. I get a list of clients
> and their contact information from my boss. Clients usually pay off their
> smuggling fees all at once after their arrival. Smuggling fees are always paid
> by families, relatives, or friends. But if any clients owe money, we will give
> them a deadline to pay up, and we won't be so friendly the next time we see
> them. If anyone becomes delinquent, we will beat him up and force him to
> pay off the balance soon. No clients dare to call the police, and I am very
> confident of this because they are all from Fuzhou, and they know that we
> can cause trouble to their families back in China as well.

It is no secret that Chinatown gang members have been hired by human
smugglers at the end of their operations to work as contract enforcement
agents. These gangsters and their collection services are the formal "social
control" apparatus in the smuggling business, which is vital for preventing
the breakdown of shared norms and expectations. The extent to which these
gangsters should be considered an integral part of the smuggling enterprise
remains an open question, however, because, in most cases, these gangsters
are not just collecting money for snakeheads but are also involved in a variety of other criminal activities. One 50-year-old subject, who claimed to
be a onetime gangster boss in New York's Chinatown, considered his job a
support service to the smuggling business:

> I am helping people to collect money owed to them. When I started out in
> 1982, I had some 30 *mazai* (soldiers) and later we grew to be more than 60.
> When some snakeheads could not collect their fees from the immigrants,
> they would turn to me and give me a list of names with contact informa-
> tion. I'd then send my *mazai* out to collect the money. Before I had my
> own people, when I was still young and strong, I was a *mazai* for the Flying
> Dragons. I went out to collect protection fees from businesses in our ter-
> ritory and also acted as a debt collector. Later I started my own group. All
> our current clients are referred by other clients. If I do my job well, I get
> referred to still more people. We also run many numbers games.

Although the gangsters represented only a small number of the subjects in this study, the linkage between human smuggling and traditional Chinese criminal organizations runs counter to what has been discussed thus far. In one case, a gangster even claimed that his organization, the Fuk Ching gang, was collaborating with other international groups in the smuggling business:

> I know how our group is doing the smuggling business. It is through a freight shipping line from Holland to the U.S. The main players in our organization have close ties with members of a criminal organization there. They are all Westerners, but we have interpreters. The Dutch connection was developed in the last two or three years. Our group has no problem transporting clients from China to Holland by boat. We control that route. We rely on the Dutch group to secure the ships. It is very expensive what we pay. These Dutch captains only listen to their organized crime group in Holland, and they are familiar with the U.S. waters and customs inspection patterns.

In another case, the 38-year-old payment collector described earlier reported that some gang fights had resulted from collection activities for snakeheads:

> I am a payment collector, so physical conflicts are unavoidable. I remember this one time back in 1996, when a smuggled client had no money to pay us, but he hired some gangsters from the Ghost Shadows to negotiate with us. We got in a fight with them, and it was a bloody event. But that was a rare incident, because if physical fights were to happen frequently, no one would want to get involved in payment collection anymore.

Exactly how much credibility to give to these gangsters and their affiliated criminal organizations is debatable. There is no way to verify the truth of their stories, particularly those told by low-level musclemen about higher-level organizational decisions and smuggling strategies. To complicate the analysis further, aside from the three debt collectors who claimed to be active at the time they were interviewed, the other six had ceased their engagement in smuggling-related activities either voluntarily or because their organizations requested it. One subject, who claimed to be a lieutenant in a New York Chinatown gang in charge of coordinating payment guarantees for prospective immigrants who collected smuggling fees upon arrival, explained why he decided to quit the business:

> Smuggling methods have not changed much over the years, but the price has gone up a lot. Back in 1995 the smuggling fee was only $30,000 to

$40,000; now it is $60,000. This is because governments in China, the U.S., and other countries are cracking down hard on smuggling activities. Especially after the Dover incident, it has just become too dangerous to stay in the business. We have other businesses, like running gambling dens, nightclubs, and karaoke bars. Our investment is diversified, and we are making more money in these other businesses.

Like an old hand in the underworld, this payment collection lieutenant claimed that his organization was careful to protect itself:

Our group members don't change normally. All key players will remain the same. If accidents happen or people die, new members will then be recruited to fill the positions. Whenever a new member joins the organization, we must be very careful in screening him, because we know the government is using informants to infiltrate our organization.

A connection between Chinese criminal organizations and transnational human smuggling did exist during the Gold Rush era. In fact, the "paper son" racket (discussed in Chapter 1) contributed significantly to the establishment of tongs in American Chinatowns (Lee 1960, 303). These clans and associations protected illegal smuggling channels, coordinated the sale and arrangement of false identification documents, settled disputes, and blackmailed anyone who might expose the racketeering activities. If the tongs in the early Chinatowns were able to gather resources to smuggle Chinese nationals into the United States, there is no reason to believe that these organizations are somehow less capable today. It is therefore logical to speculate that traditional secret societies within the Chinese communities may have *something* to do with modern-day human smuggling activities.

It is also possible that the lack of connections between human smugglers and the traditional Chinese criminal organizations could very well be an artifact of the sampling strategy in this study—the fact that only independent entrepreneurs could be reached for interviews. Smuggling activities controlled by traditional triad-type organizations may be far better concealed and guarded than those of these loosely connected enterprising individuals, and hence off limits to this study.

In sum, one clear and consistent finding of this study remains: that the vast majority of snakeheads have no standing relationship with traditional Chinese criminal organizations. Even when they do use gangsters, they use them mainly to deal with delinquent clients. Being a gangster or revealing even the slightest hint of association with the underworld is in no way an advantage in connecting with government officials, recruiting prospective clients, or even convincing other snakehead partners to include them in their operations.

Organized Crime and Trafficking in Women and Children

One area of illegal transnational migration that has received little attention either in this study or in mainstream criminology is the connection between traditional criminal organizations and human traffickers (i.e., those who transport women and children for purposes of commercial sex, brokered marriages, or indentured labor).

Propelled by global trade and improved sociopolitical conditions in many parts of the world, international migration has reached unprecedented levels, as millions leave their homes in search of better economic opportunities. However, among the regular human smugglers are those who are bent on taking advantage of the weak and vulnerable. There have been many reports of the involvement of criminal gangs in the newly independent republics of the former Soviet Union in luring and transporting young women to Western countries for prostitution (Shelley 2005; Hughes 2001). These women come from Russia, the Ukraine, and other East European countries. The economic and political turmoil that followed the collapse of the Soviet Union has been considered a leading cause for trafficking in women for commercial sex (Bales 1999). Russian organized crime groups and others, including Albanian, Estonian, Chechen, Serb, and Italian gangs, are widely believed to be involved in a host of transnational criminal activities in Europe, from firearms sales to drug trafficking, and from document fraud to money laundering. Russian organized crime in particular has begun to dominate the illicit sex industry in a number of west European countries (Miko 2004).

Trafficking in persons is counted among the main sources of illegal profits for organized crime, behind only narcotics and firearm trafficking, and it generates billions of dollars annually (U.S. Department of Justice 2003). According to U.S. government estimates, an estimated 600,000 to 800,000 people are trafficked across international borders each year, having been bought, sold, transported like commodities, and often held in slave-like conditions for sex and labor exploitation. Between 14,500 and 17,500 of these victims are thought to be trafficked into the United States annually, although no one can determine the precise number of these victims (U.S. Department of Justice 2004). Most of them are forced into prostitution or exploited as workers in sweatshops, as domestic servants, or as construction and agricultural workers. Law enforcement agencies have initiated trafficking investigations in most domestic states and territories. Prosecutions have uncovered victims transported from countries around the world, including Bangladesh, Cameroon, China, El Salvador, Ghana, Guatemala, Honduras, Indonesia, Jamaica, Mexico, Russia, Thailand, Tonga, the United States, Uzbekistan, and Vietnam (U.S. Department of Justice 2004). The following are some of the demographic characteristics of trafficked victims (U.S. Assessment 2004):

- Approximately 80 percent are female, and 70 percent of these females are trafficked for commercial sex.
- Roughly two-thirds of the global victims are trafficked intra-regionally within East Asia and the Pacific (260,000 to 280,000 people) and within Europe and Eurasia (170,000 to 210,000 people).
- The largest number of the people trafficked into the United States come from East Asia and the Pacific (5,000 to 7,000). The next highest numbers come from Latin America, Europe, and Eurasia, with about 3,500 to 5,500 victims from each region.

Trafficking in women and children from Asia correlates with the growth of sex tourism in the region. Thailand, Cambodia, and the Philippines are popular sex tourism destinations. China, especially the two border provinces of Yunnan and Guangxi, has become a major supplier of young women and children for the sex trade in Thailand because of geographic proximity. In recent decades, there has been a continued demand for women from Yunnan Province in southern Thailand (Bangkok, Pattaya, and Phuket), where brothels serve large numbers of ethnic Chinese Malayans visiting popular tourist locations (Arnold and Bertone 2002).

Governments of various nations are struggling to deal with this sinister global enterprise. The U.S. federal government has recognized the significance of this problem, as evidenced by the formation of a cabinet-level, multi-agency task force. The President's Interagency Task Force involves senior officials from the departments of State, Justice, Homeland Security, Health and Human Services, Labor, and Agriculture, and the U.S. Agency for International Development. The government provided financial support to approximately 234 anti-trafficking programs in 2003 alone, with a total investment of about $91 million going to more than ninety countries (U.S. Assessment 2004).

It seems reasonable to assume that transporting women and children across international borders, regardless of whether by force or by fraud, requires the coordinated efforts of more than individual entrepreneurs. Along any given transportation route, traffickers must maintain control of victims by intimidation, coercion, or physical force. Once victims arrive at their destination country, the underworld vice lords, together with their gangster minions, must collude with indigenous traffickers to receive and dispose of these women. Without the involvement of underworld criminal organizations, trafficking of women and children would be all but impossible.

Although the traffic in women and children has become a global phenomenon, drawing wide attention from human rights and women's organizations, few independent studies have been conducted, and thus little systematic knowledge is available on the inner workings and the social organization of traffickers. Even less is known about the possible connection between human trafficking and traditional underworld organizations. Much of the information about this illicit business comes from either news stories or reports by government or non-government organizations.

There have been a few studies on women and children as sex workers in Thailand. However, the role of organized crime or criminal organizations in the business of human trafficking remains largely unexamined. The key question here is to what extent human traffickers resemble human smugglers. They both are in the business of transporting human beings across borders. Do the organizational patterns and operational characteristics of traffickers resemble those of human smugglers, where participants are willing and pay a fee? Are human traffickers mostly freelance entrepreneurs, like their smuggling counterparts, or do they also organize themselves into gangs or task forces, engaging in one deal at a time?

Based on official sources, Richard (1999) suggested that organized Asian criminal organizations (mainly Chinese, Vietnamese, and Koreans) have played a major role in trafficking Asian females and running brothels in the

United States. However, Richard also averred that these groups, when involved in trafficking of women, tended to operate more like loose confederations of criminal entrepreneurs than like large crime syndicates controlling the entire trafficking process (1999, 13–14). Traffickers form a loose joint venture only when opportunity presents itself, although here the division of labor is fairly well developed, with such roles as recruiters, transporters, enforcers, document forgers, brokers, and brothel owners. These are the same organizational features common among the snakeheads in this study. However, without the backing of empirical data, one must treat these apparent similarities with caution.

There does seem to be at least one main difference between these two groups of entrepreneurs. Once an illegal immigrant has entered the United States, the operation is considered successful and completed; human traffickers, however, must deliver their "cargo" to the underworld bosses, who in turn disperse it to different vice establishments. Unfortunately, there are more questions than answers in current research on human trafficking. Without empirical studies, one can only speculate about what these traffickers and their organizations might be like. Because of the sinister and dehumanizing nature of the business, any empirical attempts to study human trafficking pose much greater challenges and logistical difficulties than those encountered in studying human smuggling.

CHAPTER 10

Women and Chinese Human Smuggling

Organized crime has historically been a male enterprise. However, in the context of Chinese human smuggling, it is not uncommon to find women actively involved in planning and coordinating smuggling operations. This chapter examines their unique position in this illicit enterprise. An attempt will be made to build a conceptual framework to better understand why a sizable number of women have managed to become effective and even highly successful organizers in transnational human smuggling. The success of Chinese women as snakeheads raises theoretical and policy questions. Findings from this study point to a set of unique factors in the smuggling trade that produce a niche market that allows women to participation. This kind of business environment is not commonly found in other racketeering activities. Women's prominence and their prospect of continued participation in this illicit business are hindered only by their ability to network to cultivate and maintain smuggling-pertinent resources.

The Place of Women in China

In China women were traditionally defined in reference to men; however, social inequalities based on gender have greatly diminished since the Communists took control of the country in 1949 (Whyte and Parish 1984). Touting that "women can hold up half of the sky," the Communist state mobilized more than 90 percent of urban women into the work force during the Mao era (1949–76) (Zuo and Bian 2001). This progressive social policy greatly improved the social and economic standing of women relative to men, especially in the area of basic education (Hannum and Xie 1994). In urban China, most married women are in the work force and share economic resources with their husbands at a rate higher than that of some more economically advanced countries (Entwisle and Henderson 2000). Under the Maoist slogan "same-work, same-pay" (*tong gong tong chou*), participation in paid employment is thought to be the solution to the fundamental eradication of most, if not all, social inequalities between the sexes (Zuo and Bian 2001).

Despite tremendous advances in women's employment, educational attainment, and economic status, the traditional female role of "virtuous wife and good mother" has managed to survive decades of social change under communism. Gendered role expectations and social practices still exist among both men and women (Stacey 1983; Honig and Hershatter 1988; Honig 2000; Zuo and Bian 2001). Women are supposed to be thoughtful and compassionate, and therefore take primary responsibility in household labor and child-rearing activities (Shek 1995). Bian (2002, 102), in his review of recent research on Chinese social stratification and social mobility, points out that although these "domestic" expectations do not keep women out of the labor force, the growth of market economies in the past two decades has led to increased discrimination against female workers in hiring and layoff practices and consequently exerts pressure on women to leave the workplace. In addition, in southern China, rising despotism in the private sector has made working conditions hard to endure, with heavy physical labor and long hours common (Lee 1995). In rural China, the running of a family business and its expansion rely mainly on the size of the male labor pool. While men are pursuing family business opportunities, women are left behind to tend the fields (Entwisle et al. 1995).

As privately owned businesses increasingly dominate China's fledging market economy, the state is slowly losing its influence both as an employer and as an advocate of women's rights. Women must still construct and negotiate their social and domestic roles in relation to men. Zuo and Bian (2001) argue that the persistence of gendered roles in Chinese society is attributable to the lack of real jobs outside the home that allow women to pursue fulfilling careers, opportunities to garner the same financial rewards as their male counterparts, and the autonomy necessary to freely choose between work and family. In short, women have been losing ground to men in the new market-driven economy.

This study, however, found a group of Chinese women who have managed to develop "alternative" economic opportunities by engaging in the business of human smuggling. Their gendered roles have turned out to be an asset in this illicit enterprise.

Women and Organized Crime

Women in various cultures have long participated in illicit economic activities. For example, in the 1910s, women in the Jewish community in New York's Lower East Side were active in coordinating and organizing operations like prostitution and narcotics dealing (Block 1977). Studies in recent years have examined women's active roles in the drug economy (e.g., as users, traffickers, and pushers) and related property crimes (Inciardi et al. 1993; Fagan 1994; Maher and Daly 1996; Denton 2001).

In the majority of studies that focus on the issue of gender in criminal organizations, women are mostly relegated to auxiliary roles as family members or accomplices of their male partners. In her analysis of the role of women in the Italian mafia, Siebert (1996, 143–72) described female members of the mafia family as often targets of exploitation and subordination who are excluded from the male-dominated world. Although the important role of "virtuous" mother or wife helps maintain the mafia family and its "territorial sovereignty," women's participation in mafia activities is mostly by way of complicity (Siebert 1996, 143).

Resendiz (2001) found that in professional auto-theft rings along the U.S.-Mexico border, males are introduced into the theft rings through friends, but females enter the business by way of intimate sexual relationships and family ties. Although women are active participants, most of them occupy relatively low-risk and low-paying positions in the auto-theft rings.

A few studies did find women occupying leadership positions in criminal organizations, however. For example, Dino (1998) synthesized research on the role of females in the mafia, beginning with observations of how mafia families communicate with the outside world. She found that women often play central roles in maintaining criminal organizations as they often step in to manage the clan's affairs when their male family members (i.e., their fathers, husbands, and brothers) have been arrested. Erminia Giuliano, in her fifties and a member of the 200-year-old Camorra clan, stepped up to the helm of her family's lucrative heroin trade in Naples after her father and all her brothers were imprisoned (Nadeau 2002). Although she was later arrested by the police, her rise to prominence within the criminal clan showed that under some circumstances women can assume the leadership of a major criminal organization in Italy. These women, like their male counterparts, take on the mentality of defending the family honor. As a result of their increasing involvement in mafia businesses, mothers, daughters, sisters, and nieces are now targeted for assassination and hunted through the streets— by other women (Carroll 2002). For instance, in May 2002, a 30-year-old feud between the Cava family and Graziano family in Naples erupted in a bloody shootout, except that this time it was the women who pulled the triggers (Carroll 2002).

Women and Chinese Human Smuggling

Reports of female snakeheads involved in transnational human smuggling have surfaced time and again in the press. Some of these women have come to personify the audacity and scope of illegal Chinese migration to the United States or other Western countries. For example, U.S. law enforcement officials have for years considered Sister Ping (also known as Cheng Chui-ping) a leader of an international criminal organization specializing in transporting illegal migrants from China to America, and she has been called the "mother of all snakeheads" (Barnes 2000). After evading the U.S. authorities for years by hiding in China, she was finally captured in April 2000 in Hong Kong and was extradited to the United States to stand trial for her role in the infamous *Golden Venture* incident. For more than a decade, Sister Ping's many exploits in human smuggling and money laundering made her almost legendary. Many snakeheads in the United States and China have claimed to be her associates in order to boost their otherwise obscure status and attract clients or to charge higher fees. On March 16, 2006, Sister Ping was sentenced in a federal court in New York to thirty-five years on charges of conspiring to commit alien smuggling, hostage taking, money laundering, and laundering of ransom money (Immigration and Customs Enforcement 2006).

Women have also been implicated in several high-profile human smuggling cases in the United States. In the fall of 2000, when Robert Porges, a high-powered immigration lawyer in New York City was arrested on RICO charges for colluding with human smugglers and local gangsters in immigration frauds. His Chinese wife, Sherry Lu Porges, who was also arrested, was widely believed to be the mastermind behind the scenes and responsible for recruiting and extorting illegal immigrants (*World Journal* 2000). According to one account, with her language and cultural skills, she was able to lure clients from the Chinese community to her husband's law firm, where various schemes, from fabricating stories to providing "financial guarantees," were used to help illegal immigrants obtain legal status (*World Journal* 2000). In another case, a woman, Ai Qin Chen, in Monterey Park, California, pled guilty to federal charges of conspiring with Asian organized crime groups to smuggle Chinese nationals into the country and to hire gangsters to track down the relatives in China of those who were unable to pay her smuggling fees (*Los Angeles Times* 1999).

Some of the best-known Chinese human smugglers in Europe have also been female. Following the Dover incident, Dutch law enforcement agencies launched a large-scale investigation, named Operation Opaal, and caught the alleged ring leader, a female named Chen Jing Ping (also known as Sister Ping in European Chinese communities), who was later sentenced to three years in prison and fined 12,000 euros. In addition to her alleged connection with the Dover incident, she was accused of having smuggled perhaps more than a thousand illegal Chinese immigrants to Western Europe in the course of a few years (Bulsing 2004).

It was not difficult to find female snakeheads in both the sending and the receiving communities during the course of this study. In fact, they made up 18 percent of the total sample. They were found at various points in the smuggling process. Some were successful and remained in the business for years without encountering serious setbacks; others worked as recruiters and low-level go-betweens, making occasional money for referrals.

Explaining Women's Participation in Organized Crime

Organized crime has been by definition a man-only association (Siebert 1996). Traditional Chinese triad societies have always been known as fraternal organizations (Booth 1990; Chin 1990; Chu 2000). This male-only tradition continues today. Brotherhood defines group identity and reinforces organizational cohesion. Loyalty to one's "brothers" is seared into each member's psyche through initiation rites, job titles, codes of conduct, and the hierarchical order.

Theories of organized crime have largely been built on observations of these male-only organizations. One example is the economic theory of protection developed by Gambetta (1993), who argued that organized crime, particularly in the context of the Sicilian Mafia, essentially is a business of providing protection to those who engage in high-risk transactions for which legal protection is neither available nor effective. Muscle power therefore is needed to provide assurance of smooth operations. In an analysis of organized crime in New York that is similar to Gambetta's framework, Alan Block (1980) proposed a paradigm of an extortion-protection-oriented "power syndicate." The power syndicate maximizes profits through territorial monopoly; it does so largely through its ability to evoke fear and to use violence to assert its domination. Obviously, theories derived from gender-specific criminal organizations are limited in their ability to explain women's participation in organized crime, because they explain a social milieu that precludes women from participation.

Block also proposed a service-oriented "enterprise" paradigm, which dominates the domain of such illegal businesses as prostitution, gambling, smuggling, and drug trafficking. Under this conceptual framework, crime groups survive on the margins of legally regulated economies and are mainly regulated by the same economic principles of supply and demand. Potter's analysis of the gambling business (1994) exemplifies this approach. The enterprise paradigm shifts the focus of analysis away from exclusive and male-only features toward market demands for illicit goods and services, and the responses of groups of entrepreneurs to provide them. Values such as loyalty and blood oaths, which are central to the mafia and Chinese triad fraternities, are no longer essential under this paradigm, where bonds among members of a criminal group extend no further than a mutual interest to make money.

Theories specific to women's participation in criminal organizations or organized crime are few. Some researchers have suggested that women's participation in organized crime reflects the rise of new criminal opportunities spurred by market expansion (Inciardi et al. 1993; Mieczkowski 1994); the increasing autonomy and changing roles of women (Bourgois 1989; Karstedt 2000); or an extension of women's traditional household responsibilities (Siebert 1996). However, Maher and Daly (1996, 466) have argued that recent changes in the drug economy have not made the drug markets any more accessible to women, who are still relegated to low-level auxiliary roles with few opportunities for stable income generation. Women are often used to make up for shortages of male drug dealers due to police intervention and seasonal change, or to minimize risk for drug business owners because females attract less attention and are less likely to be harassed by police (Maher 1997, 90; Siebert 1996).

Maher and Daly (1996) attributed such unequal distribution of market opportunities to continued institutional sexism in the underworld, where men prefer working with other men because of the implied or explicit violence required in this volatile and uncertain work environment. Women are thought to lack the mental and physical ability to use violence and to manage men (Steffensmeier 1983).

Although these studies have advanced the understanding of women's participation in organized criminal activities, they mostly pertain to street-level crime. Transnational human smuggling is a different type of criminal enterprise, with market conditions that are vastly different from other types of racketeering. Therefore, to explain specifically why Chinese women have risen to prominence in this illicit business, additional theoretical constructs are needed.

Female and Male Snakeheads: A Demographic Comparison

We found both similarities and patterned differences between the male and female snakeheads in this study, as shown in Table 10.1. Overall, female snakeheads were better educated than their male counterparts, with 52 percent having graduated from high school, compared with only 32 percent of the men. The sample's women were also more likely than the men to be single or divorced. Like their male counterparts, few female snakeheads held regular, salaried jobs at the time of the interviews. Most described themselves as either self-employed or unemployed.

Table 10.1. Demographics of snakehead subjects by gender

	Female		Male	
	Frequency	*Percent*	*Frequency*	*Percent*
Education				
No formal education	0	0	5	5.1
Grade school	3	14.3	26	26.3
Junior high	5	23.8	26	26.3
High school	11	52.4	32	32.3
College	2	9.5	10	10.1
Total	21	100.0	99	100.0
Marital Status				
Married	14	60.9	86	82.7
Single	6	26.1	15	14.4
Divorced/separated	3	13.0	3	2.9
Total	23	100.0	104	100.0
Age				
21–30	4	17.4	14	13.3
31–40	11	47.8	54	51.4
41–50	7	30.4	29	27.6
51 and older	1	4.3	8	7.6
Total	23	100.0	105	100.0
Citizenship/legal status				
U.S. citizen/green card holder	10	43.5	43	40.6
U.S. legal non-immigrant	1	4.3	16	15.1
U.S. illegal immigrant	1	4.3	11	10.4
Chinese citizens only	11	47.8	36	34.0
Total	23	100.0	106	100.0

NOTE: Percentages are rounded.

Gendered Paths into the Smuggling Business

Our subjects followed fairly gendered pathways into the smuggling business. For most female smugglers, family ties provided the most common route to the smuggling underworld. Many of the females entered the business through their relationships with men (mostly husbands or lovers). A woman in New York, who got into the United States by using a photo-substituted passport, told her story:

> When I first arrived in the U.S., I worked in a massage parlor for about half a year as a masseuse. Later I got to know a snakehead and became his mistress. After we lived together, I became involved in his business and have been collecting payments from his clients since.

Her experience contrasted sharply with the typical male's entry into the business, as shown in Table 10.2. The vast majority of female smugglers (about 77 percent) entered into the business by way of their friends and relatives, compared to less than 40 percent of their male counterparts. For the female subjects, personal contacts served as both their primary pathway into the business and their main source of clients. In comparison, the male smugglers tended to rely on somewhat formal arrangements for recruiting clients. Although usually introduced to the business through their male partners, women were not necessarily relegated to auxiliary roles, as one subject in New York's Chinatown described her role in the business:

> My husband was involved in the smuggling business first, so of course, I followed him into this business. My husband told me that I had more education than he did, so he let me manage all the paperwork and accounting tasks. I know I am a woman, but I think I am a strong woman.

The gendered pathway was not always the route by which women got into smuggling. A few of the female subjects ventured into the business on their own or through contacts with other snakeheads. These women, mostly divorced or separated from their male partners, needed to become economically self-sufficient. Lacking employment skills, they learned to put their

Table 10.2. Method of entry, source of clients and motives by gender

	Female		Male	
	Frequency	*Percent*	*Frequency*	*Percent*
Introduced to smuggling by				
Relatives and friends	13	76.5	36	38.7
Business associates	0	0	6	6.5
Recruited by snakeheads	4	23.5	34	36.6
Self-initiated	0	0	11	11.8
Crime group activity	0	0	6	6.5
Total	17	100.0	93	100.0
Sources of clients				
Relatives and friends	13	76.5	41	44.1
Referrals from other clients	1	5.9	13	14.0
Referral network	3	17.7	39	41.9
Total	17	100.0	93	100.0
Motivations in smuggling business				
Earn money	8	47.1	58	61.7
Help friends	2	11.8	6	6.4
Help friends and earn money	7	41.2	30	31.9
Total	17	100.0	94	100.0

NOTE: Percentages are rounded.

social networking skills to work. One of the subjects in the Los Angeles area, who specialized in marriage fraud and passport acquisition, came to America via a fraudulent marriage in 1997. Her "husband" was a habitual gambler who was desperate for money. She paid a total of $51,000 in fees for herself and her two children, which, according to her, was a bargain at the time. This mother of two had no regular job but was living comfortably in Southern California. She told us her story:

> I had no background in this business at all and didn't know anyone to begin with. For a while I was doing what I had been doing in China. My husband back in China and I used to operate a car sales business. I would find great bargains in the U.S. and ship the cars to China for resale. I remember going to auto auctions on hot summer days, wearing a hat and soaking in sweat as I inspected the cars before the auctions began. I knew few English words, but I could read the numbers. I was quite proud of myself. It was hard work, but we were doing well until I got word through my relatives in Fuzhou that my husband was cheating on me in China. He was sleeping with this young woman and even got her pregnant. I realized I could not count on him and had to become financially independent. I got into the smuggling business first solely as a recruiter by referring my friends in China to a snakehead here in the U.S.

Irrespective of how these females entered the business, money seemed to be the primary motivation. To some, money was the only reason to get involved in the business, as the former masseuse in New York's Chinatown explained:

> Look, I like this business because I can make easy money. Otherwise, why would I want to be a mistress to this snakehead, if there weren't anything for me to gain? He is twenty years older than me. Of course I am staying with him for the money. Once I got involved in the smuggling business, I quit my massage parlor job because I did not want to sell my body anymore. With this snakehead, I am starting a new life. He gives me a fixed income each month, plus I get to keep 20 percent of all payments I collect. I am quite content.

Another woman, who operated a travel agency in Los Angeles, claimed to find human smuggling exciting, because it gave her opportunities to meet people and travel. Driving a luxury car and living in an upscale neighborhood, she said that she did not have to make a living, because her husband owned an electronics manufacturing business, but she did not want to rely on her husband to give her spending money. She wanted to have her own life and to make more money:

> You know, there is an old saying in Chinese: "Sadness enshrouds day and night if a husband and his wife are short on money." Money is important to me. The funny thing is that when we did not have much money before, we tried hard to make money. Now we have a lot of money, and we are trying hard to hide it.

Not all of the snakeheads were in the business just for the money. Many said helping friends and relatives was also an important factor. However, there were marked gender differences. As Table 10.2 illustrates, more females than males wanted to help family members or relatives to come to America to have a better life. Of the women, 53 percent considered themselves to be doing good deeds and making money; only 38 percent of the males gave this rationale. As the mother of two from Los Angeles (the marriage fraud specialist) explained:

> I am helping my friends, in most cases. I have not made much money. It is hard to set up fraudulent marriages because there is not much money to be made and it takes a long time to complete a case. If you mess things up, you will lose your friends. And if you succeed, you only make a small profit. Many times I was just doing favors for my relatives and friends, without making any money. To tell you the truth, I am charging less than most other people. The people I am helping are all close to my family and friends in China; therefore I cannot charge too much.

As Chin found in his New York study (1999), illegal Chinese immigrants often consider snakeheads to be philanthropists or "normal people" who merely want to make some money. In this regard, both male and female snakeheads in this study were much the same in that they tended to have a positive opinion of themselves and of the smuggling business. As a female specialist in passport photo substitution in New York noted:

> I use my daughter's and other relatives' green cards to help people to come to the U.S. My motive is simple. I want to make money and at the same time help my relatives to come to the U.S. I consider it a good deed to be able to help them leave behind their bitter life in China. In Fuzhou they only made a few hundred Chinese yuan a month (about fifty to seventy U.S. dollars). Here they can make at least $1,000 a month. Why not help them achieve a better life!

Gender and Roles in the Smuggling Business

We found a few differences in roles and responsibilities of the two sexes in smuggling. Female snakeheads were found in most aspects of smuggling activities, undertaking active and diversified roles like their male counterparts. Some females undertook tasks that have traditionally been thought to be a man's job (e.g., escorting clients to transit points, corrupting officials, and collecting debts). A former hair salon owner in New York's Chinatown who specialized in photo substitution schemes told her story:

> My main responsibility is to collect payments from our clients or their relatives. I don't feel embarrassed about what I am doing. We help our clients to reach the U.S. and they should pay us. Otherwise, how can we pay our customers who supplied the passports to facilitate the smuggling operation? So my primary task is to collect all agreed-upon fees and that is it. Furthermore, I must do the collection myself. You cannot rely on someone else to do it for you.

Table 10.3 shows that female snakeheads are just as likely to procure passports for photo substitutions or arrange fraudulent business delegations as their male counterparts are. At the same time, both males and females can be found at the low end of the business, as recruiters for a nominal fee. Perhaps because of gendered preference, females are more likely to be engaged in arranging marriage frauds than their male counterparts, while males are more likely to be involved in tasks such as taking clients from drop-off point to safe houses or other transit locations. In general, males and females are just as likely to be independent operators in charge of specific aspects of a smuggling operation as they are to be following instructions from other smugglers for assignments. A female smuggler in Washington, D.C., said:

> I am doing this business full time now. When I just started, I was working for a snakehead and followed his instructions. Then I went independent, but I still occasionally refer out my clients to other snakeheads. I work with three to four partners, but I do a lot of things myself, such as screening clients, building contacts, and securing travel documents, and even collecting payment. I mostly use package tour groups from mainland China to Hong Kong, Singapore, Malaysia, and Thailand. The main transit point is in Thailand. Some of my clients fly to the U.S., and others arrive in Canada or Mexico first and then enter the U.S. by car.

Table 10.3. Primary specialties in smuggling business by gender

Primary Specialty	Female		Male	
	Frequency	Percent	Frequency	Percent
Photo or passport substitution	1	4.3	4	3.8
Fraudulent marriage	2	8.7	5	4.7
Fraudulent documents	4	17.4	8	7.5
Fraudulent business trips/escort	2	8.7	4	3.8
Client recruitment/screening/ deposit collection	4	17.4	26	24.5
Payment guarantee	3	13.0	2	1.9
Debt collection	4	17.4	10	9.4
Incarcerated client bailout	1	4.3	0	0
Coordinate/plan/arrange smuggling tasks	0	0	7	6.6
Muscleman	0	0	1	.9
Receive clients/collect payment	0	0	3	2.8
Transport/escort/forward clients	0	0	16	15.1
Misc. tasks—assistant to big snakeheads	0	0	8	7.5
Unable to determine	2	8.7	12	11.3
Total	23	100.0	106	100.0

NOTE: Percentages are rounded.

Male snakeheads were found taking instructions and assignments from female collaborators, and vice versa. In any smuggling operation, the ability to assign tasks is mostly tied to the responsibilities and roles a snakehead undertakes. Thus, on the one hand, if a snakehead is responsible for securing travel documents, no one else in the smuggling operation can make a move until the proper papers arrive. On the other hand, the snakehead—male or female—who is in charge of escorting clients through border checkpoints and has the proper contacts with the airport security personnel can determine when the clients will leave. There are gendered differences in the type of resources developed and controlled by males or females, but gender makes little difference in terms of who actually delivers the needed service.

There were, however, a few aspects of the smuggling business in which I found no females. These were mainly activities that clearly required the capacity for violence, such as serving as enforcers—whether to keep order on a smuggling ship or to beat up delinquent clients for failing to make payments. Females also avoided activities and social settings that they considered inappropriate or uncomfortable. A female snakehead in Fuzhou described one of these settings:

> The worst part of this business is to deal with corrupt officials. They are worse than thieves. Thieves are sneaky and maintain a low profile. These officials openly ask you for money and name their prices for their services. You don't slip them an envelope under the table. You hand stacks of cash over the table and they count the notes right there in the open. In Sichuan, for instance, my contacts in government liked to go to these teahouses first, which would cost me about 400–500 yuan (about 50–62 U.S. dollars), and a dinner later, and then they would all want to go to a sauna. These people always asked for prostitutes in these sauna places, and I'd have to pay their bills. I usually would leave after the dinner, and my male assistants would take them to those sauna places. There were a few times I had to pay thousands of yuan for those sauna excursions. My people told me they each called in two girls at once. What can you do about these people? If you want to do this business, these are the people you must kowtow to. They sometimes would tell you about their financial problems, such as remodeling their new houses, insinuating at every turn that they needed money. The going price for transferring one's residential registration is 20,000 yuan. I know the real cost for processing the documents is only about 3,000 yuan. But these officials charge me 20,000 yuan per client. Last time, I had four clients and I handed them four stacks of cash. The investment is really costly and risky. If they can't produce the documents you need, how are you going to get your money back?

Gender and Financial Returns

The earning patterns for the males and females in this study were similar. However, more females declined to report their financial gains than did their male counterparts. Half of the female subjects refused to answer questions about their profits per client and annual income from the business, compared with 34 percent of the males.

Based on their responses, both sexes appeared to stick to very similar pricing practices, charging a median smuggling fee of $50,000 per client and making the same median profit of $10,000 per case. There were a few extreme cases: one female who claimed she was making $500,000 a year, and a male who claimed to be making $2,000,000 a year. Although these figures must be taken with caution, there do not appear to be any systematic differences in the prices males and females charge for their services. It seems logical that snakeheads' pricing practices and profit margins are mostly set by market conditions and smuggling method, as opposed to gendered preferences. One female smuggler in Washington, D.C., area described how she made her money in the business:

> The by-air route is the most expensive (for the client). Sometimes my clients have to use several passports and change planes several times to get into the U.S. The size of a by-air trip is usually five–seven people, and I can make about $200,000 from each trip. But the by-sea route can handle forty to fifty . . . clients at once, which can make more than $1,000,000. But I don't get involved in that type of operation.

Female snakeheads were rarely found in maritime smuggling operations, which are the most daring and risky. About the only exception thus far was the widely publicized *Golden Venture* incident in 1993, in which U.S. law enforcement agencies alleged that Sister Ping was a principal organizer, in collaboration with one of New York's Chinatown gangs (Thompson 2000). None of the female subjects in this study were involved in arranging maritime smuggling operations. Instead, female snakeheads are more likely than their male counterparts to exploit the safest method (or the one with the highest success rate)—marriage fraud, which also garners the highest smuggling fees. At the time of this study, the going rate for a fraudulent marriage was $60,000 to $70,000 in the Fuzhou region. In comparison, other methods of smuggling, such as boat-land-air combinations, cost about $10,000 less.

The Conditional Market Perspective

Like their male counterparts, female snakeheads typically possess few marketable skills. However, as Robert Merton described in his theory of adaptation (1938, 1957), such women learn to apply available resources to create their own money-making opportunities and to bargain for a more favorable financial arrangement for themselves and their families. In this regard they are no different from their male counterparts or any other ethnic criminal organization, whose illicit enterprising activities merely reflect their collective struggle to seek and to devise survival strategies in a society where they have neither the skills nor other resources necessary for material success (Schatzberg and Kelly 1997).

Within the enterprise perspective, entering an illicit economy depends largely on access and opportunities. However, to explain the involvement of women in Chinese human smuggling, additional theoretical constructs are needed, both to specify how such opportunities have emerged and to explain the impact gender seems to bear on the business. In Figure 10.1, a diagram using the conditional market perspective is presented to make sense of the female smugglers' gendered participation in the business. This paradigm is built upon the two prerequisites necessary to participate in the business and a set of market conditions that have effectively reduced the traditional gender barriers commonly found in other criminal enterprises.

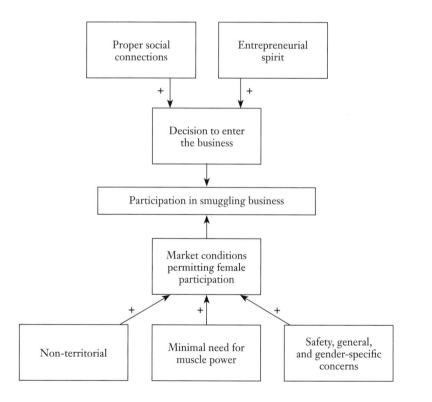

Figure 10.1. A schematic diagram of the conditional market perspective

There are two prerequisites for anyone who wants to become a snakehead:
(1) sufficient entrepreneurial spirit (i.e., courage) and (2) appropriate social
connections (i.e., resources and opportunities). The prerequisite of appropriate connections is self-evident, because Chinese human smuggling is all
about having the right connections (or *guanxi*), from recruiting clients to
securing necessary travel documents.[1] Every smuggling operation requires
a group of individuals to provide a series of services. The value of the resources a snakehead brings into a smuggling organization largely depends
on her ability to cultivate and maintain the right contacts. Connections
enable a snakehead to accomplish vital smuggling tasks. More important,
smuggling-appropriate connections open doors to further opportunities.
Although opportunities to initiate smuggling operations are constrained by
many factors (including market demand, referral networks, and law enforcement activities), those who can provide vital services reliably are likely to get
clients. Consequently, there is a continuous need to cultivate and maintain
these contacts for as long as one's smuggling scheme remains viable. As one
female subject in Fuzhou explained:

> I did many cases through Dalian (a city in northeast China). My clients went
> through South Korea and sometimes Japan to transfer to the U.S. But that
> route is dead now. My Philippine route was also dead after two of my clients
> were caught during their transfer. These routes often change, and each time
> I meet with my friends in the business, we talk about the situations on dif-
> ferent routes, and get the latest updates. You have to change your routes
> often to survive in this business. It is the nature of the business that when-
> ever a route works well, everyone wants to send their clients through the
> same route. Soon the authorities will discover this route and shut down the
> loopholes. Therefore new routes must be developed constantly.

The prerequisite of sufficient entrepreneurial spirit is easily understood,
but difficult to define. It has to do with one's willingness to take risks, de-
termination to handle unexpected events, and desire to make money on
one's own. Female snakeheads are as aware of the illicit nature of the business and cognizant of the potential risks as their male counterparts are.
Several females interviewed in this study claimed to have lost large sums of
money when they had to pay fines for clients who were detained and repatriated. Several others were discouraged by the increasing risks and decided

to quit the business. A snakehead in New York's Chinatown explained why she quit the business:

> I have never been arrested. I don't escort any of my clients into the U.S. or out of China. I have done more than a dozen clients thus far and none of them were arrested. I guess I have been lucky so far and made all this money. But my daughter, who was not in this business, was once detained in a transit country for four months. The immigration officials in the transit country accused her of carrying a fraudulent passport. The truth is that I had previously used her passport to smuggle someone else into the U.S. The passport had been altered, but it was really her passport. After my daughter's arrest, I quit the smuggling business. You can't do this illegal business for long. Now my to-go restaurant is doing quite well, and I am no longer in the smuggling business.

The entrepreneurial spirit also includes the willingness to venture into the unknown and the tenacity to see things through. The following story from one of the female snakeheads in Fuzhou illustrates this point:

> I always believe I should know each smuggling route myself as much as possible. A few years ago, I escorted a client to Vietnam through Ping Xiang City (bordering with Vietnam). The whole trip was to get her exit permit changed. We flew to Nanning (the capital city of Guangxi Province) and then took a bus to Ping Xiang. I didn't know that my own Hong Kong passport also needed a visa to cross into Vietnam. My client didn't want to cross the border without me, so we had to turn back. By then, it was late in the day, and the city was so small and poor that there were few places to eat. We were hungry so we went to a small eatery to find something to eat. The owner said there was no hot food, because the cook had already gone for the day. I asked what he could serve to fill our stomachs. He offered us instant noodles and charged us five yuan a bowl, which at that time was twenty times more than one could buy it for from a market. All he did was add hot water to the instant noodles. We were starving and had to eat. Then we wanted to find a place to settle for the night, but there were no clean hotels. So I decided to return to Nanning the same night. We took the last bus— the so-called sleeper-bus back to Nanning. The bunks in the bus were just hard boards with no sheets or pillows. It was a miserable night. It took about six hours to get back to Nanning. The city looked so dirty and backward. I had a very bad impression of that city. I later flew my client to Vietnam through Hong Kong. She entered the U.S. not long ago through Canada.

Reflecting on the traditional Chinese custom of husbands providing for their wives, a few female subjects were adamant about making a living on their own and becoming financially self-reliant. They viewed participation in human smuggling as an opportunity to bring about fundamental changes in their financial situation. One school teacher–turned-snakehead in Fuzhou described her reasons for entering this business:

> China is still a country where men are valued more than women, but I think in the cities such a mentality is not as strong as in the villages. I like to have my own business. My husband is in Chengdu and he runs a health care product company. . . . I do my own projects in Fuzhou. I like to be independent. We are a generation that cannot count on our children to take care of us when we get old. Every family has only one child. Who knows how the child may turn out and what kind of woman my son will marry. So I must make my own money. There is a cultural tradition that women should rely on their husbands for subsistence, but then these women must also behave according to their husbands' moods (i.e., *kanlianse*). If you have a good husband, maybe he will give you some money to spend. What if he doesn't give you anything? What do you have to go on if your husband leaves you for another woman? That's why I don't want to depend on anyone for my livelihood.

Niche Market Conditions

Most criminal rackets (e.g., loan sharking, gambling, fencing, and even prostitution) are controlled by men. Even in studies where women are highly visible and participate actively (such as in the drug economy), they are still confined to the margins (Maher 1997, 194; Jacobs and Miller 1998). To explain how women have been able to achieve prominence in Chinese human smuggling, one must examine the nature of the business and its particular market conditions.

Since both male and female snakeheads rely on their social networks for entry into the smuggling business, the two prerequisites of courage and resources are inadequate, albeit necessary, explanations of why women play such an active role in this enterprise. Transnational human smuggling occurs within a unique context in which gender holds significant implications in a snakehead's work. Much of this unique context is attributed to three specific market conditions.

BUSINESS WITHOUT A TURF

Human smuggling is a business that does not require a territory. Unlike most traditional racketeering activities, in which clients and business establishments are tied to specific neighborhoods, human smuggling involves mostly one-time transactions among individuals of varied backgrounds and takes place in various locations. The combination of the clandestine nature of the business and the limited clientele dictates that the human smuggling business does not lend itself to any stable geographical boundaries. Without a turf or a few city blocks that a smuggler can claim as his or her home territory, competition for or protection of one's business becomes unnecessary. Thus far, there have been no stories of turf fights among snakeheads. No smuggling organizations are been found attempting to drive away competitors from the village or city blocks where they operate. Competition among individual snakeheads of either sex to gain market share or to control client sources is unheard of. Chinese human smuggling has thus far remained an open-entry enterprise (Zhang and Chin 2002b).

Without a turf, and with transactions conducted in secrecy among only the individuals directly involved, the business of human smuggling possesses two essential attributes that render the issue of gender less salient. First and foremost, the use of violence to protect one's territory is of little relevance. The ability to control volatile situations through violence is probably the most important defining element that relegates women to the margins in most illicit economies (Maher 1997, 194). However, if an enterprise is non-territorial, the masculine identity constructed around interpersonal violence becomes irrelevant.

Second, as long as the patron-client relationships remain dyadic and transactions secretive, snakeheads can retain total control over their own resources, which makes competition unlikely. Any snakehead, male or female, who can provide the needed services can remain a viable partner, with little fear of being cut out by unscrupulous competitors. Although a potential client could theoretically talk to different snakeheads to compare prices and inquire about their smuggling methods, few snakeheads know enough details of the entire smuggling operation to make such a comparison possible. Furthermore, a snakehead does not make a move until a down payment has been made, and once that happens, the client most likely will stick with his or her smuggler to the very end, successful or not. With little chance to compete for clients, physical violence is of little use.

GUANXI: THE ULTIMATE ASSET IN HUMAN SMUGGLING

In most traditional Chinese organized crimes, such as extortion and gambling, the ability and willingness to use violence for instrumental purposes has been a prerequisite as well as a hallmark of successful and sustained operations. As Chin (1996) illustrated in his study of Chinatown gangs, many strategies, ranging from shootouts to rambunctious behavior, can be used to drive away rival gangs or to subdue unwilling store owners. However, human smuggling for the most part relies on *guanxi*, or personal connections. Although guarding safe houses and maintaining order onboard smuggling vessels require physical intimidation, in most transactions muscle power is of little use.

This is not to say that female smugglers are incapable of applying physical measures to enforce their contracts. They just don't do the physical job themselves. A snakehead in Los Angeles admitted that she had used a Vietnamese gangster as a debt collector. In one incident, she said, a young Vietnamese woman became scared of the marriage fraud in which she was to "marry" a Chinese client and decided to quit the deal midstream. This snakehead told how she resorted to the threat of violence to resolve the situation:

> I hired a gangster to pay her a visit. The guy was a member of a Vietnamese black society, and he worked out a payment plan for her to pay back the original deposit I gave her, plus more. I charged her twice the amount of the deposit she took from me for backing out of the deal. Because my debt collector had to take half of whatever was collected, I had to double the amount of money she owed me to cover my loss. Besides, all the middlemen who referred her to me also had to return the fees I paid out. That's the rule.

SAFETY AS AN OVERRIDING CONCERN

Transnational human smuggling often involves treacherous routes through multiple countries. Migrants are often subjected to unsanitary and crowded living conditions, vehicle breakdowns, and the constant fear of unscrupulous smugglers and fellow immigrants waiting to take advantage of them (McCarthy 2000). In Chin's survey of 300 illegal immigrants in New York, he documented numerous stories of unruly enforcers physically and sexually abusing female immigrants (Chin 1999).

Concerns over health and safety during the transportation are pervasive among prospective migrants. These concerns can be divided into two categories: general and gender-specific. On the one hand, *general concerns* refer to the widespread anxiety among would-be migrants about the safety of the smuggling process because of the horror stories often reported in the news or passed around as gossip in the villages. Personal safety is typically among the first few questions the clients raise or the snakeheads address. Snakeheads typically use past successful cases to illustrate their capability and safety records, and try to talk their clients into believing that treacherous and perilous journeys somehow do not present a problem this time around. For instance, in interviews in July 1999 in Tijuana, where 177 illegal Chinese immigrants were detained by the Mexican authorities, subjects reported that their snakeheads had never warned them how hard it would be to travel across the Pacific in a small cargo boat in summertime. One subject reported:

> The boat was rocking so much we couldn't sleep and were constantly throwing up. For days I could not keep anything down in my stomach. It was miserable. For the two weeks on the boat, no one took a shower. The fresh water was for drinking and cooking only.

Gendered preferences in the choice of snakeheads emerge amidst concerns over safety and travel conditions. Female snakeheads were generally thought to be more considerate and attentive to welfare and safety issues. Illegal migrants often saw female snakeheads as motherly figures who were more likely than male snakeheads to be concerned about travel conditions. Motivated by the desire to help friends and relatives, female snakeheads were more likely to construct their work identity in accordance with gendered cultural expectations and therefore take safety issues more seriously than do their male counterparts. This gendered preference for female snakeheads was reported by undocumented Chinese immigrants in the United States and prospective clients in China, who considered female snakeheads easier to work with and definitely less likely than males to resort to violence or to expose female clients to possible sexual exploitation.

This preference for female snakeheads is more than a simple reflection of the general Chinese expectations of gendered roles and responsibilities in social interactions. It is also the product of the collective knowledge of many illegal immigrants who have experienced differences in the ways male and female snakeheads handled their clients. Sister Ping, the so-called mother of all snakeheads, is an example. She was highly regarded in the smuggling community in New York's Chinatown for her concern about her clients' safety and travel conditions. She demanded that her underlings and affiliated street gangsters not mistreat her clients, because they were her customers just like those who frequented her store in Chinatown (Barnes 2000). A male snakehead in New York described his impression of Sister Ping this way:

> People in the community do not consider Sister Ping a criminal. In fact, she is highly regarded, because she has never used force to collect smuggling fees. Some of her clients who could not come up with the balance were set free to work. She allowed these people to work first and pay her later. Not only that, she is known for her humbleness and generosity. Whenever she invited people to dinner or lunch, she would make sure everybody would eat well. She would rarely eat herself, but would busy herself with serving her guests.

On the other hand, *gender-specific concerns* over personal safety are especially noticeable among female clients. Concerns about sexual abuse and exploitation rank as the highest concerns among prospective female migrants.[2] Female clients are at the mercy of their smugglers, not only for personal safety but also for protection from sexual assaults by either their male handlers or male clients. There have been many stories in the news media and in research reports about female migrants being raped and assaulted en route to the United States. Chin (1999) reported that sexual exploitation was particularly rampant in boat-based smuggling operations, where women were trapped in close living quarters with men over extended periods of time. Most female snakeheads in this study claimed to be keenly aware of the particular risks for their female clients and were eager to offer their strategies to deal with them. One subject in New York's Chinatown said that she made sure such things would never happen to her clients:

> Of course I have heard many horror stories on those smuggling boats. When you have men and women sleeping close together for such a long time, sexual assaults are bound to occur. I always suggest that woman clients should always take the air route and never get on a boat. These things will never happen to my clients. I have transported more than a dozen clients and all of them are either relatives or friends from my own village.

None of the snakeheads in this study admitted to have ever permitted sexual assaults on female clients, but a few male snakeheads hinted that such incidents had occurred. One snakehead in Los Angeles, who was responsible for receiving and forwarding clients and guarding safe houses, noted:

> Snakeheads usually separate male and female clients into different compartments on a boat or into different rooms in safe houses. We usually warn male clients not to touch the females, but sometimes a few of them just can't control themselves. The most we can do is to warn the males not to do it again after the fact. What else can we do? Our clients usually stay in the safe houses for very short periods of time and only for transit purposes.

Because of these gender-specific concerns, female clients usually preferred female snakeheads to male. It is not clear whether such gendered preference has successfully averted sexual abuse or improved travel conditions, as many smuggling operations are carried out by male and female snakeheads collaborating with one another. However, it was clear during this study that both prospective migrants and snakeheads were cognizant of these unspoken gendered cultural expectations and conducted their activities accordingly.

Another issue related to safety concerns was the perceived trustworthiness of female snakeheads in business transactions. One interviewer for this study in Fuzhou, after talking to several female snakeheads, had this to say:

> Women tend to be more reliable and better trusted by clients. The main reason is that female snakeheads are local people and tend to be stable. These women often live in the same township as their clients and are most likely known to others, have a reputation, and have children and a house. It is easier to find these women than their male counterparts. Men are far more transient than women. Clients are afraid of being cheated. Knowing where the snakehead lives means a lot to prospective clients. I have never heard of any female snakeheads being accused of having defrauded their clients.

In a business full of uncertainties and hazards, when gendered cultural expectations are compared with a successful reputation, a female snakehead can command significant respect and attract attention beyond her "home territory." Sister Ping is a case in point. For years before her arrest, many snakeheads, male and female, in Fujian and the United States claimed to be working for her or to be part of her circle of friends. These claims, most of them false, were nothing more than a scheme to boost their otherwise obscure status in the smuggling community in order to attract clients or to charge higher fees. No male Chinese snakeheads have ever ascended to the status in the smuggling community in North America that was enjoyed by Sister Ping. And for that matter, the most highly regarded snakeheads in Europe, as far as the law enforcement agencies and the news media are concerned, have also been female.

Although women are receiving increasing attention in the literature on organized crime, there is as yet limited empirical evidence to suggest that they have made significant inroads into the criminal underworld. Instead, women's participation in various illicit economies may best be attributed to the shifts and changes in the gendered organization of market sectors that afford new and different opportunities for women. Transnational human smuggling is one such market sector. Female snakeheads take advantage of their social connections to advance their financial interests and their self-proclaimed goodwill to assist friends and relatives. Although female snakeheads are easy to find, it would be a mistake to claim that, unlike other racketeering activities, the business of human smuggling is an "equal opportunity employer."

Because of the unique features of the smuggling market, gendered preferences and cultural expectations as reflected in prospective migrants' choice of snakeheads have created more opportunities for women's participation than other illicit economies afford. Maher (1997, 168) has argued: "opportunities for participation in the informal economy are not empty slots waiting to be filled by those with the requisite skills." The gendered preference is not a market determinant that can propel women to eventually surpass their male counterparts for market dominance. Far from it: the majority of snakeheads are still men, whose social contacts and smuggling networks consist mainly of other men. Since the resources vital to smuggling operations (e.g., producing travel documents, arranging transportation means, or paying off border security personnel) are mostly controlled by men, the resources to cultivate and sustain profitable smuggling channels are therefore not equally distributed between the sexes. Although all smugglers must overcome the same challenges (e.g., finding reliable referrals and securing timely delivery of smuggling services), females must face additional challenges, among which are unequal distribution of the social resources required to build smuggling networks in the first place. The unequal distribution of resources that leads to restricted market opportunities for women is a major factor that effectively limits their access to the illicit economy and prevents them from exploiting the gendered preference for women to a greater extent.

Little is known about how female smugglers affect transnational human smuggling as a result of their gender and their unique operational attributes. This study has merely made a rudimentary attempt to explore why some women have been successful in an underworld traditionally dominated by men. It is the intent of this study to alert other investigators to the fact that something about the business of transnational human smuggling is unique and allows both men and women to take advantage of emerging opportunities.

CHAPTER 11

The Future of Chinese Human Smuggling

Suffice it to say that illegal human smuggling will always exist to some degree. It is perhaps only realistic to recognize illegal immigration as a permanent feature of the U.S. political and social landscape. As Kwong (1997) has pointed out, in China illegal migration is more of a labor issue than an immigration problem, and as long as the American economy demands cheap labor, there will be jobs for illegal immigrants and a market for human smugglers. Attempts to stop illegal immigration are likely to fail as long as other, broader socioeconomic conditions persist. Those who do not qualify for legal immigration or do not want to wait to become eligible to immigrate legally will seek the services of smugglers. Enterprising agents will provide these services, as long as there is a market demand for them. Although authorities consider these entrepreneurs criminals, migration researchers prefer to consider them as facilitators or brokers "who offer a range of services, some of which may be in breach of law, while others may be perfectly aboveboard" (Pieke et al. 2004, 195). These professionals enable family members, relatives, friends, and others from the same or neighboring townships to form a continuous flow of immigrants, some legal and others illegal.

The Pressure to Leave China

News reports have for some time claimed that the lure of the Gold Mountain is losing its luster, as fewer illegal Chinese migrants seem to be arriving (Tempest 1995; Chen 2003). In addition to the hardship of the journey and the high smuggling fees, newly arrived immigrants also complain to their families at home about long hours of menial labor, homesickness, and a dim future in the United States. Making a comfortable living, albeit with less money, in a red-hot economy at home and in a familiar culture has become an attractive alternative to working twelve hours a day, seven days a week, in a foreign country (Chen 2003). Townships around Fuzhou are lined with busy factories that produce everything from Nike shoes to consumer electronics to plastic toys (Hood 1997). With the current smuggling price of $60,000 or more, the cost-benefit ratio no longer tips absolutely toward America. Growing job opportunities at home in China are beginning to dampen the enthusiasm of would-be migrants still waiting in line for a chance to go to America.

Although such reports may hold some truth and reflect a more realistic picture of current sentiment about going abroad, the United States remains a strong magnet to the vast majority of Fujianese, particularly those living in the counties surrounding Fuzhou, from which large numbers of people have already emigrated. Smuggling is not as feverish as it was in the early 1990s, but the desire to go to the United States is just as palpable. While eagerly waiting for his son to become a U.S. citizen so he would be eligible to apply for immigration, one prominent community figure in a township in Lianjiang County explained why America continues to symbolize hope and opportunity:

> There are still many people waiting to be smuggled to the U.S. Let's face it: It is all about money. What is there to do in this place? Nothing! No industry, no commerce in this area. There is practically nothing to do. There is not much land either, and all the farm work is now contracted out to laborers from poorer neighboring counties or provinces. No one wants to do hard

farm work that makes little money. Everywhere you go, you see the success of those whose family members live overseas.

A few years ago, this community leader's wife had "divorced" him, "married" a U.S. citizen, and immigrated to the United States with their two children. He was the only member of his family still in Lianjiang. Walking around his township, he pointed out that all the prominent buildings were constructed with foreign money. Living by himself in a five-story building also built with money sent from abroad, he predicted that emigration to Western countries, both legal and illegal, would continue for many years to come. As for himself, he said he could hardly wait to start his life anew in the "land of gold":

> In our township, we have as many people living abroad as are living here. Most of those abroad are in the U.S. Other countries include Japan, Argentina, Hong Kong, and Spain. There are still many people waiting in the pipeline to go to the U.S. We are talking about the second and third generations. They were only kids in the 1990s during the high tide of illegal emigration. Now they are old enough to be smuggled. Currently we have about 400 people in this township between the ages of eighteen and thirty-five, unmarried. The price for a fraudulent marriage (*jiajiehun*) is $62,000. It is getting expensive now, but people still want to go. If you have a solid snakehead, you will have no problem setting your price. People are more worried about smuggling channels not being reliable than the price being too high.

It would be naïve to assume that China's fast-growing economy will take care of illegal emigration to America. Far from it—most smugglers interviewed in this study predicted that the demand for illegal emigration would remain strong for decades to come. As the average price of an illegal journey to the United States indicates, those who are smuggled into America are not China's poor. A college-educated, illegal Chinese immigrant who came by way of Mexico in 2004 explained his motive:

> Back in China, even if you want to work hard there is no place for you to work, because there are so many people out of jobs and waiting for employment. If you work in a restaurant in the U.S., you can make $1,500 to $2,000 a month. Here in this restaurant, the owner provides food and lodging. I practically have no other expenses of my own. So I can save all my money each month and send it home. One year's work here in the U.S. can

earn as much money as I would for ten years in China. The main problem in China is that there is no social security. When there is no safety net, people are afraid of spending money. Once you are out of money, you are out of luck. The government is not going to save you when you are out of money. In the U.S., there is a safety net, and people can spend as much as they make and more. This is important, as people in China have no sense of security. No one knows what's going to happen when they get old. If I work here for a few years, and even if my application for political asylum is rejected, I can still return to China with enough money to last the rest of my life.

These same sentiments are common among law enforcement officials and snakeheads alike in China. Frequent official crackdowns in China and the tightening of immigration and border control procedures in the United States after the events of 9/11 have thus far failed to dampen the desire to emigrate. A ranking police official in Fuzhou once said:

> Illegal emigration by Chinese to other countries does not hurt China by any means. By the year 2010, there will be about 1.6 billion people in China. I believe our government is willing to allow as many people to leave the country as possible. Right now, almost all the border gates are wide open for people to leave—that is, if other countries will let you in.

One snakehead in Los Angeles recently predicted that the demand for illegal border crossing into the United States would never subside and said that snakeheads should not feel bad about what they do:

> I still have many people in my home town, Guantou (a township in Lianjiang County, north of Fuzhou), who want to come here. The line is endless. There will always be people who want to come to the U.S. I don't see an end to this. But the average age of the newcomers is getting younger. They are mostly in their twenties, early twenties. We came here in our thirties. So there is a big difference. I don't feel bad about being in this business. I am helping these people and making money in an honest way.

Combating Illegal Migration, Chinese Style

The Chinese government has greatly intensified its efforts to halt illegal transnational migration activities in recent years. It has, among other things, collaborated with foreign governments to improve information sharing and conducted joint investigations of criminal activities. China has repeatedly stated its official position against illegal migration and periodically launched campaigns to crack down on human smuggling. China's Border Patrol Armed Police (or *wujing*) likewise have stepped up inspection activities at checkpoints and seaports. In 2003, for instance, Chinese police arrested and imprisoned 774 snakeheads who organized human smuggling activities (Li 2004). The government's actions against snakeheads are becoming increasingly severe. The official Xinhua News Agency (2004) reported that a snakehead was sentenced to life in prison for smuggling fifty-one people across the border (mostly headed for Japan), and his personal possessions, including two cars and a laptop computer, were confiscated.

China's policy toward population migration is at odds with itself, reflecting a multitude of competing needs in its fast-growing, export-dependent economy. The nation suffers from a vast, impoverished interior, has a large unemployed and under-employed transient population, is surrounded by many poor countries, and is constantly subject to complaints from the international community (mostly industrialized countries). On one hand, in response to mounting diplomatic pressures, the proud, image-conscious central government in Beijing demands that regional governments take measures to curtail the flow of emigrants through unlawful channels. Illegal movement in and out of the country suggests a lack of control at the nation's borders, something that does not sit well with a communist government. On the other hand, within China itself there is a growing illegal immigrant population. This is unprecedented; China historically has been a supply country for population migration to all corners of the world. China's growing economy has softened many forms of government control that date from the Mao era, and this has greatly increased commerce and trade within the country as well as with other nations. Rapid economic progress has all but washed away the traditional residential registration system (or *hukou*); in turn, millions from the interior of China were uprooted and sent toward the coastal provinces. The vibrant private sector in this red-hot competitive market economy determines labor and wage relations in contemporary China. Unionization is unheard of, and the government doesn't always uphold protection of workers' rights and benefits. Such an economic environment invites exploitative labor practices in which employers have few restrictions to undercut wages and benefits. The cheapest labor does not always come from the interior of the country, however. In recent years, Chinese authorities have noticed an increase in immigration from neighboring countries, especially North Korea (McDonald 2004). Some 300,000 North Koreans reportedly live in China. In a recent crackdown on illegal border crossings, 16,300 illegal North Korean immigrants were repatriated (Agence France-Presse 2004). In a five-month operation between October 2003 and March 2004, law enforcement agencies arrested 5,286 stowaways and 444 snakeheads for illegal immigration, and another 16,000 illegal foreign immigrants were caught when police inspected hotels, rented houses, religious places, and public entertainment spots (Reuters 2004). To manage these transient populations, domestic and foreign, China is busy watching its own borders and building a previously nonexistent immigration and work-permit system, which few employers presently care to follow.

China has its hands full dealing with its own growing illegal immigration problems as it simultaneously attempts to address complaints from many industrialized countries in the West. Washington, D.C., for example, periodically expresses its unhappiness about the large number of illegal Chinese immigrants currently held in detention in the United States. Homeland Security Secretary Michael Chertoff claimed that China has been slow and reluctant to cooperate with the U.S. government in repatriating its citizens (Jordan 2006). China took back only 800 of its citizens in 2005. In the meantime, some 39,000 Chinese migrants have been denied immigration to the United States and are waiting to be repatriated (Jordan 2006).

Beijing periodically orders Fujian Province to undertake massive crackdowns on human smuggling activities, particularly after major events abroad that cost illegal immigrants their lives, such as the *Golden Venture* disaster on New York's Long Island in 1993, the Dover catastrophe in England in 2000, and the Morecambe Bay tragedy in 2004, when more than a dozen illegal Chinese immigrants drowned in swift tides while harvesting cockles (Tyler 2004).

Fujian's law enforcement agencies share anti-smuggling responsibilities. The Border Patrol Armed Police operate under the control of the provincial Public Security Bureau. County governments have anti-smuggling units within their police forces. Fujian Province has three specialized anti-smuggling units, one within the provincial Department of Public Security, one within the Fuzhou Municipal Police, and another within the Zhangzhou Municipal Police in southern Fujian Province. Law enforcement officials

interviewed in China for this study all claimed that their agencies are serious about stopping illegal emigration activities (or *tousidu*). In one interview
with officials from Lianjiang County, an officer claimed that his department
was, indeed, taking human smuggling seriously. Because of Lianjiang's notoriety as a sending community, the local police are often under strict orders
from the provincial government to identify, locate, and arrest snakeheads.
This officer described an ongoing crackdown at the time of the interview:

> We have established a list of about a hundred snakeheads and distributed the
> roster to all district police stations. Every station director is held responsible
> for catching all the identified snakeheads in their jurisdictions within a year.
> Anyone who can't catch them all or account for their whereabouts will be re-
> leased of his official duties, and be placed on the task force full time to catch
> the snakeheads. After a period of time, if any station director still can't catch
> or account for all the snakeheads within his jurisdiction, he will be stripped of
> his official title and re-assigned. The pressure is tremendous, and this is the
> number one duty now for all *tousidu*-disaster counties (i.e., counties where
> illegal migration is rampant). So far, more than half of those on our list have
> been caught. The county government has established the ten most wanted
> snakeheads and offered 50,000 yuan for the arrest of anyone on the list.
> The efforts made by the local government are sincere and real. Tremendous
> pressure has been placed on local police stations with jurisdictions over the
> snakeheads' listed residences. Although many of the blacklisted snakeheads
> are small-time players, our superiors believe whoever is involved in organiz-
> ing and coordinating smuggling activities should be arrested.

Increased law enforcement crackdowns have made a significant impact
on the smuggling business. Many subjects in this study reported a decrease
in or complete cessation of their smuggling activities because of intense law
enforcement scrutiny. Some reported decreased success rates in smuggling
operations and an increase in the number of people caught, a fact they offered as a main reason for the major increases in smuggling fees. One snakehead in Fuzhou, who specialized in acquiring foreign passports for photo
substitutions, explained why it was difficult to find snakeheads to talk about
the smuggling business:

> Police are arresting a lot of snakeheads these days. I can tell you there are
> still many people who want to go overseas and there are still a lot of snake-
> heads. But no one talks about this openly anymore. They don't know you so

why should anyone tell you anything about their business. Even if you are a potential client or another snakehead who wants to form a smuggling partnership, the normal procedure now is to refer you to some mutual friends. No snakeheads will talk to strangers anymore.

In contrast to the many complaints the subjects in this study made about their current smuggling business, a few recalled how easy it once was. A 36-year-old snakehead in Brooklyn, New York, reminisced:

> I began smuggling immigrants in 1989 from mainland China to Hong Kong, and then onward to the U.S. We mostly used freighters to smuggle them out. It was so easy back then for people to go to the U.S. It was actually more difficult to get them out of the mainland into Hong Kong. We were most afraid of being caught by the coast guard police in Hong Kong and we gave our passengers all forged identification cards. I did this for five years and never got caught, but now it is a very different game. Both the Chinese and the Hong Kong governments have tightened their security procedures. Hong Kong is no longer an easy transit point. That's why many people in this business either send their clients elsewhere or directly from mainland China to the U.S. The U.S. government is also cracking down hard. I believe this business is going to end pretty soon.

Some snakeheads interviewed in this study remained optimistic about the future of human smuggling, but many see the end coming. A snakehead in Fuzhou described recent changes in his business:

> In the past, you could make a lot of money without having to worry about being arrested. You could also move a large number of people out simultaneously by boats. Now it is a completely different game. Both the U.S. and Chinese authorities are becoming very aggressive in cracking down on human smuggling, and that means you must spend a lot of money to bribe the security checkpoint officials (or *maiguan*) and the costs have increased dramatically. Besides, our clients are more likely to be arrested now, and be deported and fined heavily. Before, the deportees were sent to Beijing from overseas where they were fined about one to two thousand yuan. Now, they are sent to Fuzhou directly and are fined between 30,000 to 50,000 yuan. We have to pay the fines for our own protection and that's why nine out of ten snakeheads are losing money nowadays. We are like gamblers.

Many more snakeheads have slowed down their smuggling activities or gone dormant as law enforcement activities accelerate, in both Fujian and the United States. One subject in Fuzhou, who had been running a successful photo-substitution operation and then switched to arranging business delegations, became nervous after a series of successful operations:

> It is becoming more and more difficult lately. Police are cracking down. I didn't handle any case last year because I felt tense about the whole situation. I only do a few cases every once in a while to earn a living, and I am not greedy. Some people like to take big risks and want to make tons of money, but they are also the ones who get arrested or go bankrupt if something goes wrong.

In its eagerness to present the nation as forward-looking and progressive, and in response to the growing wealth and demand for leisure activities among its populace, the Chinese government in recent years has standardized procedures to facilitate citizens' application for various travel documents. Traveling overseas has become routine, particularly to countries and regions known as major transit points in the transnational human smuggling business. For instance, travel agencies widely promote package tours to Thailand, Singapore, Malaysia, Hong Kong, and Macau to anyone who can afford the price. At the same time, China is also busy courting overseas Chinese to participate in its economic development. Many of these overseas Chinese were once clients in the human smuggling trade. Official recognition of their accomplishments lends legitimacy to these former illegal migrants of humble backgrounds who have risen to positions of high social status. One of the research associates in this study observed from his interactions with snakeheads in the field:

> The examples are easy to see. Those who left China years ago as illegal immigrants now have returned as U.S. citizens and are respected by the villagers and government officials alike. These people are just laborers or low-class small business owners in the U.S., but they get to meet with high-ranking regional and local government officials upon return from overseas, and even dine with them. The drastic changes in financial and social status of these village people serve as a powerful example for others to emulate.

Rags-to-riches stories are plentiful, and people in the villages seem impressed and at times awed at how one's fate and fortune can be transformed so completely and miraculously simply by moving to a faraway country. One snakehead in Fuzhou reflected on the nation's love-hate relationship with the illegal population migration:

> Chinese officials' reaction to human smuggling has always been like this: if you succeed, you are a king; if you fail, you are a bandit. If you can make it to America and make a lot of money, these government officials will know where to go when they need money for local construction projects. They will go to the families of these overseas Chinese for donations. If you are arrested and repatriated, then will they impose heavy fines on you, from 10,000 to 30,000 yuan. Like this relative of mine, who was arrested twice and fined both times. I said to him, "You have no choice but to keep on trying." On his third try, he made it to the U.S. And when the local government was working on the new Changle International Airport, they came to my relative's home and asked for a 1,000 yuan donation. I told the officials to go ask their Public Security colleagues for donations, because they had made some much money from those fines.

The Priority of Human Smuggling to Law Enforcement

Amidst many other pressing social problems, law enforcement agencies in China typically do not perceive illegal emigration as a threat to social order. Many even hold a fairly benign view of those involved in smuggling activities. One police representative in the Fujian provincial government, whose primary responsibility was conducting and coordinating anti–human smuggling activities, revealed that most of his colleagues shared this view:

> It (human smuggling) is not predatory, neither evading any government taxes nor harming anybody in this country. These people just want to find a good job and make some money. They are the same as those laborers from Sichuan Province who are working in Fuzhou. The only difference is the existence of a border. These people are not harming anybody, and they even pay their way to a foreign country. I have deep sympathy for them. These are hard working people who just want to make a better life than what they have here. However, the Ministry of Foreign Affairs in Beijing is under a lot of diplomatic pressure, and they pass the pressure to the Ministry of Public Security, which in turn passes it on to us.

This widely shared viewpoint undoubtedly influences where law enforcement agencies draw the line in their pursuit of smugglers and illegal migrants. Although few deliberately disobey orders from above or set free detained suspects, some officers have taken the liberty of letting through smuggling boats or have simply turned a blind eye. One businessman in Fuzhou said:

> I used to work for the police. Once, I discovered a smuggling boat headed for the U.S. but I let it go. Why? Because I don't think going to America is a crime. If you go to the U.S., you will have respect back home, and you can send money back and help your homeland in many ways. For example, many farmers often don't have money to buy fertilizers and they can always turn to people with relatives in the U.S. for a loan. Besides, if you are a laborer in America, people don't look down on you. Here, if you are just an ordinary worker, you will always be humiliated by government bureaucrats.

Transnational human smuggling can probably be controlled most effectively by authorities in migrant-sending countries. Unfortunately, the Chinese government these days faces far greater social and political challenges than this benign irritant that at worse can only cause occasional embarrassment. Consequently, it is no surprise to find that law enforcement agencies at all levels in Fujian have invested little in anti-smuggling efforts. According to one source, at the time of this study the provincial department of Public Security operated only a three-person unit, which was charged with overseeing and coordinating anti–human smuggling activities in the entire province. This unit had neither a budget nor administrative procedures in place by which to recognize and measure its effectiveness. An official from this unit complained that there were few reasons or incentives for them to work on anti-smuggling activities:

> For anyone who works at the provincial government level, there are absolutely no financial incentives. Worse, we are actually afraid of doing too much, because we have no staff and receive no rewards from the fines collected from the cases we have assisted in solving. The more cases we work on, the more we stretch ourselves. It is very hard work. For local and regional law enforcement agencies, there is a system of financial incentives. For each fine collected, a certain percentage is remitted to the agency responsible for solving the case. We don't have the resources and people to work on any large cases. And we don't want to work on large cases. It is already too much police work on something that really doesn't affect public safety in any way.

Other branches of the government seem to share the same view on human smuggling. Few government officials, at least in Fujian, have been able to point out specifically how human smuggling activities may harm the nation or the larger society, other than to create an image problem for the central government in Beijing. Lacking adequate public support and moral outrage, government officials often find it hard to justify the energy and resources invested in combating this problem. On the contrary, they have been quick to list the specific benefits China stands to receive from its exported labor force. One police official in Fuzhou shared his view on this issue:

> This benign view towards illegal emigration is why human smuggling has never been a priority for law enforcement agencies in China. Local officials in Fuzhou will do something only if there is pressure from the central government in Beijing, and China will do something only if there is pressure from the international community. Crackdowns on human smuggling activities are like parents spanking their children in public. The purpose is simply to show others that they are doing something to their wayward children. They never really intend to hurt their kids. Sometimes we do take harsh measures against snakeheads when there is a major incident, like when we discovered more than one hundred migrants who were suffocated to death underneath the deck of a fishing boat. If we take actions, ordinary folks are going to say, "Look, the communists nowadays are so incompetent that they are not even doing anything after this kind of disaster." Normally, we just overlook the problem of illegal outflow of people, because it is beneficial to our country, and to the United States.

Townships with large numbers of registered residents living abroad usually attract close scrutiny from higher levels of governments. Branches of the local village government are also under pressure to crack down on "human smuggling activities," which, to most law enforcement officials and civilians, refers to maritime smuggling only. People who use "legitimate" channels to leave the country are generally viewed with no disdain whatsoever. One local township government leader in Lianjiang County said:

> Leaving the country by boats on the open seas is illegal. We do not allow anyone to engage in this type of smuggling activities. It is also dangerous. But some are still doing it. If a total of five people are caught doing maritime smuggling activities, our village government will not be eligible for awards of any sorts from the county government. We will also be denied of

other government benefits. When we talk about combating human smuggling activities, we are talking about these maritime operations. Fraudulent marriages, tourist visas, or business visas (i.e., B1 or B2) involving legitimate documents are not viewed the same as illegal emigration (or *tousidu*). Both police officers and civilians share this understanding.

Such selective interpretations of the effects of illegal emigration appear to be widely shared by officials in law enforcement and other government agencies in Fuzhou and elsewhere in China, and are reflected in their pursuit of smuggling facilitators. One law enforcement official said:

> Fake marriages are not illegal human smuggling. It is impossible to prove anyone's intention in such cases. As long as you have real paperwork, you are not doing *tousidu*. Officially, these cases are not pursued by law enforcement agencies in China. They are not discussed in the same breath as maritime operations. They are legal. The same is true of all other legal exits with proper visas to third countries.

The decline of boat-based smuggling activities has improved the overall perception of the smuggling business. Because of many interceptions by the United States on the high seas, pilots of smuggling boats have to seek less desirable ports in Latin America and then transport the passengers across arduous routes overland. Not many would-be immigrants are willing to travel on crowded boats and endure weeks of hardship on the high seas. More and more snakeheads are exploiting "legitimate" channels to move their clients to transit countries first before reaching their destination countries. One law enforcement official in Fuzhou said:

> Most snakeheads have improved their smuggling methods, abandoning the old primitive maritime operations in the old days in favor of more "civilized" measures such as using the air-route. They are paying more attention to the safety and comfort of the migrants.

Going After the Big Fish

For years, U.S. anti-smuggling policies and strategies have focused on tracking down and arresting "big" snakeheads. However, where these people actually live is the subject of some speculation. Although subjects in this study reported that "big" snakeheads usually would not deal with clients directly, preferring instead to coordinate from behind the scenes, they also believed that these big players lived away from the action, perhaps on the other side of the Pacific Ocean. The majority of the subjects in this study and law enforcement officials in China said that most big snakeheads were overseas Chinese who would control smuggling operations remotely from outside the country. One ranking police officer in Lianjiang County Police Department said:

> I don't think big snakeheads get involved in operational details. They are mostly in the U.S. and control smuggling operations from there. At most, they might be in Taiwan or Thailand. Here in Fujian, snakeheads here are mostly low-level operatives who have little knowledge of an entire operation.

A ranking police official working directly in the anti-smuggling unit under the provincial Public Security Bureau concurred with this observation. He said all the police could catch were little snakeheads working for their bosses overseas. Most of the arrests made in and around the sending communities were recruiters or low-level organizers, who often would rather be smuggled out themselves. He said:

> In the past year and half, we caught no snakeheads, but snake tails. They were low-level operatives. There was only one big snakehead, a Fuzhou native who was living in Thailand. He arranged a tour group of thirty people and managed to get their passports in Yunnan Province. He could have pulled it off. However, he became greedy and shortchanged the travel agency that helped him get the passports. Someone tipped off the police and an investigation ensued. He was arrested and received seven years in prison. We have caught some snakeheads at home, not many, and all small-time operatives. We can't catch big ones. We don't have any informants and no one is willing to tell us anything. If no one tells us anything, we don't know where to look for snakeheads.

It seems logical to assume that most big snakeheads must be either U.S. citizens or green card holders because they need to travel freely between the United States and China. Consequently, their primary residence is likely to be outside China. Of the fifty-two subjects we interviewed in the United States, 81 percent were either U.S. citizens or permanent residents. One subject said, "Most snakeheads I know are either U.S. citizens or green card holders. If there is a problem with their operations, they immediately leave China. There is no way that Chinese authorities can catch these people."

Even so, being a U.S. citizen or green card holder does not preclude a snakehead from spending most of his or her time in China, where most smuggling activities are planned and initiated. U.S. anti-smuggling officials repeatedly claimed that big snakeheads usually resided in China because of the familiar cultural environment, the client base, and the flexible environment for financial transactions. Since most smuggling recruitment and operations take place first in China, big snakeheads are also likely found in China.

These contradictory claims concerning the whereabouts of snakeheads only illustrate the complexity and clandestine nature of this underground enterprise. Not only are the whereabouts of big snakeheads difficult to determine, but the very definition of "big snakehead" is problematic. U.S. law enforcement agencies have developed a list of so-called big snakeheads, as have their Chinese counterparts. However, rarely have the two sides reconciled the lists or agreed on who should be included. To further complicate the matter, the big names on an official "wanted" list do not necessarily reflect the prevailing views of the smuggling community. Sister Ping was a case in point. Despite the fact that U.S. authorities for years considered her the "mother of all snakeheads" (Barnes, 2000, 48), several subjects in this study claimed that she was probably more successful in her underground banking business than in smuggling illegal migrants. These snakeheads, who were active at the time of this study, disputed Sister Ping's reputation as a big snakehead and questioned her actual capability. One snakehead in Fuzhou said:

> Sister Ping got in the smuggling business early when few others were aware of it. But her reputation was inflated far beyond her actual capability. She was successful for a while in the early 1990s, but her days are gone. I know people in Fuzhou who are far more successful than Sister Ping. She is probably better known for her underground banking business than human smuggling.

It may be futile to determine who qualifies as a big or small snakehead. Not all who have attracted the attention of authorities are big players in the business. In general, snakeheads who have developed connections in various governments and stable contacts in transit countries are likely to engage in continuous operations, and can thus be viewed as big snakeheads. Other smugglers, such as those who live in or near the sending communities, are probably low-level operatives because of their limited ability to travel, form extensive alliances, and develop smuggling routes. One police official in Lianjiang explained:

> The snakeheads on our pursuit list are provided by police agencies elsewhere that have caught illegal migrants trying to leave China. From these detainees' testimonies, the names of those who helped them are provided to the Lianjiang County Police. However, most snakeheads we have arrested are local residents who were only recruiters or some front-end players. Those working behind the scenes at remote locations or in transit countries are out of our reach.

A local government official from a township in Lianjiang County concurred with this observation:

> Intelligence on snakeheads is typically provided by those who are caught while being smuggled, either at border crossings or some transit countries. The local county government officials receive a list of people who have been repatriated. Interrogations will be conducted by government officials to obtain the names of the snakeheads who helped the villagers to leave the country. These names obtained during the interrogations will then be forwarded to the concerned local police branches.

If catching snakeheads is difficult, successfully prosecuting any of them is even more challenging. One law enforcement official in Lianjiang County elaborated:

> Even when you catch a few snakeheads, it is hard to prosecute them. The old doctrine of "confession leads to leniency, while denial brings harsh punishment" no longer works anymore. We are talking human rights these days and must follow proper procedures to convict a criminal. The new mantra among criminal suspects goes like this: "Confession leads to a sentence long enough for the floor of the jail to rot through. Denial lets you go home in time to celebrate the New Year." Without confessions, we have little to go on about collecting the evidence and the case becomes dead-ended. Therefore, even if snakeheads are caught, few can link them to any smuggling organization. We will be lucky just to get enough evidence to charge the arrested snakeheads individually.

Those who are caught attempting to leave China illegally or in transit countries are typically repatriated back to the townships of their registered residences. They are usually fined and occasionally face short-term sentences in jail. One law enforcement agency official in Lianjiang County explained the process:

> After repatriation, illegal migrants are kept in the Border Patrol's "education camp" for about two weeks. After that, they will be released once they pay 20,000 yuan in fines. Otherwise, they will be moved to a labor camp (or *laojiao*) and detained from one to three years.

Although there are some regional variations in how repatriated migrants and their snakehead handlers are penalized, law enforcement agencies in Fujian Province have been under tremendous pressure from Beijing to deal harshly with arrested snakeheads. As the ranking police official in Fujian's provincial Public Security Bureau quoted earlier explained:

> The provincial government leaders and people from the central government in Beijing have held many meetings. Many regional ordinances have also been passed to increase the penalty for smugglees as well as smugglers. Not long ago, we had a training workshop on anti-smuggling. In Fuzhou, if you are caught trying to emigrate illegally, you will be fined 10,000 yuan plus one year in prison for the first time. For the second time, you can be imprisoned for two years. Third time, three years in prison. In the past, only financial penalties were imposed on those who were caught. Now, prison terms have been added.

Official Corruption: A Major Obstacle to Anti-Smuggling Efforts

A frequent topic of all conversations with the snakehead subjects in this study was official corruption. The Chinese term for it, *maiguan*, has become so common that even ordinary people in Fujian who are not involved in the business know what it means. Human smuggling would not be possible without involvement, either direct or tacit, of government officials. One research contact in Fuzhou, who claimed to be well connected with snakeheads as well as law enforcement officials, made it clear:

> Just think about it. How is it possible that so many people have been smuggled out of China by boat? Wouldn't you find it odd that our coastline is so loosely guarded that thousands upon thousands could easily pass through? Of course, corruption is the key. Only the small snakeheads get caught. The real big ones are immune to most law enforcement efforts. They will never

get caught. Just imagine, if you work for the police and have taken a few hundred thousands yuan from me, wouldn't you make a phone call to me if I were close to danger?

Even law enforcement agency representatives are aware of the widespread corruption at checkpoints in coastal or border provinces. One police representative in Fuzhou said:

I know official corruption exists and most people know it is there. It is an open secret, but no one knows who gets what and where. No one will tell you. At an anti-smuggling training workshop not long ago, the instructor openly ridiculed those who were escorting or allowing illegal migrants through checkpoints for a fee. He quoted a list of fees for various services, and 30,000 yuan per person was the bottom line.

He insisted that at his level (the provincial government office) there was no way for anyone to profit from anti-smuggling operations. He continued:

We don't see any money at our level. All fines are paid at a designated bank (Bank of Agriculture) into a government account, and the offenders bring back a receipt. But local police forces have much more latitude in handling money. There are also formal procedures to reward local police agencies with a portion of the fines they collect from arrested illegal emigrants.

Chinese authorities have indeed attempted to address the problem of official corruption at border checkpoints, have streamlined border patrol functions, and have increased central government oversight in recent years. In the past, for instance, repatriated emigrants and their snakeheads were handed directly to their respective local authorities. This often led to quick release or lenient punishment. Now the Border Patrol Armed Police keep all arrested smugglers and repatriated smugglees jailed before sentencing. Only when a case has been formally charged do the Armed Police transfer the suspect to court. Despite the fact that many snakeheads and would-be smugglees claim that international airports along China's coast are full of corrupt officials, the significant increase in prices for bribery (or *maiguan*) in recent years is a clear sign of growing difficulties. Now all ports have some form of mandatory rotation of personnel, and document inspectors are periodically reassigned to other functions or posts. Places such as Guangdong Province, once a prime location for exiting China, are now used less often because of the frequent rotation of checkpoint inspectors.

Some snakeheads, however, disagree that corruption is as common or serious as it has been alleged to be. Instead, they subscribe to a more benign view of how smugglers seek assistance at crossing points. One snakehead in Fuzhou explained:

> I have known enough of these people (border checkpoint officials) to tell you that they know better than to take bribes. Few of us will openly ask them to violate the law. I don't think bribing one's way through a security checkpoint or buying a passport is a common occurrence. But I do know government officials also have friends and these friends may buy them expensive meals and treat them with lavish perks that only wealthy business people can afford, for instance, eating at an exclusive restaurant, paying for their sauna and massage (including prostitutes). In return, when these wealthy friends have relatives (or friends) who are leaving the country, their border checkpoint contacts will be notified to provide special treatment—escorting them through or notifying inspectors on duty that their friends are coming through so that these travelers will be expedited through inspection.

Other law enforcement officials seem to concur that openly assisting snakeheads is rare, but skirting the law or going easy on friends does happen from time to time. One senior police instructor from the Fujian Provincial Police Academy also contested the notion that corruption was rampant at exit checkpoints:

> I just find it hard to believe that snakeheads can bribe their way through so many checkpoints at airports or border checkpoints, because most inspectors watch each other and often work in pairs. It will be hard to get away with covert activities for long, especially when so many people are supposedly involved in a smuggling scheme. How can one be sure that when an internal investigation takes place, other accomplices in the scheme won't sell out first?

Challenges for U.S. Policy Makers

America has been stuck in the illegal immigration quagmire for decades. The 1986 Immigration Reform and Control Act (IRCA), enacted under the Reagan administration, which attempted to solve the illegal immigration problem once and for all, has only made the situation worse. None of IRCA's intended goals have been realized. Instead, twenty years later the growth of the illegal population has practically exploded, and employers continue to hire illegal immigrants with impunity. A recent study by the Pew Hispanic Center estimated the number of illegal immigrants in the United States to be close to 12 million in March 2006; the number continues to grow at a steady pace, with no sign of relief in sight (Passel 2006). Growth has averaged more than 500,000 per year since 2000, with more than one-third having arrived five or less years previously (Cearley 2004; Passel 2006).

Fixing the nation's borders and immigration system is no easy task. Many U.S. policy makers have tinkered with the system for decades, only to find that the problem of illegal immigration not only persists but has actually grown. The events of 9/11, the War on Terror, and the swelling population of undocumented immigrants have besieged legislators and policy makers on Capitol Hill with regard to the nation's immigration and border control problems. No one knows exactly how many foreign nationals enter the United States illegally, or arrive legally and then overstay their visas. The bulk of the illegal population in the United States consists of Mexican nationals. However, millions of foreign nationals enter the country under various visas each year, and immigration authorities have little idea of when they leave, and how many of them actually leave before their visas expire.

The nation's policies towards illegal immigration, which have sustained the smuggling enterprise, have for decades reflected U.S. ambivalence on the subject. In August 2004, rather than take a smuggler's speedboat across the Florida Straits, a Cuban woman shipped herself in a wooden crate on a DHL cargo plane that flew from the Bahamas and landed at Miami International Airport (Diaz 2004). Though she was Cuban, she had landed on U.S. soil, and was allowed to stay. Had she been caught on a raft floating toward the U.S. coast, she would have been repatriated. The so-called "wet-foot, dry-foot" policy towards Cubans allows those who touch U.S. soil to stay, while sending home those intercepted at sea. Other foreign nationals have not been afforded such a privilege. In March 2004, for example, a Dominican stowaway was sent home after he flew to Miami hidden in the wheel well of an American Airlines jet (Ovalle 2004).

Although those may be uncommon ways of illegal entry into the United States, hundreds of thousands of foreign nationals exploit its porous ports and borders. A study in central Mexico found that one-third of those who attempted illegal entry into the United States were never detected, and that more than 80 percent of illegal migrants entered the United States with the help of smugglers (Cornelius 2005a). The majority of illegal immigrants in the United States entered through clandestine channels, rather than over-staying their visas. According to one U.S. government estimate, 59 percent of the illegal immigrants in the country were clandestine entrants; in 2004, the General Accounting Office put the figure at 73 percent (Cornelius 2005b). These figures point to the obvious fact that human smugglers are very much an integral part of illegal immigration.

For decades the United States has struggled to decide how best to con-trol the unregulated influx of illegal immigrants across its borders. Debates in Congress and among the public alike flare over how the nation should deal with the illegal immigrant population. Suggestions range from arrest-ing and deporting them, to the less harsh withholding of social services, to allowing them temporary work permits, to making them legal residents. These debates took on an increased urgency after 9/11. U.S. immigration and border patrol agencies have been chastised and ridiculed for many years for failure to protect the nation's borders and for their inability to screen out undesirable elements from the masses of foreign visitors. Conservative crit-ics and policy makers call for drastic measures to shore up immigration and border control functions, while special interest groups, particularly those that represent ethnic minorities, civil rights groups, and even high-tech in-dustries, caution against racial profiling and offer competing as well as con-flicting proposals.

Increased concern over the lack of control of the U.S.'s borders has brought about legislation and administrative measures to tighten immigra-tion, both legal and illegal. The Bush administration asked for $64 million to upgrade technology to assist with border protection and $10 million to develop and deploy unmanned aerial vehicles to patrol the borders (Gam-boa 2004). In a rare primetime broadcast on May 15, 2006, President Bush announced his plan to send 6,000 National Guard troops to bolster patrols along the U.S.-Mexican border, citing urgent national security requirements and America's basic sovereign right.   The social and legal ramifica-tions will be hard to ignore if the influx of illegal immigrants from such a vast country as China were to continue unchecked, but it is unlikely that the U.S. government can successfully block illegal entries without creating significant economic and political side effects. Tens of millions of non–U.S. citizens enter the country each year. To successfully single out and detain those who intend to overstay their visas or cross the border illegally would require a massive effort.

Few authorities in China believe the recent changes along the U.S. borders will have any long-term impact on illegal immigration. The United States remains a strong magnet for migrants from around the world. Scholars have written many books about the problem of illegal immigration and illegal aliens as a major threat to national security and a heavy burden to the U.S. welfare system (see Brimelow 1995; Malkin 2002; Graham 2004). However, only a handful of them have examined the relationship between the underground U.S. economy and the extent to which the mainstream American society has come to rely on illegal immigrants to maintain their lifestyles (see Massey et al. 2002).

Many Chinese law enforcement officials blame U.S. immigration policies and border control practices for human smuggling. As long as the American ethos supports the principles of a competitive market economy, supply will follow demand. Many Americans have become accustomed to a lifestyle made possible by illegal immigrants, who provide an incredibly wide range of services, from baby sitting and landscaping to construction and hospitality services. Chinese human smugglers are only one small group of entrepreneurs who have cashed in on America's appetite for cheap goods and services. When Chinese snakeheads are added to the long list of human smugglers of other nationalities, it is not hard to see the challenges that U.S. policy makers face and the consequences they must be prepared to accept. One police official in Fuzhou said:

> The outflow of Chinese migrants is very much affected by the immigration policies of various receiving countries. Here are some of the key factors that affect the flow of smuggling activities: U.S. political asylum practices, immigration officials' attitudes toward smuggled Chinese, the number of deportations, and changes in new immigration laws. The number of snakeheads being arrested in China is definitely not going to affect the smuggling trade. This problem will continue to exist. It is going to get worse. This is probably just the beginning. There are so many people here who are unemployed. They have no choice but to try their luck somewhere else, and that means going abroad.

COMBATING ILLEGAL CHINESE IMMIGRATION:
POLICY IMPLICATIONS

For the most part, U.S. efforts to combat illegal immigration by Chinese nationals have been ineffective. This is true, partly attributable to insufficient guidance from empirical research, and somewhat attributable to a deeply rooted institutional inability to fight ambiguous enemies. Because most U.S. law enforcement strategies are built on the outdated assumption that formal crime syndicates such as the triads are behind smuggling operations, they are ill-suited to dealing with the actual situation, in which masses of entrepreneurs form temporary alliances and engage in criminal activities only sporadically.

The challenge is to recognize that illegal migration is no unitary act but consists of different configurations in selecting destinations and choosing travel routes and types of transportation (Pieke 1999, 19). Concerns about illegal Chinese migration have been on the rise in different parts of the world, particularly in Europe, where many countries (such as England, Italy, Hungary, France, and Germany) have either experienced a rapid increase in the number of Chinese immigrants, or live in fear of massive waves of Chinese immigrants (Pieke 1999). The direct overland link between Europe and China through Russia makes this route easier and more attractive than crossing the vast waters between the United States and China.

Many recommendations have been made about what to do with the nation's broken immigration system, from erecting fences and jailing repeated border crossers (Brimelow 1995) to militarizing the borders altogether and overhauling the asylum system (Malkin 2002). However, decades of debate in the public and political arenas have produced few legislative solutions, let alone effective ones. For decades, for example, illegal immigrants from around the world have exploited the U.S. asylum system. Chin (1999) found in his extensive field work in New York that the large majority of Chinese asylum claims were fraudulent. However, the ideology-driven U.S. asylum system does not seem capable of judging the veracity of numerous applicants who have filed petitions on such grounds as the inhumanity of China's one-child policy (e.g., with forced abortions or employment discrimination for having more than one child) and religious persecution (e.g., for practicing Falun Gong, a religious sect combining principles of Buddhism and Taoism that is considered subversive by the communist government). More recently, some Chinese asylum seekers have claimed that they were persecuted by the Chinese government for harboring North Korean migrants who escaped their country's brutal Stalinist regime.[1] To change the asylum system means U.S. policy makers must explain to their constituents the contradictions in their publicly stated convictions. As Brimelow (1995, 238) lamented, the most powerful and wealthy nation in the world seems incapable of defending its own borders and establishing a consistent national identity.

Massey et al. (2002) likened America's current efforts to curtail illegal immigration to trying to fix complex machinery by adding new levers and springs here and there simply because they may "look good." These solutions over the years have produced a host of unintended consequences. For instance, in 1994 the U.S. Department of Justice launched Operation Gatekeeper to control rampant illegal border crossings between San Diego, California, and Tijuana, Mexico (U.S. INS 1998). However, Operation Gatekeeper's significant increase in the number of Border Patrol agents, construction of fences, and introduction of high-tech ground sensors and infrared scopes only pushed illegal migrants away from busy suburban routes into more desolate canyons farther east. As a result, illegal immigrants died by the hundreds while attempting to cross this harsh terrain. Civil rights organizations such as the American Civil Liberties Union and the California Rural Legal Assistance Foundation charged that the U.S. government knowingly and deliberately diverted illegal border crossers into places of mortal danger that led to the deaths of hundreds seeking to enter the United States to find jobs or to reunite with their families (California Rural Legal Assistance Foundation 1999). Amnesty International also condemned Operation Gatekeeper's practices, citing many incidents of human rights violations (Amnesty International 1998).

While pundits, politicians, and community activists engage in a never-ending discourse on how to fix the nation's immigration system, law enforcement agencies must continue their battles in the trenches. Armed with a knowledge of the inner workings of human smuggling groups and their operational characteristics, policy makers perhaps can devise new strategies or improve the existing ones. The following are a few possibly effective strategies:

- *Stop searching for the big fish.* The traditional law enforcement strategy of looking for "godfathers" in human smuggling organizations should be abandoned. Much of law enforcement's anti–human smuggling energy has been spent on tracking down and arresting the "mother of all smugglers," Sister Ping, and other so-called big snakeheads, when in reality most smuggling groups consist mainly of loosely affiliated, enterprising agents. Because mounting empirical evidence suggests that non-traditional criminals are responsible for transporting the majority of Chinese nationals, law enforcement resources should be redirected to deal with these small groups of entrepreneurs. The various market and socio-legal constraints dictate that not only are there few big snakeheads, but few last in this business.

• *Focus on disrupting smuggling networks.* A hierarchically structured criminal organization can be best dealt with by removing its leadership (i.e., going after the big fish). Small entrepreneurial groups such as human smuggling organizations, however, are most sensitive to the disruption of resources. The removal of links along a transportation route will severely disrupt or even terminate an operation. This book has devoted much space to explaining how human smuggling networks operate and how snakeheads deal with one another. The series of one-on-one relationships between and among members of a smuggling organization are a product of operational requisites designed to minimize risk and manage market uncertainties. By employing various defensive measures to mitigate the risks inherent in this business, snakeheads also expose their Achilles heel—that to complete an entire operation, all links in the network must succeed in fulfilling their individual functions. If law enforcement agencies fully understand and appreciate the intricacies and vulnerability of these dyadic relationships, a great deal of success can be achieved simply by removing any one individual smuggler in the chain. Once a snakehead is arrested, all smuggling operations going through this person will either fall apart or be put on hold for a protracted period while other partners, now disjointed, spend time and resources to reconnect the chain.

• *Improve international collaboration.* A logical extension of the focus on disrupting smuggling chains is to increase international cooperation between governments. Effective anti-smuggling strategy requires international collaboration not only between sending and receiving countries, but also with transit countries. Liaison offices for intelligence sharing and joint operations can prove much more effective than the efforts of any one nation fighting on its own. An extensive international network of drug enforcement agencies has already been established to foster global anti-drug collaborations. The U.S. Drug Enforcement Agency has a liaison office in China, and the two countries routinely collaborate in transnational drug trafficking investigations. There is no reason that similar structures cannot be established to monitor and manage human smuggling and trafficking activities, particularly in light of the potential of smuggling networks to be used by terrorist organizations wanting to move their members to target nations.

- *Monitor and control legitimate businesses.* Any comprehensive anti-smuggling strategy planning cannot ignore the fact that human smugglers exploit the same channels that ordinary visitors and business people use to arrive in the United States. The auxiliary services that enable the regular and legitimate movement of foreign nationals in and out of the country are also vital to the success of smuggling operations. They are no less important to smugglers than the services provided by corrupt officials in China. These services—provided by lawyers, paralegals, travel agencies, temporary employment agencies, and other business entities—are used by snakeheads to arrange legal business documents, establish business entities, and provide coverage for their smuggling activities. It is only prudent to monitor these service providers to prevent and minimize their possible collusions.

- *Be wary of traditional triad societies.* This study did not find sufficient evidence to suggest the systematic involvement of traditional Chinese organized crime groups in transnational human smuggling operations. Nor did I find sufficient evidence to prove that triad-type organizations are *not* involved in human smuggling. The real danger for law enforcement is the possibility that independent task forces of entrepreneurs may join hands with the more stable criminal organizations. There are no logistic obstacles that prevent the development of a coalition between triad societies and Chinese smuggling groups. Perhaps it is only a matter of time before the two find each other in the underworld marketplace. It would be prudent for law enforcement agencies to monitor members of either criminal group engaging in continued business collaborations.

Future Research on Illegal Chinese Human Smuggling

Findings from empirical research can provide fresh insights that may stimulate discussion about legislative reform and the enforcement of immigration laws. The need to study Chinese human smuggling organizations goes beyond mere intellectual curiosity. It bears direct implications for U.S. immigration policy at all levels. Illegal immigration in any organized fashion disrupts and interferes with legal and regular population movement and undermines the integrity of a nation's immigration system. Undocumented immigrants increasingly exert pressure on social services in local communities, from health care to schools. Furthermore, illegal immigrants already in the country are most likely to seek methods, legal or not, to become legal residents, and doing so in turn affects the flow of legal immigration.

As Massey (1999) pointed out, wage differentials, market failures, and segmentation of labor markets are likely to accelerate with the globalization of commerce. With the recent collapse of many totalitarian regimes, the proliferation of telecommunication devices and improvements in transportation have greatly reduced the barriers and distance between countries, thus making the logistics of coordinating and moving people around the world easier than ever.

Future studies need to monitor and examine methods that human smugglers currently use to transport their clients into the United States. Countermeasures and policies can then be formulated. Researchers need to provide a detailed description of the interrelationships among the physical, economic, and socio-psychological dimensions of illegal Chinese immigration. Knowledge of these dimensions can help policy makers develop appropriate social service programs such as medical care, mental health care, housing, education, and crime prevention. The civil penalty and employer sanction provisions of the Immigration Reform and Control Act must also be re-examined. Research into the origins and processes of smuggling operations, as well as the common destinations of undocumented Chinese, should shed light on such issues as the employment of illegals, the capacity of immigration agencies to control borders, and the informal economies of settlement communities. The problem of human smuggling has long strained the resources of the U.S. immigration and welfare systems. Short of militarizing the borders, human smuggling is likely to continue unabated, until and unless strong disincentives and opportunity-blocking measures are enacted equally and simultaneously.

Epilogue

Over the years, I have often wondered why anyone would want to spend tens of thousands of dollars, a huge fortune by any Chinese standard, just for the privilege of working twelve hours a day in a noisy and dust-filled garment factory or the smoke-darkened, greasy kitchen of a Chinese restaurant, while enduring years of homesickness in almost total social isolation. During my many trips to China in recent years, I saw few men and women between the age of eighteen and forty-five (people of prime working age) in the streets of the sending communities around Fuzhou. Elderly people were caring for young children whose parents were probably slaving away on the Lower East Side of Manhattan or in some Chinese buffet in the middle of America. China's booming economy seemed to have skipped these villages. There were no visible manufacturing businesses in these villages, which were still surrounded by rice paddies and vegetable fields. I heard again and again that the people tending the fields were not locals, but peasants from other provinces or the mountainous counties in the north where land was scarce and few jobs were available. One local government leader once described the severe gaps in the village demographic composition with most able-bodied men having gone abroad:

> The emigration started in 1978 in my village, and reached the peak between 1992 and 1994, which was when the term "$18,000 sisters-in-law" (or *wanbasao*)[1] was coined to describe the large number of married women who were left behind by their husbands. We now have three surpluses and one shortage in our population—women, children, and senior citizens far outnumber men of working ages. Our fields are tended by transient laborers from the interior counties or other provinces. The entire village is mostly supported by money from abroad. Our children are learning English and preparing themselves to go to America.

People in these sending communities are equally gripped by the craze to get rich like the rest of China, except that their dreams and ambitions are pinned on their migration to the United States or other Western countries. In interview after interview, I have learned that the ostensible prosperity in these communities has been sustained mainly by remittances from abroad. Almost every other household in these townships seems to be receiving money from abroad. More than a decade ago in Changle County alone, as much as $100 million was sent home annually from abroad (Tempest 1995). Most residents in Lianjiang and Changle have either leased their land to others or hired farmhands from the interior of Fujian or other, poorer provinces. There simply is not enough money to provide a living commensurate with the rising local standard. Local people would rather play mahjong and drink tea all day long than tend the fields. These villages have become entirely dependent—economically, socially, and psychologically—on their family members overseas.

Newly constructed houses, standing four or five stories tall with metal-framed windows and ornate exterior decorations, showcasing what could become one's home if the family were in America, line the roads leading from the Changle International Airport to Fuzhou, contrasting sharply with the remaining shabby-looking dwellings built with red-clay bricks and tiles. Only overseas Chinese (or *huaqiao*) can afford such dream houses in these rural townships. With no viable business ventures or public pension systems to count on, parents rely on their sons to earn enough to build them a house and to support them during their remaining years. Their sons, in turn, will expect their own children to do the same. This is more than their way of building an insurance policy. This is a cultural tradition that has been passed on from one generation to the next. It is important for residents of these local townships to have overseas family members, or a means to go overseas themselves. Migration is a sign of and an avenue for success and upward social mobility (Liu 1997; Li 1999). Owning a stand-alone, multi-story building is the most powerful statement one can make about one's wealth and social standing in Fujian or elsewhere in China. Earning money in the United States has come to symbolize one's metamorphosis from a low-class peasant into a member of the upper crust. To be able to get there is to turn dreams into reality, and to stay behind is a sign of laziness and lack of ambition.

It has become apparent that the flow of emigration, legal or illegal, has been directed and sustained by this collective desire and tradition. For generations, young males have followed in their parents' footsteps to foreign lands, not only to find better jobs, but also to carry on a tradition of migration (Thuno 1999). Their home town provides a source of ambition as well as reminding them of their familial obligations. Working long hours and earning less than minimum wage thus become acceptable because these illegal immigrants realize that whatever they earn in America can produce financial security and social status back home. Emigration to them "is couched as much in the language of self-sacrifice for the family's survival and prosperity as in terms of personal ambition, adventurism, and success" (Pieke et al. 2004: 195). To these villagers, if following the tradition and fulfilling their familial obligations require them to skirt the law and thumb their nose at the Chinese and U.S. governments, so be it.

Appendix A: Research Sites

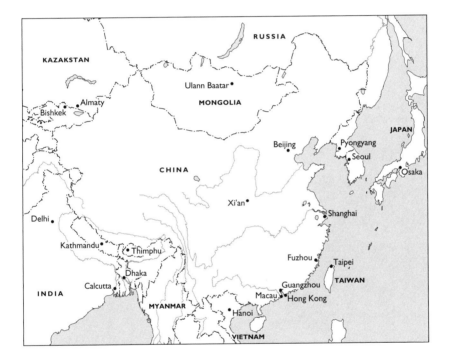

Map of China

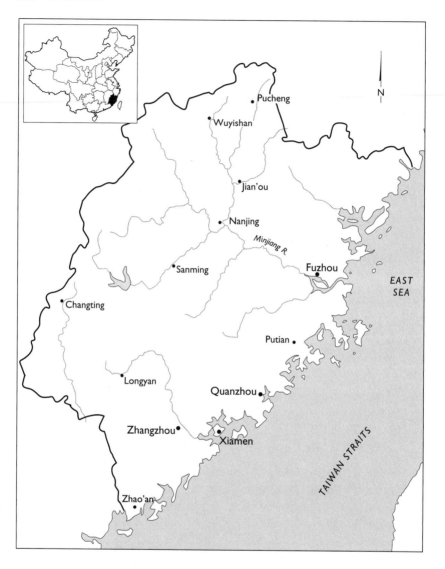

Map of Fujian Province

Appendix B: Research Method

OVERVIEW

This book is based mainly on a study funded by a grant from the National Institute of Justice, U.S. Department of Justice. Data collection from this study took place from 1999 through 2001, using a variety of collection strategies: face-to-face interviews, field observations, and the gathering of relevant documents and press reports. The research team consisted of Ko-lin Chin of Rutgers University and me, and a team of researchers in Fuzhou, China, where the vast majority of Chinese illegal immigrants originate. Researchers from both countries independently conducted in-depth interviews and field observations. Both sides used the same set of core questions in their interviews. U.S.-based interviewers familiar with local Chinese communities assisted with the interviewing. Further details on the methodologies used in this study are given below.

We interviewed a total of 129 individuals (so-called "snakeheads") in the United States and China. These were people directly involved in recruiting, organizing, and transporting Chinese nationals illegally into the United States. We conducted additional interviews with key informants who were familiar with the smuggling business or whose close friends or relatives were snakeheads, and with law enforcement officials in anti-smuggling details both in China and the United States.

SITE SELECTION

Our research took place in three primary locations: New York City, Los Angeles, and Fuzhou. New York was included because many undocumented

Fujianese eventually settled in that city's Chinatown (U.S. Senate 1992; Myers 1994). It is the most common destination for illegal immigrants from Fujian Province. The community is a well-established social and commercial center for newly arrived Chinese immigrants (Kwong 1987). It is situated on the lower east side of Manhattan in an area known as Little Italy, surrounded by City Hall and the East River.

Los Angeles is another major port of entry and gathering point for illegal Chinese immigrants (Chin 1999). It has become a major final destination, especially for non-Fujianese immigrants. Chinese communities in Los Angeles are located about fifteen miles east of downtown Los Angeles along the I-10 freeway corridor that extends twenty miles and spreads across such cities as Monterey Park, Alhambra, West Covina, Roland Heights, and Diamond Bar.

For smuggled Chinese who fly to the United States, the Los Angeles International Airport is a popular entry point. Illegal Chinese who are smuggled across the Mexico-U.S. border usually arrive in Los Angeles before they are transported to New York or other parts of the country. Those who come by sea usually arrive in Los Angeles. Its many container yards are often used for unloading illegal human cargo.

Fuzhou, with a population of more than 5.4 million, is located in the northern coastal area of Fujian Province, which directly faces Taiwan across the Taiwan Strait. The city consists of five districts and eight counties. The communities sending the most illegal immigrants are the villages of Mawei, Changle, Tingjiang, Lianjiang, and Fuqing, all along the coast within a forty-mile radius of Fuzhou. U.S. law enforcement agencies have estimated that up to 90 percent of all illegal Chinese immigrants in America start from this region (Hood 1994).

SUBJECT SELECTION AND DATA COLLECTION

Human smugglers, commonly known as "snakeheads" in China and in overseas Chinese communities, are defined in this study as those who help people enter the United States illegally for a fee. Because little was known about the smuggler population and random sampling was not feasible, we adopted an ethnographic approach to our subject population.

The snakeheads in our study are all self-identified human smugglers residing in either China or the United States. We conducted two types of interviews with them: formal and informal. Formal interviews involved one-on-one conversations around a predetermined set of open-ended and structured questions. Informal interviews usually took place in restaurants or at other social gathering places, where formal inquiries into clandestine business were neither feasible nor socially acceptable.

We made frequent trips to conduct field observation in the Chinese communities in New York and Los Angeles. We also made several trips to the sending communities in the villages outside Fuzhou; there, the majority of the households had either immediate family members or close relatives overseas, mainly in the United States. We stayed in these sending communities and talked to villagers about their family members overseas. We also visited local English language schools that were preparing prospective immigrants or the children of those already in the United States for their eventual trip to America, and we observed daily events and interactions on the street.

The final phase of the data collection involved gathering relevant literature, including published books and articles on illegal Chinese immigration and smuggling activities, government documents, news reports and feature articles published in English and Chinese language media around the world (mostly from Hong Kong, China, Taiwan, the United States, Canada, and Australia), as well as unpublished manuscripts and conference papers.

Because human smuggling is a highly secretive criminal activity and snakeheads face constant threats from law enforcement, we encountered significant difficulties in recruiting subjects who would agree to be interviewed. During the course of data collection and field observations, we made numerous time-consuming and costly efforts to cultivate personal relationships, either directly or through our field contacts, with prospective subjects. We often spent days in Fuzhou waiting for prospective subjects to meet with us for a few brief hours. Many of these conversations produced little useful information. Others occurred in locations where it was impossible for us to probe sensitive topics. We made frequent trips to Los Angeles and New York to meet with interviewers who assisted us with field activities. We often felt that we were collecting more receipts than useful data. Particularly after the Dover incident (McAllister 2000), many of our subjects and others with whom we had ongoing relationships went into hiding or declined to speak with us. Scheduled interviews were canceled, pager numbers were suddenly out of service, and phone calls went unanswered. Despite the many obstacles, however, we have collected enough data to provide a rare peek into the secret world of human smugglers and to provide an understanding of their social organizations.

SUBJECT PROTECTION

We recruited subjects in this study through multiple methods. Some were part of our own social circles, while others were part of our interviewers' or collaborators' social circles. Still others were referred to us through the snowballing technique (i.e., one subject refers to another). If a potential subject appeared willing to be interviewed, he or she would be invited to meet a member of the research team in person. At the informal meeting, an interviewer would explain the study to the potential subject. We took several measures to ensure the cooperation and comfort of our prospective respondents.

- Potential smugglers were screened to ensure that only willing and candid participants were recruited.
- The questionnaire was pilot-tested beforehand to make sure subjects would be comfortable providing answers to most of the questions.
- A nominal fee was offered as an incentive to our subjects for their participation.[1]
- All interviews were recorded anonymously, and no identifiable information was collected.
- The interviews were conducted in the subject's own dialect (e.g., Mandarin, Cantonese, or Fujianese).
- The subjects were assured repeatedly that their participation in the study would not lead to investigation by any authorities. In addition, the data collected in this study were not accessible to persons other than members of this research team.

These procedures worked well in the field, with no adverse consequences befalling any of our subjects because of our research activities. In all cases, the subjects were informed of the intention and identity of the research staff. No deception was used in any of the interviews. All of our assistants, including our Chinese research collaborators, were trained in human subject protection issues.

VALIDITY AND RELIABILITY

A study of this nature poses many challenges in terms of validity and reliability (see Jacobs 1996; Jacobs and Wright 1999). After all, our subjects had little to gain by telling us about their business and much to lose if the information they provided wound up in the hands of law enforcement officials. Thus we employed several strategies to increase the validity and reliability of the data.

Our focus was on building trust and confidence in our subjects. We spent many months in the field, meeting and talking to the smugglers. Skeptical at first, many eventually were convinced that our guarantee of anonymity and confidentiality was sincere. As college professors, our profession garners special prestige and respect in the Chinese culture, and many of our subjects were delighted to impart their expertise to us once their suspicion subsided.

Another factor that helped us earn the trust of potential subjects was that we had cultivated many personal contacts (or *guanxi*) in our previous research projects in Chinese communities. Using our social resources and native language ability to help our subjects deal with mainstream society (e.g., to explain how the school system works in the United States or help them fill out official forms), earned us several friends who later provided valuable information about smuggling operations. After all, human smuggling is essentially a business built upon a myriad of *guanxi*. By tapping into this common cultural practice, we were able to gain the trust and confidence of our subjects. Still, our efforts to build trust with human smugglers were limited by budgetary and time constraints.

The interviewers in this study also provided us with vital access to a wider smuggler population through their extensive networks in the Chinese communities. The four interviewers (two in New York and two in Los Angeles) recruited for this project were themselves involved in smuggling activities at one time. They were able to reach a much larger population through their direct connections in their communities. Because they knew the subjects personally, spoke their dialects, and even lived in the same communities, it took them much less time to build enough trust and confidence to allow interviews to take place.

Internal validity was further strengthened by our cross-checking answers obtained from formal interviews (with a consistent protocol of semi-structured questions) against those from informal interviews and from our field observation. Most of the questions in our questionnaire were designed to reflect the knowledge of human smuggling activities we had accumulated in our previous fieldwork. Unlike studies in other empirical settings (e.g., the world of drug dealers), where we paid money for each interview and where easy cash may have motivated respondents to answer questions in an anticipated manner consistent with the goal of the project (Jacobs et al. 2000), in this study few of our subjects took money from our interviewers. Therefore, they had no financial incentive to lie to us. Furthermore, because all of the formal interviews and most of the informal interviews were conducted on a one-on-one basis, it would be all but impossible for our subjects to conspire to mislead us.

Although the possibility that some of the subjects lied to us or distorted certain facts can never be ruled out, we felt confident that the methods we employed in this study (semi-structured interviews, informal conversations, and field observations) were probably the most viable entrance into the world of human smuggling. Researchers who have assessed the quality of offender self-report data have concluded that semi-structured interviews represent one of the best ways to obtain valid information about crime.

However, reliability was more problematic in this study, in which much of the information was based solely on confidential interviews or conversations. Holding repeated interviews or conversations over time with the same subject was not only unrealistic, but also prohibitively expensive. The fact that responses from our subjects (based on both formal interviews and informal conversations) were repetitive and patterned gave us a measure of confidence that the data were reliable. Still, such repetition could have resulted from the artifact of the sampling design itself (Jacobs 1996). Therefore, findings from this study must be interpreted with caution.

There are many limitations in the use of personal contacts and the snow-ball-sampling technique vis-à-vis external validity (Biernacki and Waldorf 1981). We used a quasi-quota sampling method to generate the sample of human traffickers. To make the study sample more representative, we strove to (1) interview smugglers that specialized in different stages of smuggling operations (e.g., recruiters, transporters, and debt collectors); (2) recruit subjects at multiple sites (i.e., New York, Los Angeles, and Fuzhou); (3) include smugglers who specialized in different trafficking schemes (e.g., fraudulent marriages, business delegations, and passport substitution); and (4) solicit information from both active and retired smugglers.

Finally, we pre-tested the questionnaire and the structure of the questions with our research contacts in China and with a small, selected number of individuals in the smuggling business. All interviews followed a semi-structured format, combining structured items with forced choice and open-ended items. The structured questions were used to capture common elements suitable for statistical analysis such as demographics, common tasks in the different smuggling operations, and certain financial aspects of the business. Many other questions were open ended. Most interviews were conducted in an informal and non-threatening manner, allowing the interviewer discretion over how and when to ask sensitive questions while remaining true to the research questions' intent. In other cases, our interviews were in essence informal conversations with the subjects that took place in hotel lobbies, restaurants, or their living rooms. During these interviews, we mixed research questions with social conversation.

ADDITIONAL SOURCES OF DATA

In addition to the three-year NIJ study, we also drew materials from our independent research on illegal Chinese immigration and other criminal activities over the past decade. Most notably, we borrowed from the study by Chin and Kelly (1997) that interviewed 300 undocumented Chinese immigrants in New York's Chinatown. The study, which resulted in a book by Chin (1999), explored the reasons for immigration, immigration patterns, and the seriousness of the problem of illegal Chinese immigration; it also touched upon the social organization of Chinese human smuggling and the nexus between human smugglers, organized crime, and official corruption.

Finally, we extensively reviewed empirical studies and papers on Chinese migration by other researchers. We also examined relevant news stories, feature articles, and reports from government agencies and non-government organizations from both English and Chinese language sources.

LIMITATIONS OF THIS STUDY

Several limitations in the data collection methods that we used may ultimately affect the interpretation of the findings. One is the access afforded the research team largely through a network of personal connections. Despite extensive, deliberate efforts to locate a wide variety of smugglers, we were limited in the selection of the subjects and their referral networks for the most part to the initial contacts in our own personal networks, and therefore our findings could very well be systematically biased. It is possible that our referrals led us to smuggling networks that were composed of smugglers who were more honorable, upstanding, less violent, and more often worked at it part-time. For instance, the lack of evidence to substantiate links between triad-type criminal organizations and the human smuggling trade could be an artifact of limited access—the fact that only part-time, moonlighting "non-criminals" were located, and not serious, well-organized professionals. Because of this access limitation, it is impossible to rule out the role of traditional criminal organizations and their relationships with big snakeheads in the smuggling business.

Another limitation of this study was that the organizational features of Chinese human smuggling rings, as presented in this book, were built upon data gathered from individuals who were not all part of the same organization. Describing a human smuggling organization in this manner may be like the proverbial blind man trying to describe an elephant. Organizational features had to be inferred from data provided by individuals who in their smuggling affiliations were unrelated to one another. We made no attempt, for obvious ethical and safety reasons, to infiltrate a smuggling group and follow an entire smuggling operation from start to finish. Therefore, we pieced together the "smuggling organization" as a whole from fragmented descriptions from multiple individuals. Although some distinctive "roles" were derived from the information provided by the subjects, it was not possible to get an in-depth look at the components of one complete organization. The lack of hierarchical relations and of evidence of well-organized smuggling organizations in our data may be a result of the sampling technique rather than an actual finding.

Finally, regardless of what strategies we employed to gain confidence or how successful we were in convincing the subjects of our sincere intent to protect their identity, we cannot be certain of the extent to which these snakeheads gave honest answers. As all researchers of sensitive topics must do, we relied on multiple sources of information and our intuitive understanding from direct field observations. Much more research is needed to substantiate the findings in this study and to improve our understanding of these versatile groups of entrepreneurs in transnational illicit enterprises.

Notes

1. The exact origin of the term "snakehead" remains unclear, although it has been widely used in China and Chinese communities overseas since the late 1980s to brand anyone involved in organizing or coordinating the transportation of people into another country without going through legal immigration channels. We made many attempts and inquiries in this study to determine the origin of this term, but to no avail. Illegal immigrants and snakeheads alike knew little about how the term first came about. Those who write about Chinese smuggling understand the term mostly as a figurative description of the clandestine process of human smuggling, which resembles the movement of a snake (Burdman 1993a; Chin 1999). The earliest documented use of the term was in 1981, in a United Press International story about Hong Kong-based mobsters involved in smuggling illegal immigrants from mainland China into the British colony (United Press International 1981).

2. It should be noted that although Chinese may have been the first immigrants to enter the United States illegally, by the early 1900s many more immigrants from other countries chose the border as an alternative to undergoing immigration inspection at a U.S. port (Lee 2003, 169–70). Syrians, Greeks, Hungarians, Russian Jews, Italians, and some "maidens" from France, Belgium, and Spain were the main groups entering through Canada and Mexico.

3. In early June 1993, a rickety smuggling vessel was deliberately beached on the Rockaways, off Queens, New York, after no transfer boat showed up to ferry the illegal immigrants ashore. Gangsters on the Panama-registered freighter urged the 286 illegal immigrants onboard to jump and swim to "freedom." Many did, but ten of them drowned.

4. I asked residents of Fuzhou and surrounding counties about family members who were living abroad at the time of the survey. The questionnaire was attached to the national census, and local public security personnel provided assistance in carrying out the survey. We retrieved information about when the overseas relatives left China, and where they went, from local residential registration records. However,

families sometimes ignore the government requirement to cancel an overseas relative's record of residence. Therefore, the estimate (or underestimate) includes only
those known to the Public Security agencies.

5. I obtained this information from a presentation made by an intelligence officer from the U.S. Border Patrol and a representative of the U.S. Marshal at the 7th
Working Group Meeting on Project Bridge, an international conference on transnational human smuggling, held by Interpol in Lyons, France, February 25–26, 2004.

6. In June 2000, a Dutch-registered truck arrived from Belgium at Dover, a
major channel port in the English county of Kent, and was pulled over for customs
inspection. Found inside the truck's container were the bodies of fifty-eight illegal
Chinese immigrants, all apparently dead from asphyxiation. There were two sur-
vivors. Prior to boarding the ferry, the Dutch driver had closed the container's air
vent to avoid detection by immigration authorities. The incident triggered a massive
international manhunt for the handlers behind the operation. The driver was sentenced to fourteen years for his part in the incident.

7. This information is from an interview in February 2005 with a U.S. Homeland Security agent who was working on anti-smuggling details.

CHAPTER 2

1. Sister Ping (a.k.a. Cheng Chuiping) was probably the best-known and the
most respected snakehead in the Fujianese community, both at home and abroad.
Over the years, both illegal immigrants and snakeheads who knew her had only good
things to say about her. Her business practices were widely regarded as fair and ethical. She was often viewed by the subjects in this study as a principled smuggler who
treated her clients with respect and care.

CHAPTER 3

1. Illegal immigrants from Mexico, once apprehended by border patrol or immigration officials, are typically repatriated immediately. However, illegal immigrants
from countries other than Mexico (or OTMs) are often afforded an opportunity to
plead their cases in front of a federal judge. Because of limited detention facilities,
the majority of OTMs are released on bail with a promise to show up in court on
their scheduled dates. Once released from detention, most of them simply vanish
into America's vast ethnic enclaves and start working in the underground economy.

CHAPTER 4

1. This information was provided by a representative of the Belgian Federal
Police during a presentation at the Interpol's Project Bridge conference in Pula,
Croatia, on June 4 and 5, 2003.

2. This information was provided by a Finnish law enforcement representative

during a presentation at the Interpol's Project Bridge conference in Pula, Croatia, on June 4 and 5, 2003.

3. This information was provided by a representative from the airport police of Zurich during a presentation at the Interpol's Project Bridge conference in Pula, Croatia, on June 4 and 5, 2003.

4. The information was obtained at the 7th Working Group Meeting on Project Bridge, organized by the Interpol at its headquarters in Lyons, France, on February 25 and 26, 2004.

CHAPTER 5

1. The credit-ticket system was essentially a mutual aid practice with a capitalist twist. The relatives and friends of overseas Chinese and sometimes Chinese fraternal associations provided emigrants with tickets on credit for the voyage abroad. These indebted migrants were then obligated to repay the fare out of their future earnings upon arrival at their destination, often with a high interest rate (Campbell 1969).

2. A "mirror transfer" is a financial practice employed by overseas Chinese in which no actual money is sent from one country to another. For instance, an immigrant in America who wants to send money to relatives in China gives the money to an underground banker, who in turn makes a phone call to tell his or her business associate in China to deliver the equivalent amount in Chinese yuan or in U.S. dollars. Conversely, families in China can also send money to the United States by giving the money to someone in China, who in turn calls his or her contact in the United States to deliver the money. No actual transfers take place through the legitimate banking system. Individuals and small businesses often use this mechanism to move funds. It is safe, efficient, and less expensive than commercial banks. Friends and relatives often offer such money transfers to one another free of charge.

3. In the 1990s, Sister Ping was a household name in the Chinese human smuggling community. To U.S. law enforcement agencies, she was a ruthless underworld boss in New York's Chinatown, the "mother of all snakeheads," and a cut-throat underground banker. But to her clients, she was almost a goddess, who was eager to help her less fortunate countrymen to seek a better life in America (Barnes 2000). Her Chinese name was Cheng Chuiping, but she was affectionately called Big Sister Ping (or Yi Ping Jie) both in her hometown in Fujian and in New York's Chinese community. After being indicted in connection with the ill-fated Golden Venture incident, she fled the country and went into hiding in her native Fujian for several years. In April 2000, she was arrested in Hong Kong with the help of local authorities. After three years of legal maneuvering, she was extradited back to the United States to stand trial. Her saga finally came to an end on March 16, 2006, when she was sentenced to thirty-five years for conspiring to commit alien smuggling, hostage taking, money laundering, and trafficking/laundering ransom proceeds (Immigration and Customs Enforcement 2006).

CHAPTER 6

1. Figures on apprehension of illegal border crossers are from the Office of Public Affairs, U.S. Border Patrol, Department of Homeland Security.

2. Smuggling fees quoted in the news media and government reports tend to vary significantly, depending on their sources. Many factors affect the overall price in smuggling, such as the choice of transportation, travel distance, accommodations, method of entry, and, most important of all, law enforcement activities. Human smugglers in the San Diego/Tijuana region usually charge about $2,000 per person to bring a Mexican migrant from south of the border to Los Angeles, a distance of about 150 miles (Cearley 2004). Smuggling fees overall have increased steadily in recent years, mainly because of increased law enforcement activities along the border such as Operation Gatekeeper, which initiated the construction of border fences, installation of high-tech surveillance equipment, and the hiring of additional patrol agents.

3. One major expense not included here is expenditures for food and lodging for illegal immigrants during transportation or at transit points. Depending on the number of transit points (which range from one to nine) and the duration of the stay (from a few days to a few months), the expense may range from a few hundred to several thousand dollars per migrant.

CHAPTER 7

1. The F-2 visa scheme is essentially a variation of the common marriage fraud. In this case, foreign students are approached and offered a hefty fee to cooperate in the marriage scheme. Because foreign students often spend years in the United States pursuing academic degrees, petitions to bring along their spouses are usually granted by U.S. consulates overseas.

CHAPTER 8

1. A portion of this chapter was previously published in a paper by Sheldon X. Zhang and Ko-lin Chin, Enter the dragon—Inside Chinese human smuggling organizations, in *Criminology* 40 (4) (2002): 737–68.

2. The Senate bill (S.754—104th Congress) was introduced by Edward Kennedy, D-Mass., on May 3, 1995; it sought to amend the Immigration and Nationality Act to more effectively control U.S. land borders, prevent the employment of illegal aliens, expedite the removal of illegal aliens, provide wiretap and asset forfeiture authority to combat alien smuggling and related crimes, and increase penalties for human smuggling activities. The full text can be found at the Library of Congress website: thomas.loc.gov/cgi-bin/query/D?c104:./temp/~c1040FzrWD::

3. From the late 1980s to mid-1990s, many smugglers attempted to recruit clients through legitimate business fronts, such as immigration service agencies, overseas employment agencies, and matchmaking services. While some of these fronts

are still in operation, few of the snakeheads in this study used this method to recruit clients. Most relied on referrals from friends and relatives.

4. The conclusion that the smuggling market was fragmented and smuggling groups were often isolated from one another received validation from ranking law enforcement representatives from the Fujian Provincial government. An official in charge of anti-smuggling operations in the province said that he had never heard about Sister Ping. The community contact who accompanied this police official during the interview had not heard about her, either. Although it was possible that the official was withholding information, it was unlikely that his non-police friend would want to cover up for him. This community contact was well connected to members of the smuggling community in Fuqing, another county south of Fuzhou, who introduced us to several subjects for interviewing. He was smuggled to Japan himself years ago and made a small fortune there before returning to Fuzhou to open a supermarket and several other businesses. Most likely, any information about Sister Ping and her smuggling operations was confined to circles of people connected to her native township.

CHAPTER 9

1. This chapter is a revision of a previously published paper by Sheldon X. Zhang and Ko-lin Chin, The declining significance of triad societies in transnational illegal activities—A structural deficiency perspective, *British Journal of Criminology* 43 (3) (2003): 469–88.

CHAPTER 10

1. *Guanxi* translates simply as "relationships" or "connections," but it is often a complex social protocol. To a Chinese, the term has a meaning similar to the American idiom "pulling strings." A person's social standing can often be defined by the extent of one's *guanxi*. The practice of *guanxi* is a never-ending process of giving and receiving favors and often becomes the binding element in one's social network. The concept is so pervasive and fundamental to the way Chinese think and deal with one another that it amounts to an essential feature distinguishing the Chinese mindset from that of the West.

2. In an unpublished survey of the three coastal counties adjacent to Fuzhou in 2000, researchers in Fujian Province found that in a sample of 1,636 people who left for the United States by various methods, 43 percent were women. Although this survey does not distinguish between legal and illegal means of emigration, the figure nonetheless reveals the large percentage of women in the emigrant population.

CHAPTER 11

1. Based on personal interviews with special agents in the Bureau of Customs and Border Patrol in 2005.

EPILOGUE

1. The term refers to the many women whose husbands were smuggled out of China for a fee of $18,000 in the early years of illegal emigration. These women stayed behind, looking after the elderly, rearing the young, and living off the remittances sent by their husbands. There were so many of these women in the region that a male prostitute industry emerged to cater to them. Nowadays, the term simply refers to married women with overseas husbands who are on the lookout for sexual adventures.

APPENDIX B

1. Prospective subjects were offered $75.00 each for a completed interview, as budgeted in the grant proposal. This fee was significantly higher than those in any of our previous projects involving primary data collection. However, the amount turned out to be far from sufficient to entice potential subjects to come forward. Those who agreed to talk to us mostly refused to accept the payment. Those who declined to be interviewed said the money was not worth the risk or their time.

Glossary

Chinese words and phrases used in this book are presented in pinyin transcription and in simplified characters. Following the literary translation, an interpretation or explanation of the phrase in context is provided in parenthesis.

baiping（摆平）Appeasing all parties (paying bribes to all officials involved in a smuggling operation so no one becomes upset about being left out).

bianjian（边检）Border inspection (immigration or border control checkpoints or inspectors).

chongguan（冲关）Dashing through the checkpoint (trying one's luck with a falsified passport to pass U.S. immigration inspection).

chuguo（出国）Going abroad.

dailou (in Cantonese)（大老）Gangster boss.

diaobao（调包）Switching bags (assuming the identity of a person as printed in a passport).

diaoxialai（掉下来）Dropping to the ground (failure of an air-route operation and capture of the passenger).

duirentou（对人头）Matching human heads (matching a genuine passport, with a valid visa, with a look-alike client).

fuyuan（复员）Being discharged from one's military career and returning home.

gongan（公安）The Police or the Public Security Bureau.

guanxi（关系）Connections.

guxiang（故乡）One's hometown.

huantianshu（换天书）Changing the heavenly book (altering a passport).

huaqiao（华侨）Overseas Chinese.

hukou（户口）A residential or household registration.

jiajiehun（假结婚）Marriage fraud.

kanlianse（看脸色）Watching someone's face (being mindful of someone's mood and behaving accordingly).

laojiao（劳教）Education through labor (a common form of legal punishment that takes place in labor camps, where prisoners are supposedly reformed through hard physical work).

maiguan（买关）Buying the security checkpoint (paying a bribe to secure one's passage through a security checkpoint).

mazai（马仔）Foot soldiers (enforcers from a Chinatown gang).

peidu（陪读）Accompanying someone to study abroad (usually the spouse of a foreign student, who qualifies for an F-2 visa to enter the United States).

renminbi（人民币）People's currency (the official name of the currency used in mainland China, abbreviated as RMB).

shatou（杀头）Chopping off one's head (replacing the photo in the passport).

taitou（抬头）Lifting one's head (as soon as the airplane takes off, the smuggling transaction is completed).

tong gong tong chou（同工同酬）Same work, same pay (a woman who does a man's job should get a man's pay).

tousidu（偷私渡）Clandestine and private trespass (an official term for illegal international migration).

tuqi（土气）Dirt-like smell (looking or behaving like a country bumpkin).

wanbasao（万八嫂）$18,000 sisters-in-law. (A term that emerged in the early 1990s, referring to women whose husbands were smuggled out of the country for a fee of $18,000. These women stayed behind, looking after the old and rearing the young, and living off the remittances sent by their husbands. There were so many of them in some regions that a male prostitute industry emerged to cater to them. Nowadays, the term refers to women with husbands overseas who are looking for sexual adventure.)

wujing（武警）Armed Police (the military branch of the national police force, responsible for all border checkpoint security and inspection and for border patrol).

yuan（元）The most common unit of Chinese currency, worth about U.S. $.12 at the time of the study.

References

Abadinksy, Howard. 1990. *Organized crime*, 3rd ed. Chicago: Nelson-Hall.

Adler, Patricia A., and Peter Adler. 1983. Shifts and oscillations in deviant careers: The case of upper-level drug dealers and smugglers. *Social Problems* 31 (2): 195–207.

Agence France-Presse. 2004. Hundreds of human-traffickers arrested in China border crackdown. March 24. web.lexis-nexis.com.

Amnesty International. 1998. United States of America: Human rights concerns in the border region with Mexico. AI Index: AMR 51/03/98. May 20. web.amnesty .org/library/Index/engAMR510031998.

Arnold, Christina, and Andrea M. Bertone. 2002. Addressing the sex trade in Thailand: Some lessons learned from NGOs. *Gender Issues* 20 (1): 26–27.

Asimov, Nanette, and Pamela Burdman. 1993. Baja coast now most convenient back door to U.S. *San Francisco Chronicle*, April 29, A9.

Associated Press. 1999. Six indicted for alleged smuggling of illegal aliens. May 7. http//:web.lexis-nexis.com.

———. 2004. Chinese illegal immigrants tortured in Greece for ransom money. March 10. http//:web.lexis-nexis.com.

———. 2005. L.A. port authorities discover 32 men and boys from China in ship's containers. January 16. http//:web.lexis-nexis.com.

Bales, Kevin. 1999. *Disposable people: New slavery in the global economy*. Berkeley: University of California Press.

Barlett, Donald L., and James B. Steele. 2004. Who left the door open? *Time*, September 20, 51–66.

Barnes, Edward. 2000. Two-faced woman. *Time*, July 31, 48–50.

Bian, Yanjie. 2002. Chinese social stratification and social mobility. *Annual Review of Sociology* 28: 91–116.

Biernacki, Patrick, and Dan Waldorf. 1981. Snowball sampling. *Sociological Methods and Research* 10: 141–63.

Black, David. 1992. *Triad takeover: A terrifying account of the spread of triad crime in the West.* London: Sidgwick & Jackson.

Block, Alan A. 1980. *East side, west side: Organizing crime in New York, 1930–1950.* Cardiff: University College Cardiff Press.

Block, Alan A., and William J. Chambliss. 1981. *Organized crime.* New York: Elsevier.

Block, Alan A., and Frank R. Scarpitti. 1986. Casinos and banking: Organized crime in the Bahamas. *Deviant Behavior* 7 (4): 301–12.

Block, Ann. 1977. Your mother's in the mafia: Women criminals in progressive New York. *Contemporary Crises* 1 (1): 5–22.

Bolz, Jennifer. 1995. Chinese organized crime and illegal alien trafficking: Humans as a commodity. *Asian Affairs* 22: 147–58.

Booth, Martin. 1990. *The triads: The Chinese criminal fraternity.* London: Grafton.

———. 1999. *The Dragon syndicates: The global phenomenon of the triads.* New York: Carroll & Graf.

Bourgois, Philippe. 1989. In search of Horatio Alger: Culture and ideology in the crack economy. *Contemporary Drug Problems* 16 (4): 619–49.

Boyd, Alan, and William Barnes. 1992. Thailand an open door for illegal passages. *South China Morning Post,* June 22, 6.

Bozic, Sonja. 2004. Project bridge. Paper presented at the 7th Working Group Meeting of Interpol's Project Bridge, Lyons, France.

Brazil, Eric, Malcolm Glover, and Larry Hatfield. 1993. Daring smuggler lands 250 in city. *San Francisco Examiner,* May 24, A1.

Bresler, Fenton. 1981. *The Chinese mafia.* New York: Stein & Day.

Brimelow, Peter. 1995. *Alien nation: Common sense about America's immigration disaster.* New York: Random House.

Bulsing, Jan. 2004. Information and analysis center: People smuggling. Paper presented at the 7th Working Group Meeting of Interpol's Project Bridge, Lyons, France.

Burdman, Pamela. 1993a. Huge boom in human smuggling: Inside story of flight from China. *San Francisco Chronicle,* April 27, A1.

———. 1993b. How gangsters cash in on human smuggling. *San Francisco Chronicle,* April 28, A1.

———. 1993c. Web of corruption ensnares officials around the world. *San Francisco Chronicle,* April 28, A8.

———. 1993d. China cracks down on smuggling. *San Francisco Chronicle,* November 19, A1.

California Rural Legal Assistance Foundation. 1999. CRLAF and ACLU file petition charging that deadly U.S. border enforcement strategy violates international human rights obligations. www.aclu-sc.org/attach/i/Intl_CivLib _Report_1999.pdf.

Campbell, Persia C. 1923. *Chinese coolie emigration to countries within the British Empire.* Reprinted New York: Negro University Press, 1969.

Carroll, Rory. 2002. Women: The rise of the godmothers. *The Guardian,* May 28, Features section, 10.

Castillo, Eduardo E. 2004. Current, ex-government workers arrested in migrant traffic ring. *San Diego Union-Tribune,* March 24, A3.

Cearley, Anna. 2004. Pressures continue on a bolstered border. *San Diego Union Tribune,* July 11, A1.

Ceska Tiskova Kancelar (Czech News Agency). 2004. Czech people smugglers given prison sentences in Germany. March, 9. web.lexis-nexis.com.

Chen, David W. 2003. Lure of America fades for many in China. *San Diego Union Tribune,* September 7, A17.

Chesneaux, Jean. 1972. *Popular movements and secret societies in China, 1840–1950.* Stanford, Calif.: Stanford University Press.

Chin, Ko-lin. 1990. *Chinese subculture and criminality: Non-traditional crime groups in America.* Westport, Conn.: Greenwood Press.

———. 1996. *Chinatown gangs: Extortion, enterprise and ethnicity.* New York: Oxford University Press.

———. 1999. *Smuggled Chinese: Clandestine immigration to the United States.* Philadelphia: Temple University Press.

———. 2003. *Heijin: Organized crime, business, and politics in Taiwan.* Armonk, N.Y.: M. E. Sharpe.

Chin, Ko-lin, and Robert Kelly. 1997. *Human snakes: Illegal Chinese immigrants in the United States.* Final report, Grant SBR 93-11114, Law and Social Science Program, National Science Foundation.

Chin, Ko-lin, Sheldon Zhang, and Robert Kelly. 1998. Transnational Chinese organized crime activities. *Transnational Organized Crime* 4 (3–4): 127–54.

Chin, Tung Pok, and Winifred C. Chin. 2000. *Paper son: One man's story.* Philadelphia: Temple University Press.

Chu, Yiu-kong. 2000. *Triads as business.* London: Routledge.

Cornelius, Wayne A. 2000. Death at the border: The efficacy and unintended consequences of U.S. immigration control policy, 1993–2000. Working Paper No. 27. San Diego: Center for Comparative Immigration Studies, University of California San Diego. www.ccis-ucsd.org/PUBLICATIONS/wrkg27new.pdf.

———. 2005a. Thinking out loud/immigration; there's no point in flailing at this piñata; scapegoating Mexico is easy, but it doesn't get us anywhere. *Los Angeles Times,* May 29, M3.

———. 2005b. Controlling "unwanted immigration": Lessons from the United States, 1993–2004. *Journal of Ethnic and Migration Studies* 31 (4): 775–94.

Cressey, Donald R. 1969. *Theft of the nation: The structure and operations of organized crime in America.* New York: Harper & Row.

Denton, Barbara. 2001. Property crime and women drug dealers in Australia. *Journal of Drug Issues* 31 (2): 465–85.

Diaz, Madeline Baro. 2004. Cuban mails herself to Miami, and to freedom airport: Workers find woman alive in crate. *South Florida Sun-Sentinel*, August 26, A1.

Dillon, Richard H. 1962. *The hatchet men: The story of the tong wars in San Francisco's Chinatown*. New York: Coward-McCann.

Dino, Alessandra. 1998. Women, mafia and ways of communication [in Italian]. *Rassegna Italiana di Sociologia* 39 (4): 477–512.

Dobinson, Ian. 1993. Pinning a tail on the dragon: The Chinese and the international heroin trade. *Crime and Delinquency* 39 (3): 373–84.

Dubro, James. 1992. *Dragons of crime: Inside the Asian underworld*. Markham, Ontario: Octopus.

Eager, Marita. 1992. Patten in tough stand against illegals. *South China Morning Post*, July 18, 3.

Engelberg, Stephen. 1994. In immigration labyrinth, corruption comes easily. *New York Times*, September 12, A1.

Entwisle, Barbara, and Gail E. Henderson, eds. 2000. *Redrawing boundaries: Gender, households, and work in China*. Berkeley: University of California Press.

Entwisle, Barbara, Gail E. Henderson, Susan E. Short, Jill Bouma, and Fengying Zhai. 1995. Gender and family businesses in rural China. *American Sociological Review* 60 (1): 36–57.

Fagan, Jeffrey. 1994. Women and drugs revisited: Female participation in the cocaine economy. *Journal of Drug Issues* 24 (1/2): 179–226.

Freedman, Dan. 1991. Asian gangs turn to smuggling people. *San Francisco Examiner*, December 30, A7.

Fritsch, Jane. 1993. One failed voyage illustrates flow of Chinese immigration. *New York Times*, June 7, A1.

Gambetta, Diego. 1993. *The Sicilian mafia: The business of private protection*. Cambridge, Mass.: Harvard University Press.

Gamboa, Suzanne. 2004. Border security official: Illegal immigration may be declining. *Associated Press*. March 30. web.lexis-nexis.com.

Gaudette, Karen. 2002. Missing Chinese girl turns up on east coast with kin. *San Diego Union-Tribune*, August 4, A3.

Gold, Jeffrey. 1995. Chinese gang accused of racketeering. *The Record*, March 23, A5.

Goldstone, Jack. 1997. A tsunami on the horizon? The potential for international migration from the People's Republic of China. In *Human smuggling—Chinese migrant trafficking and the challenge to America's immigration tradition*, ed. Paul J. Smith, 48–75. Washington, D.C.: Center for Strategic and International Studies.

Graham, Otis L., Jr. 2004. *Unguarded gates—A history of America's immigration crisis*. New York: Rowman & Littlefield.

Gross, Gregory. 1996. Smugglers of illegal immigrants become special targets. *San Diego Union-Tribune*, March 21, A21.

Hannum, Emily, and Xie Yu. 1994. Trends in educational gender inequality in China: 1949–1985. *Research in Social Stratification and Mobility* 13: 73–98.

Harris, John R., and Michael P. Todaro. 1970. Migration, unemployment, and development. *American Economic Review* 60 (1): 126–42.

Hervocek, Sam Howe. 2000. Deadly choice of stowaways: Ship containers. *New York Times*, January 12: A1.

Honig, Emily. 2000. Iron girls revisited: Gender and the politics of work in the Cultural Revolution, 1966–1976. In *Re-drawing boundaries: Gender, households, and work in China*, ed. Barbara Entwisle and Gail E. Henderson, 97–110. Berkeley: University of California Press.

Honig, Emily, and Gail Hershatter. 1988. *Personal voices: Chinese women in the 1980s*. Stanford, Calif.: Stanford University Press.

Hood, Marlowe. 1994. The Taiwan connection. *The Los Angeles Times Magazine*, October 9, 20.

———. 1997. Sourcing the problem: Why Fuzhou? In *Human smuggling—Chinese migrant trafficking and the challenge to America's immigration tradition*, ed. Paul J. Smith, 76–92. Washington, D.C.: Center for Strategic and International Studies.

Hughes, Donna. 2001. The Natashas trade: Transnational sex trafficking. *National Institute of Justice Journal* 246 (January): 9–15.

Human Smuggling and Trafficking Center. 2005. *Fact sheet: Distinctions between human smuggling and human trafficking*. www.usdoj.gov/crt/crim/smuggling_trafficking_facts.pdf.

Immigration and Customs Enforcement. 2006. Sister Ping sentenced to 35 years in prison for alien smuggling, hostage taking, money laundering and ransom proceeds conspiracy. *News Release*, March 16. www.ice.gov/pi/news/newsreleases/.

Inciardi, James A., Dorothy Lockwood, and Anne E. Pottiger. 1993. *Women and crack-cocaine*. New York: MacMillan.

Interpol. 2003. *Summary of the meeting on Project Bridge* (on June 4–5 at Pula, Croatia). Lyons, France: Interpol.

———. 2004. *Fact sheets—People smuggling: Challenge and response*. www.interpol.int/Public/ICPO/FactSheets/.

Jablon, Robert. 1999. 30 Chinese arrested for illegal entry to U.S. *San Diego Union Tribune*, December 30, A3.

Jacobs, Bruce A. 1996. Crack dealers and restrictive deterrence. *Criminology* 34 (3): 409–31.

Jacobs, Bruce A., and Jody Miller. 1998. Crack dealing, gender, and arrest avoidance. *Social Problems* 45 (4): 550–69.

Jacobs, Bruce A., Volkan Topalli, and Richard Wright. 2000. Managing retaliation: Drug robbery and informal sanction threats. *Criminology* 38 (1): 171–98.

Jacobs, Bruce A., and Richard Wright. 1999. Stick-up, street culture, and offender motivation. *Criminology* 37 (1): 149–73.

Jacobs, James B., Coleen Friel, and Robert Radick. 1999. *Gotham unbound: How New York City was liberated from the grip of organized crime*. New York: New York University Press.

Jacobs, James B., and Lauryn P. Gouldin. 1999. Cosa Nostra: The final chapter? *Crime and Justice* 25: 129–89.

Jennings, Andrew. 1993. From Marx to the mafia. *New Statesman and Society* 6 (252): 18–20.

Johnston, Ian. 2004. Scandal of the Chinese cockle-pickers who died for only 11p an hour. *Scotland on Sunday*, February 8, 1.

Jones, Maldwyn Allen. 1992. *American immigration*. Chicago: University of Chicago Press.

Jordan, Lara Jakes. 2006. China not accepting citizens, U.S. says. *San Diego Union Tribune*, March 15, A8.

Karstedt, Susanne. 2000. Emancipation, crime and problem behavior of women: A perspective from Germany. *Gender Issues* 18 (3): 21–59.

Kenney, Dennis J., and James O. Finckenauer. 1995. *Organized crime in America*. San Francisco: Wadsworth.

Kinkead, Gwen. 1992. *Chinatown: A portrait of a closed society*. New York: Harper Collins, 1992.

Kleinknecht, William. 1996. *The new ethnic mobs: The changing face of organized crime in America*. New York: Free Press.

Kwong, Peter. 1987. *The new Chinatown*. New York: Hill & Wang.

———. 1997. Forbidden workers: Illegal Chinese immigrants and American labor. New York: New Press.

Lau, Angela, and Sandra Dibble. 1999. Illegal Chinese immigrants found in Baja— At least 82 have been detained. *San Diego Union Tribune*, August 25, A3.

Lee, Adam. 1992. Macau drives against illegals. *South China Morning Post*, September 2, 7.

Lee, Ching Kwan. 1995. Engendering the worlds of labor: Women workers, labor markets, and production politics in the south China economic miracle. *American Sociological Review* 60 (3): 378–97.

Lee, Erika. 2003. *At America's gates: Chinese immigration during the Exclusion Era, 1882–1943*. Chapel Hill: University of North Carolina Press.

Lee, Rose Hum. 1960. *The Chinese in the United States of America*. Hong Kong: Hong Kong University Press.

Leung, Edward. 1999. Chinese triads. Paper presented at the 2nd International Conference for Criminal Intelligence Analysts, London.

Li, Hao. 2004. *Joint effort targets human smuggling*. www.beijingportal.com.cn/.

Li, Minghuan. 1999. To get rich quickly in Europe: Reflections on migration motivation in Wenzhou. In *Internal and international migration—Chinese perspective*, ed. Frank N. Pieke and Hein Mallee, 181–98. Surrey, U.K.: Curzon.

Liang, Zai, and Wenzhen Ye. 2001. From Fujian to New York: Understanding the new Chinese immigration. In *Global human smuggling: Comparative perspectives*, ed. David Kyle and Rey Koslowski, 187–215. Baltimore, Md.: Johns Hopkins University Press.

Liddick, Don. 1999. The enterprise "model" of organized crime: Assessing theoretical propositions. *Justice Quarterly* 16 (2): 403–30.

Liu, Xin. 1997. Space, mobility, and flexibility: Chinese villagers and scholars negotiate power at home and abroad. In *Ungrounded empires: The cultural politics of modern Chinese transnationalism*, ed. Aihwa Ong and Donald Nonini, 91–114. New York: Routledge.

Lorch, Donatella. 1992. A flood of illegal aliens enters U.S. via Kennedy: Requesting political asylum is usual ploy. *New York Times*, March 18, B2.

Los Angeles Times. 1999. Smuggler of Chinese pleads guilty. March 5, B3.

McAllister, J.F.O. 2000. Snaking toward death. *Time*, July 03. www.time.com/time/europe/magazine/2000/0703/snaking.html.

McCarthy, Terry. 2000. Coming to America. *Time*, May 1, 42–45.

McDonald, Joe. 2004. 43 Koreans climbed embassy fence in China. *San Diego Union Tribune*, September 30, A14.

McIllwain, Jeffrey S. 1997. From tong war to organized crime: Revising the historical perception of violence in Chinatown. *Justice Quarterly* 14 (1): 25–52.

McIllwain, Jeffrey S. 2003. *Organizing crime in Chinatown: Race and racketeering in New York, 1890–1910*. Jefferson, N.C.: McFarland.

Mackenzie, Peter W. 2002. Strangers in the city: The *hukou* and urban citizenship in China. *Journal of International Affairs* 56 (1): 305–20.

Maher, Lisa. 1997. *Sexed work: Gender, race, and resistance in a Brooklyn drug market*. Oxford, U.K.: Clarendon.

Maher, Lisa, and Kathleen Daly. 1996. Women in the street-level drug economy: Continuity or change? *Criminology* 34 (4): 465–92.

Mahler, Sarah. 1995. *American dreaming: Immigrant life on the margins*. Princeton, N.J.: Princeton University Press.

Malkin, Michelle. 2002. *Invasion: How America still welcomes terrorists, criminals, and other foreign menaces to our shores*. Washington, D.C.: Regnery.

Marotta, Gemma. 1997. The anti-mafia inquiries in the VIII and IX legislatures. *Sociologia* 31 (3): 163–210.

Marquis, Christopher, and Glenn Garvin. 1999. Panama smuggling scandal erupts: Top officials accused of helping Chinese sneak into the U.S. *San Diego Union Tribune*, August 28, A15.

Martin, Romano. 1992. *Multinational crime*. Newbury Park, Calif.: Sage.

Massey, Douglas S. 1988. International migration and economic development in comparative perspective. *Population and Development Review* 14 (3): 383–414.

———. 1999. Foreword to *Smuggled Chinese: Clandestine immigration to the United States*, by Ko-lin Chin. Philadelphia: Temple University Press.

Massey, Douglas S., Joaquin Arango, Graeme Hugo, Ali Kouaouci, Adela Pellegrino, and J. Edward Taylor. 1993. Theories of international migration: A review and appraisal. *Population and Development Review* 19 (3): 431–66.

———. 1998. *Worlds in motion: Understanding international migration at the end of the millennium.* Oxford, U.K.: Clarendon.

Massey, Douglas S., Jorge Durand, and Nolan J. Malone. 2002. *Beyond smoke and mirrors: Mexican immigration in an era of economic integration.* New York: Russell Sage Foundation.

Massey, Douglas S., and Rene Zenteno. 1999. The dynamics of mass migration. *Proceedings of the National Academy of Sciences* 96 (8): 5328–35.

Merton, Robert K. 1938. Social structure and anomie. *American Sociological Review* 3: 672–82.

———. 1957. *Social theory and social structure.* Glencoe, Ill.: Free Press.

Mieczkowski, Tom. 1994. The experiences of women who sell crack: Some descriptive data from the Detroit Crack Ethnography Project. *Journal of Drug Issues* 24 (1–2): 227–49.

Miko, Francis T. 2004. *Trafficking in women and children: The U.S. and international response.* Washington, D.C.: Congressional Research Service, Library of Congress.

Miller, Jody. 2001. *One of the guys: Girls, gangs and gender.* New York: Oxford University Press.

Morawska, Ewa. 1990. The sociology and historiography of immigration. In *Immigration reconsidered: History, sociology, and politics,* ed. Virginia Yans-McLaughlin, 187–239. New York: Oxford University Press.

Morgan, W. P. 1960. *Triad societies in Hong Kong.* Hong Kong: Government Press.

Mydans, Seth. 1992. Chinese smugglers' lucrative cargo: Humans. *New York Times,* March 21, A1.

Myers, Willard. 1994. Transnational ethnic Chinese organized crime: A global challenge to the security of the United States, analysis and recommendations. Testimony of Willard Myers, Senate Committee on Foreign Affairs, Subcommittee on Terrorism, Narcotics and International Operations, April 21.

———. 1996. The emerging threat of transnational organized crime from the east. *Crime, Law and Social Change* 24 (3): 181–222.

Nadeau, Barbie. 2002. Ladies of the mob: Chalk up a macabre victory for feminism. *Newsweek* (International Edition), June 17, 27.

National Intelligence Council. 2000. *Global trends 2015: A dialogue about the future with nongovernment experts* (NIC 2000–2002). www.cia.gov/nic/NIC_globaltrend2015.html.

Ngai, Mae M. 1998. Legacies of exclusion: Illegal Chinese immigration during the Cold War years. *Journal of American Ethnic History* 18 (1): 3–35.

Nikiforov, Alexander S. 1993. Organized crime in the west and in the former USSR: An attempted comparison. *International Journal of Offender Therapy and Comparative Criminology* 37 (1): 5–15.

Offley, Ed, and Joel Connelly. 1999. U.S., Canada casting high-tech net to catch smugglers of Chinese. *San Diego Union Tribune*, October 8, A29.

O'Neill, Mark. 2002. China warns of 20 million urban jobless. *South China Morning Post*, April 30, 1.

Ovalle, David. 2004. Stowaway found on plane at Miami International Airport. *Miami Herald*, March 5. www.latinamericanstudies.org/dominican-republic/stowaway.htm.

Passas, Nikos. 2000. Global anomie, dysnomie, and economic crime: Hidden consequences of neoliberalism and globalization in Russia and around the world. *Social Justice* 27 (2): 16–44.

Passas, Nikos, and David Nelken. 1993. The thin line between legitimate and criminal enterprises: Subsidy frauds in the European community. *Crime, Law and Social Change* 19 (3): 223–43.

Passel, Jeffrey S. 2006. *The size and characteristics of the unauthorized migrant population in the U.S.: Estimates based on the March 2005 current population survey*. Washington, D.C.: Pew Research Center. pewhispanic.org/files/reports/61.pdf.

Pieke, Frank N. 1999. Introduction: Chinese migrations compared. In *Internal and international migration: Chinese perspectives*, ed. Frank N. Pieke and Hein Mallee, 1–26. Surrey, U.K.: Curzon.

Pieke, Frank N., Pal Nyiri, Mette Thuno, and Antonella Ceddagno. 2004. *Transnational Chinese—Fujianese migrants in Europe*. Stanford, Calif.: Stanford University Press.

Piore, Michael. 1979. *Birds of passage: Migrant labor in industrial societies*. Cambridge: Cambridge University Press.

Posner, Gerald. 1988. *Warlords of crime: Chinese secret societies—the new mafia*. New York: McGraw-Hill.

Potter, Gary W. 1994. *Criminal organizations: Vice, racketeering, and politics in an American city*. Prospect Heights, Ill.: Waveland.

Resendiz, Rosalva. 2001. Taking risks within the constraints of gender: Mexican-American women as professional auto thieves. *Social Science Journal* 38 (3): 475–81.

Reuter, Peter. 1983. *Disorganized crime: The economics of the visible hand*. Cambridge, Mass.: MIT Press.

Reuters. 1999. China refugees found on Canadian island. *San Diego Union Tribune*, August 13, A17.

Reuters. 2004. Thousands nabbed in China crackdown on stowaways. *Dateline Beijing*, March 24. lexisnexis.com/.

Rhoads, Edward J. M. 2002. "White labor" vs. "coolie labor": The "Chinese question" in Pennsylvania in the 1870s. *Journal of American Ethnic History* 21 (2): 3–32.

Richard, Amy O'Neill. 1999. *International trafficking in women to the United States: A contemporary manifestation of slavery and organized crime*. Center for the Study of Intelligence. www.cia.gov/csi/monograph/women/trafficking.pdf.

San Diego Union Tribune. 1998. China-Canada-U.S. smuggling route shut. December 11, A17.

Savona, Ernesto U. 1990. A neglected sector: The economic analysis of criminality, penal law and the criminal justice system. *Sociologia del Diritto* 17 (1–2): 255–77.

Schatzberg, Rufus, and Robert J. Kelly. 1997. *African-American organized crime: A social history.* New Brunswick, N.J.: Rutgers University Press.

Shek, Daniel T. L. 1995. Chinese adolescents' perceptions of parenting styles of fathers and mothers. *Journal of Genetic Psychology* 156 (2): 175–91.

Shelley, Louise. 2005. Russian and Chinese trafficking: A comparative perspective. In *Human traffic and transnational crime: Eurasian and American perspectives,* ed. Sally Stoecker and Louise Shelley, 63–77. New York: Rowman & Littlefield.

Siebert, Renate. 1996. *Secrets of life and death: Women and the mafia.* Trans. Liz Heron. New York: Verso.

Skeldon, Ronald. 2000. *Myths and realities of Chinese irregular migration.* IOM Migration Research Series, No. 1. Geneva, Switzerland: International Organization for Migration.

Smith, Dwight C., Jr. 1975. *The mafia mystique.* New York: Basic Books.

———. 1980. Paragons, pariahs and pirates: A spectrum-based theory of enterprise. *Crime and Delinquency* 26 (3): 358–86.

Soto, Onell R. 2006. Case against 2 sailors detailed—document say old port of entry was used to smuggle immigrants. *San Diego Union-Tribune,* February 3, B2.

Soudijn, M.R.J. 2006. *Chinese human smuggling in transit.* The Hague: BJU Legal Publishers.

Stacey, Judith. 1983. *Patriarchy and socialist revolution in China.* Berkeley: University of California Press.

Stark, Oded. 1991. *The migration of labor.* Cambridge, U.K.: Basil Blackwell.

Stark, Oded, and David Bloom. 1985. The new economics of labor migration. *American Economic Review* 75 (2): 173–78.

Steffensmeier, Darrell. 1983. Organization properties and sex-segregation in the underworld: Building a sociological theory of sex differences in crime. *Social Forces* 61 (4): 63–101.

Stevens, Todd. 2002. Tender ties: Husbands' rights and racial exclusion in Chinese marriage cases, 1882–1924. *Law and Social Inquiry* 27 (2): 271–305.

Stille, Alexander. 1995. *Excellent cadavers: The mafia and the death of the first Italian republic.* New York: Pantheon Books.

Tam, Bonny. 1992. 198 illegals arrested in Tin Shui Wai. *South China Morning Post,* September 8, 2.

Taylor, Edward. 1992. Remittances and inequality reconsidered: Direct, indirect, and intertemporal effects. *Journal of Policy Modeling* 14 (2): 187–208.

Tempest, Rone. 1995. Chinese exodus apparently slowing. *Los Angeles Times,* October 23, A17.

Thompson, Roger. 2000. Fukienese alien smuggling. Paper presented at the annual Southeast Regional Asian Crime Symposium, Clearwater, Florida.

Thuno, Mette. 1999. Moving stones from China to Europe: The dynamics of emigration from Zhejiang to Europe. In *Internal and international migration: Chinese perspectives*, ed. Frank N. Pieke and Hein Mallee, 159–180. Surrey, U.K.: Curzon.

Tsai, Shih-shan Henry. 1983. *China and the overseas Chinese in the United States 1868–1911*. Fayetteville, Ark.: University of Arkansas Press.

Tyler, Patrick E. 2004. 19 Die as tide traps Chinese shellfish diggers in England. *New York Times*, February 7, A3.

United Nations. 2000a. *Protocol against the smuggling of migrants by land, sea and air, supplementing the United Nations convention against transnational organized crime.* www.unodc.org/pdf/crime/final_instruments/383e.pdf.

United Nations. 2000b. *Protocol to prevent, suppress and punish trafficking in persons, especially women and children, supplementing the United Nations convention against transnational organized crime.* www.unodc.org/pdf/crime/final_instruments/383e.pdf.

United Nations. 2002. *International migration report 2002*. New York: United Nations, Department of Economic and Social Affairs Population Division.

United Press International. 1981. Mobsters smuggle immigrants from China. September 7. www.wordspy.com/words/snakehead.asp.

U.S. Assessment. 2004. *Assessment of U.S. activities to combat trafficking in persons.* An analytical review by several Cabinet agencies of the U.S. Government's anti-trafficking activities. www.usdoj.gov/crt/crim/wetf/us_assessment_2004.pdf.

U.S. Commission on Immigration Reform. 1994. *U.S. immigration policy: A report to Congress.* Washington, D.C.: U.S. Government Printing Office.

U.S. Department of Justice. 2003. *Trafficking in persons report, 2003.* www.state.gov/g/tip/rls/tiprpt/2003.

U.S. Department of Justice. 2004. *Report to Congress from Attorney General John Ashcroft on U.S. government efforts to combat trafficking in persons in Fiscal Year 2003.* www.usdoj.gov/ag/speeches/2004/050104agreporttocongresstvprav10.pdf.

U.S. Immigration and Naturalization Services (U.S. INS). 1998. *Operation gatekeeper: New resources, enhanced results.* uscis.gov/graphics/publicaffairs/factsheets/opgatefs.htm.

U. S. Senate. 1978. *Report of the joint special committee to investigate Chinese immigration.* Washington, D.C.: Government Printing Office.

U. S. Senate. 1992. *Asian organized crime.* Hearings before the Permanent Subcommittee on Investigations of the Committee on Governmental Affairs, October 3 to November 6, 1991. Washington, D.C.: U.S. Government Printing Office.

Van-Duyne, Petrus C. 1997. Organized crime, corruption and power. *Crime, Law and Social Change* 26 (3): 201–38.

Wang, Jun. 2003. Residency rules loosened. *Beijing Review* 46 (44): 26.

Wang, Zheng. 1996. Ocean-going smuggling of illegal Chinese immigrants: Operation, causation, and policy implications. *Transnational Organized Crime* 2 (1): 49–65.

Whyte, Martin King, and William L. Parish. 1984. *Urban life in contemporary China.* Chicago: University of Chicago Press.

Williams, Phil. 1994. Transnational criminal organizations and international security. *Survival* 36 (1): 96–113.

Williamson, Oliver E. 1975. *Markets and hierarchies: Analysis and antitrust implications.* New York: Free Press.

Wong, K. Scott. 1998. Cultural defenders and brokers: Chinese responses to the anti-Chinese Movement. In *Claiming America—Constructing Chinese American identities during the Exclusion Era,* ed. K. Scott Wong and Sucheng Chan, 3–40. Philadelphia: Temple University.

Wong, K. Scott. 2000. Introduction: Paper lives. In *Paper son: One man's story,* by Tung Pok Chin and Winifred C. Chin, xi–xx. Philadelphia: Temple University.

Woods, Audrey. 2000. Deaths of 58 smuggling victims prompt major British inquiry. *San Diego Union Tribune,* June 20, A8.

Xinhua News Agency. 2004. "Snakeheads" boss given life term in prison, March 19. www.chinadaily.com.cn/english/doc/2004-03/19/content_316413.htm.

Zahniser, David. 2004. 2 Indicted on Smuggling Charges. *Copley News Service,* Dateline Los Angeles, March 9. usinfo.state.gov/regional/ea/chinaaliens/innewsmar04.htm.

Zhang, Sheldon. 1997. Task force orientation and dyadic relations in organized Chinese alien smuggling. *Journal of Contemporary Criminal Justice* 13 (4): 320–30.

Zhang, Sheldon, and Ko-lin Chin. 2002a. *The social organization of Chinese human smuggling: A cross national study.* Final report to the National Institute of Justice, U.S. Department of Justice. Grant number 1999-IJ-CX-0028.

———. 2002b. Enter the dragon—Inside Chinese human smuggling organizations. *Criminology* 40 (4): 737–68.

Zhang, Sheldon, and Ko-lin Chin. 2003. The declining significance of triad societies in transnational illegal activities. *British Journal of Criminology* 43 (3): 469–89.

Zhang, Sheldon, and Mark Gaylord. 1996. Bound for the golden mountain: The social organization of Chinese alien smuggling. *Crime, Law and Social Change* 25 (1): 1–16.

Zhou, Min. 1992. *Chinatown: The socioeconomic potential of an urban enclave.* Philadelphia: Temple University Press.

Zhu, Liping. 1997. *A Chinaman's chance—The Chinese on the Rocky Mountain mining frontier.* Niwot, Colo.: University of Colorado Press.

Zuo, Jiping, and Yanjie Bian. 2001. Gendered resources, division of housework, and perceived fairness: A case in urban China. *Journal of Marriage and Family* 63 (4): 1122–34.

REFERENCES CITED FROM CHINESE LANGUAGE SOURCES

Chang, Mung-yuen. Facts about Hong Kong triad societies. *Wide Angle Magazine*, May 1991, 30–39.

Chen, Chang-fung. 1986. *The emergence and decline of the Bamboo United Gang.* Taipei: Shing Ho.

Chen, Yi-mei. 1986. A survey of the winners of the most recent legislative race. *China Times Weekly* 459 (14): 20–27.

Chi, Chung-shien. 1985. *Gangs, election, and violence.* Taipei: Jiao Dian.

China Times. 1994. The number of lost passports quadruples last year. June 14, 4.

Fujian Ribao. 1993. Harsh punishment for snakeheads; human smuggling must stop. June 9, 1.

Liu, Yi-hung. 1995. It's time to discuss the legality of the anti-hooligan law. *China Times*, July 21, 23.

Wang, Kaijie. 1999. Chinese illegal aliens swamped Guam, taking Washington by surprise. *World Journal*, April 25, A1.

World Journal. 1993. Human smuggling gangs may be indicted under RICO. June 20, B1.

———. 1999. More than 100 illegal Chinese immigrants detained in less than two months. May 16, A1.

———. 2000. Lawyer colluding with snakeheads: Wife of Robert Porges suspected to be the mastermind. September 21, A3.

Index

Note: Page numbers followed by *f*, *m*, or *t* indicate figures, maps, or tables, respectively.

Adler, Patricia A., 153
Adler, Peter, 153
Afghanistan, xiii
Air, entry by, 11; checkpoints for, 55–57; demand for, 13, 51; departure arrangements for, 51–58; duration of travel for, xiv; methods used for, 77–79
Albania, 162, 178
American Civil Liberties Union, 231
Amnesty International, 231
Amsterdam, Netherlands, 140
Argentina, 72
Arrest, snakeheads' fear of, 136–37
Arrival, main U.S. cities for, 85
Asylum, *see* Political asylum
Australia, 65

Bail, 56, 85
Baiping (appeasing all parties), 58
Balladares, Ernesto Perez, 66
Banks, 149–50
Beatings, *see* Violence
Belgium, 66, 80
Bian, Yanjie, 183, 184
Bianjian (border inspection checkpoint or inspector), 56, 255
Big snakeheads, 23–25, 108, 129, 220–22, 231–32
Black, David, 155
Black Eagles, 160
Block, Alan, 187

Boarding pass swapping, 77–78
Boat, entry by, *see* Maritime smuggling
Bolivia, 24
Border inspections, 55–58, 121–23, 224–26
Border Patrol Armed Police (China), 212, 213, 225
Born-to-Kill, 161
Brazil: big snakeheads in, 24; illegal immigrants from, xiii; stranded migrants in, 71; transit through, 141
Bribery, 55–58, 114, 119–24. *See also* Corruption
Brimelow, Peter, 231
British Columbia, Canada, 12
Bulgaria, xiii
Burma, 58, 60. *See also* Myanmar
Bush administration, 228
"Business delegations," 13, 33, 34, 46, 50–51, 59, 84, 120

California Rural Legal Assistance Foundation, 231
Cambodia, 65, 141
Cameroon, 67
Canada: collaborators in, 65; detention in, 13, 57; entry from, 7–8, 11–13, 67, 249*n*2; entry into, 72; maritime smuggling in, 50; as staging area, 65, 140
Cargo containers, *see* Container ships, smuggling on
Cargo trucks, 79–80
Changle City, China, 139
Changle County, China, 236